ALMOST
PARADISE

As they pulled into the driveway, Mark noticed Ted's new silver Porsche parked there, along with the blue Audi station wagon. The estate was eerily quiet, except for ravens crowing high in the trees. The phone was ringing inside the house, someone still trying to reach Ted. Mark walked up to the large garage door and knocked loudly but there was no response. It was opened slightly. He swung it wide and stuck his head inside.

"Ted?" Mark shouted into the house.

There was no answer.

Mark pulled on one of the gloves and stepped inside. Milton donned the other and followed. The air in the house was warm and stale. They moved to the main stairway and cautiously walked up the carpeted steps as Mark continued to call Ted's name. At the top landing, Mark approached the master bedroom and then, with a gasp, froze. . . . They hurried back down the stairs and out the way they came. Mark's face was pale. He was breathing heavily, fear and shock in his eyes. To his right, the sun was setting like a fire behind the trees. Night was coming. Mark pulled off the glove, took out his cell phone, and called 911. When the dispatcher asked where the emergency was, Mark finally had to utter the words that made it real.

Ted had been murdered.

"A fast-paced account."
—*Publishers Weekly*

St. Martin's Paperbacks Titles
by Kieran Crowley

SLEEP MY LITTLE DEAD

BURNED ALIVE

THE SURGEON'S WIFE

ALMOST PARADISE

The Murder of Multimillionaire
Ted Ammon in the Hamptons—
America's Playground of the Rich and Famous

KIERAN CROWLEY

St. Martin's Paperbacks

ALMOST PARADISE

Copyright © 2005 by Kieran Crowley.

Cover photo of house by Jeffrey P. Gibbons; Photos of Generosa Ammon, Ted Ammon, and Danny Pelosi © Polaris Images.

All rights reserved. No part of this book may be used or reproduced in any manner whatsoever without written permission except in the case of brief quotations embodied in critical articles or reviews. For information address St. Martin's Press, 175 Fifth Avenue, New York, NY 10010.

Library of Congress Catalog Card Number: 2004054942

ISBN: 0-312-99913-5
EAN: 80312-99913-1

Printed in the United States of America

St. Martin's Press hardcover edition / March 2005
St. Martin's Paperbacks edition / November 2005

St. Martin's Paperbacks are published by St. Martin's Press, 175 Fifth Avenue, New York, NY 10010.

10 9 8 7 6 5 4 3 2 1

For my parents, William and Mary Crowley

CONTENTS

ACKNOWLEDGMENTS

This book is based on hundreds of interviews and several thousand pages of documents—including police reports, court papers, court transcripts, and other documents and information gathered over more than two years. There are no fictional or "composite" characters in this book, although some of the people involved in this incredible drama have requested anonymity. Their names are denoted by an asterisk (*) the first time they appear. Certain events, sequences, and conversations were necessarily reconstructed from a synthesis of all the evidence available at the time this book went to press, which was before the trial.

First, I would like to thank my editors at St. Martin's Press, Charles Spicer, Jr., and Joseph Cleemann, for all their assistance.

My deep thanks go also to my literary agent, Jane Dystel, a lovely lady who fights for me in the publishing world, listens patiently to my problems, and occasionally holds my hand by e-mail.

I wish to thank my editor at the *New York Post,* Jesse Angelo, for allowing me to take time off to write this book. I am also grateful to the *Post*'s chief librarian, Laura Harris, and her diligent staff for ferreting out clippings and other information. I want to thank *Post* real estate columnist Braden

Keil, who did great work with me on several stories on the case and got his first taste of the game afoot. I particularly want to express my gratitude to tenacious *Post* freelance reporter and author Lisa Pulitzer, who teamed up with me on many stories on the case and uncovered a wealth of information. Photo editor David Boyle was key in obtaining the great pictures for this book and I thank him and Dave Johnston, who got it all together. My thanks go also to several *Post* photographers who supplied some of the fine photos for this book, including Mary McLoughlin, Steven Hirsch, and Veronique Louis. I would especially like to thank my colleague Bob Kalfus for his excellent shot of Danny Pelosi with his wife's remains, an instant tabloid classic.

Several of Generosa Ammon's family members, including Marjorie Mize Legaye, Edwina Moran, and Albert Legaye, Jr., rekindled their bittersweet memories and helped me piece together Generosa's broken childhood. Frances Thomas and her daughter Mary Beth Lindsay were kind enough to share their remembrances of the years Generosa lived with them, as were Julie Vogel and her father, Dick Vogel. They have my appreciation for helping me to understand the good, the bad, and the ugly about Generosa's past.

Thanks to Tom Carson of the Marine Exchange of Southern California, who was able to obtain obscure, fifty-year-old shipping news for the Port of Long Beach and Los Angeles. The town of East Hampton provided interesting historical information, and Mayor Paul Rickenbach helpfully supplied his own memories and experiences.

I tender my thanks to Generosa and Ted Ammon's friend and neighbor Jurate Gazikas, herself a journalist. Michael Schnayerson of *Vanity Fair* magazine was helpful at the start of this project and I tip my hat to him.

Sarah Donley, an excellent landscaper, was kind enough to speak to me about her worst client. Jeffrey P. Gibbons is obviously a fine architect, based on his work at 59 Middle Lane, and I thank him for his constructive contributions and his photographs. John Kundle lent a helping hand by giving me an education in the workings of the burglar alarm and the video surveillance system he installed in the murder house.

I am eternally grateful to private detective Marie Schembri for all her help. She is an original and resourceful private eye who was deeply affected by the unexpected murder of her client. She helped me because she wanted the story told and justice done—and she graciously consented to being unmasked in the book. She and her operative, Taylor Baldwin, have hoped for a resolution in the case almost as much as Ted Ammon's family.

Generosa Ammon's lawyer Michael Dowd was also very helpful, as well as Mrs. Ammon's surrogate court attorney, Gerry Sweeney, who also rendered assistance.

I am very grateful to Suffolk's "go-to-guy," lawyer Edward Burke, Jr., who defended Danny Pelosi before and after he became infamous. I also appreciate the help of Pelosi's criminal lawyer, Paul Bergman, a scholar and a gentleman; and, of course, attorney and law school academic Gerald Shargel, a well-known murder defender and wry wit. Pelosi's surrogate court lawyer, James Spiess, also has my thanks.

Danny Pelosi was a source for parts of this book and I thank him for all of his help. He told me that he cooperated because he was not involved in the murder and had nothing to hide. He did, ultimately, withhold several things, but he insisted that they were key, secret elements of his defense— which could not be revealed to the prosecution before a possible trial. I also thank his friend Alex Mawyer, Pelosi's sister Barbara Lukert, and their friend Joanne Matheson.

Obviously, using a murder suspect as a source meant that I spent a great deal of time trying to confirm his claims with other sources. In many cases, other witnesses or sources could be found to corroborate his remembrances. But in several cases—particularly in regard to his alibi or to conversations that Pelosi had with people who are now dead—it was not always possible to get full corroboration. He maintained his complete innocence, insisting that he neither killed Ted

Ammon nor was involved in any way with any murder plot.

There are many other people I would like to thank by name but cannot because they requested pseudonyms or are not mentioned in the book. Thank you for your invaluable aid.

Law enforcement personages do not play major roles in this book because a grand jury was investigating the murder during the time I wrote it. Police and prosecutors are bound by the law that makes it a crime to reveal what happens in the grand jury room. However, I must thank the Suffolk County Homicide Squad commander, Detective Lieutenant Jack Fitzpatrick, for the meager assistance he was able to provide, within the law. Likewise, Suffolk District Attorney Thomas Spota, along with his communications director, Bob Clifford, also have my gratitude for providing access to public documents and records. In the same vein, Suffolk Surrogate Court Judge John Czygier, Jr., and court clerk Michael Cippolino should also be mentioned for pointing me toward useful public files.

This book could not have been written without the love and help of my family—a very understanding group. I thank my mother-in-law, Tess Nemser, for her loving support, babysitting, and even her meatballs. My father-in-law, Al Nemser, is the wisest man I know, as well as a lawyer, and I, as always, am grateful for his legal advice, his help, and his matchless sense of humor. My sister-in-law, Kathy Nemser, also dispensed legal advice, along with unfailing support and encouragement. The only family member who was not particularly supportive of the project was my daughter, Ariel, who is now happy that this book is finished, so I can spend more time playing with her.

My wife, Riki, is my first and best editor and was instrumental in the completion of this book. Once again, she set aside her art career to help me, which was the art world's temporary loss and my gain. Words cannot express my gratitude to her, so I won't try.

PROLOGUE

Mark Angelson looked out the window of the corporate helicopter as it lifted off the pad and banked over the roiling East River. The investment banker's own worried face, topped by thinning silver hair, looked back at him from the thick Plexiglas. It was late October but it was a warm, sunny afternoon with cotton clouds in a crisp, cerulean sky. The Monday evening rush hour was building on the roadways beneath them as thousands of cars snaked over the bridges, out of Manhattan, through the Midtown Tunnel, and on to the Long Island Expressway and other routes to the suburbs. As they climbed higher, Mark watched the sun dip behind the glinting Manhattan skyline. The aircraft flew over Queens and then over the south shore of Nassau County and then into Suffolk, as it sped above the fish-shaped immensity of Long Island, just thirty minutes to the Hamptons, the exclusive summer enclave of the wealthy and well-known elite of the city. Below and to the right was the Atlantic Ocean. The barrier beaches stretched away toward the horizon ahead, toward Montauk Point. Seated next to Mark was Milton Macias, the chauffeur for Ted Ammon, Mark's wealthy senior partner and boss at the investment firm of Chancery Lane Capital in Manhattan. Both men wore somber expressions as the chopper began its descent over a darkening sea.

That morning, Milton Macias had driven Ted's BMW to his East Ninety-second Street town house to pick him up for the usual drive to his office, but, for the first time, he was not there. Ted had driven out to his East Hampton mansion for the weekend but had not answered any phone calls since Saturday night. Mark and Ted were partners and close friends who spoke to each other every day. When Ted had not answered calls on Sunday, Mark thought it was a bit odd. But Ted sometimes played the part of Hamlet and went off by himself to think. Then Milton called Mark and told him that he did not know where Ted was.

When he was still unreachable that Monday morning, Mark called around to family and friends, his dread deepening as each person, ignorant of Ted's whereabouts, added his or her worry to his. When Ted failed to pick up his kids after school for his visitation time with them, Mark knew in his heart that something had happened to his best friend. Ted loved his twins, Alexa and Gregory, more than anything else in the world. But because of Ted's past vanishing acts, Mark still hesitated to involve the police, hoping that Ted would suddenly pop up, so he could yell at him for disappearing without a word. Mark decided that he and Milton would fly out east to Ted's estate.

Tall, talented, and athletic, Ted had achieved great wealth by being one of the "Barbarians at the Gate" leveraged buyout specialists who acquired RJR Nabisco in history's largest hostile corporate takeover. But Ted was no barbarian. He was charming, handsome, and a good father and friend. He was also a philanthropist and the president of Jazz at Lincoln Center. That week, he had lunch with former president Bill Clinton, for whom he had been a fund-raiser.

During the helicopter flight from Manhattan, Mark and Milton did not talk about what they would find. They knew that Ted was in trouble, but neither wanted to use the words that might somehow make it real. They both knew about Ted's wife, Generosa—her bizarre behavior, wild temper, and the threats she had made against Ted. Mark had begged

Ted to get a bodyguard, but Ted had just laughed it off. Ted and Generosa were nearing the end of a long, vicious divorce and custody battle that had limped on for more than a year.

The former Generosa Rand was California blond, beautiful, and an intense overachiever; she was a designer, real estate developer, and artist. She was the driving force behind the building of the East Hampton house; it was her favorite place, her best creation. But 59 Middle Lane had been transformed into a cursed symbol, a battleground in the war of the Ammons, because Ted refused to let her have it in a divorce settlement, which drove Generosa to frequent and disturbing fits of rage. The twins had been caught in the middle of the domestic warfare for far too long, a situation that was due to end in just a few days with the signing of the final divorce papers.

When the helicopter touched down at the East Hampton Airport, Milton got a cab and he and Mark were driven to the Ammon estate, which was near the beach and not far from the lavish compound of comedian Jerry Seinfeld. As they slowed on Middle Lane, Mark looked out the window at the imposing residence, his stomach tightening with anxiety. The mansion, framed by large, hanging trees, was disguised as a quaint, gabled English country cottage, with a curved-eyebrow attic window in the center of the shingled roof. An expanse of blooming yellow flowers in front shimmered under a cool breeze. It was perfect, ideal, a home where beautiful, thriving people who had everything came to relax. How could something that had started out so right between two incredible, talented people have gone so far wrong?

As they pulled into the driveway, Mark noticed Ted's new silver Porsche parked there, along with the blue Audi station wagon. The estate was eerily quiet, except for ravens crowing high in the trees. The phone was ringing inside the house, someone still trying to reach Ted. Mark walked up to the large garage door and knocked loudly but there was no response. It was open slightly. He swung it wide and stuck his head inside.

"Ted?" Mark shouted into the house.

There was no answer. Milton produced a pair of work gloves.

Mark pulled on one of the gloves and stepped inside. Milton donned the other and followed. The air in the house was warm and stale. They moved to the main stairway and cautiously walked up the carpeted steps, as Mark continued to call Ted's name. At the top landing, Mark approached the master bedroom and then, with a gasp, froze. There was dark, brown blood everywhere, on the white walls, the white sheets, and pools of it on the rope-colored rug. In the middle of it, Ted's naked, bloody body was terribly twisted into a fetal position on the sisal carpet beside the bed. Mark backed away from the scene of slaughter, and they hurried back down the stairs and out the way they had come. Mark's face was pale. He was breathing heavily, fear and shock in his eyes. To his right, the sun was setting like a fire behind the trees. Night was coming. Mark pulled off the glove, took out his cell phone, and called 911. When the dispatcher asked where the emergency was, Mark finally had to utter the words that made it real.

Ted had been murdered.

PART ONE

Roots

1

GENEROSA: PRAYERS AND SECRETS, 1955

Babe and her girlfriend were all dolled up in bright, attractive summer dresses, with makeup, red lipstick, and nylons, their high heels clicking on the pavement as they walked to the nightspot. The place was jumping, the dance music audible from out front, thumping drums, bass, and saxophone. Babe fiddled with her ring finger, which felt naked without her wedding ring. The warm, June night air was fragrant with flowers, salt air, and leaded-gasoline fumes. In the nearby harbor of Long Beach, California, more than a dozen ships were docked. Hundreds of seesawing steel oil rigs clanged at the mouth of the bay, sucking the black liquid up from under the muddy bottom of the Los Angeles River.

The women walked in the front door and were hit with a warm blast of noise, cigarette smoke, and beer. Everybody inside was laughing, flirting, having a great time. There was no such thing as AIDS. It was 1955. Doctors made TV commercials for cigarettes.

Half of the men in the nightclub were wearing uniforms from a dozen different countries. Babe was a sucker for a man in a uniform. After she and her friend had ordered drinks, a couple of sailors walked over. One of them smiled at Babe. It was a nice smile. He was tall and blond in his summer whites, his blue eyes set off by the tanned, olive

skin of his clean-shaven face. Nervously brushing at her
wavy blond hair, she smiled back at the handsome sailor. He
extended his hand to Babe and she placed her hand in his.
She was surprised when he took her hand and kissed it. In
deeply accented English he asked her to dance, then led her
onto the dance floor. Babe was over thirty-five, a woman
with three children, but she blushed, warming the cheeks of
her pretty, round face. She hoped he would not guess her
true age as they danced. She asked his name.

"Generoso," he replied.

In halting English, he told her he was a sailor in the Italian navy and that his ship had just docked.

"Gen-er-o-so?" she pronounced the unfamiliar name.

He asked her name. Babe told him her real name: Marie.

"Marie," he repeated, nodding his head like a Continental
gentleman.

In short, awkward sentences that he had practiced aboard
his ship, he told Babe he liked her. He also said that he liked
America and Hollywood, just thirty miles and a world away
from the waterfront bar. Babe told him that she did not live
in Hollywood, but nearby, right in Long Beach. After their
dance, they had more drinks with Babe's girlfriend and the
other sailor and then danced some more. He kissed her and
offered to see her home.

She took his arm as they strolled along the sidewalk toward her place. The dark green blades of the palm trees
clacked gently in the sea breeze, slicing up the white moon-
light. They entered Babe's dark apartment and she turned on
the lights. He took her in his arms and kissed her again,
deeper. Neither could understand what the other was saying,
but they didn't need words. Soon the words melted into sighs
and the ardent strangers turned out the lights and made love
in the dark.

Babe was born Marie Therese Legaye in the Roaring Twenties, the child of a California farmer and his wife. She was an
adorable child but moody and sometimes confused. Babe

was very religious, and when she was a young woman, she entered a convent. After a year under vows, she decided that being a nun was not her true vocation. She rejoined the world during World War II and made up for lost time. Babe became a party girl, dating and drinking and dancing whenever she could. She seemed to have no ambition and was alternately listless or active. Some people in the family wondered if she might be what was then called a manic-depressive.

When Babe's father died, ownership of the family ranch passed to her mother. When her mom died of cancer a few years later, she left the farm to Babe but made her older brother, Al, the executor of the will. He set up a trust fund and purchased oil stock so that there would be money to take care of Babe. Al became a rich wheeler-dealer businessman. Babe floundered and, eventually, had only what Al gave her.

Babe became a war bride, marrying a man named Lynne Thomas. They partied hard, which was fine, until they had children. Charles came first, and then Marie Therese followed in 1945. Everyone called them Chuck and Terry. Babe continued to carouse and refused to let motherhood stop the party. She often left her babies home alone, unfed and in stinking diapers, and went out dancing and drinking. Not surprisingly, the marriage fell apart, ending in divorce.

Chuck was eventually parceled out to relatives but Terry was sent to a foster home, forgotten and cut off from the family for years. As soon as she could, at age nineteen, she escaped into marriage.

Babe married another soldier, Clarence Rand. In 1953, they had a daughter, Dolly, who became the victim of the same neglect and abandonment as Babe's earlier children. Clarence, a disabled war veteran, later went into a veterans' hospital and would not get out any time soon. Their marriage also ended. Babe kept Dolly with her but often left her at her brother's place, with his wife, Edwina, who had four kids of her own to look after. Babe had left Dolly there the night she met her Italian sailor.

· · ·

Babe's romance with Generoso at her Long Beach apartment was passionate but brief. In just over a week, he was gone. She went to see him off at the dock and he kissed her goodbye, leaving her with a photograph of him in his uniform, and a scribbled mailing address in Italy.

The next month, she woke up nauseated and she knew that she was pregnant. She wrote Generoso and told him about her condition. There was no answer. She wrote several times and waited for a reply but she never received one.

Babe gave birth to that fourth child, her third daughter, Generosa Jomary Rand, in Long Beach, California, on March 22, 1956. She gave the baby her husband's last name, Rand. It was easier to keep the secret of the child's paternity because Babe was a married woman although she did not live with her husband. She adored her new daughter but soon returned to her hard partying habits. The family did not use Generosa's first name, which she had gotten from the sailor whose existence was a family secret. Some called the new baby Gen, but most called her by her middle name, Jomary, or simply Jo. A cute, chubby child with blond hair, she was a friendly, happy kid. Generosa and her older sister Dolly played well together and became close, especially when their mother would go off on a spree and leave them alone.

In 1960, when Generosa was four and Dolly was seven, they moved with their mother into a new house with their uncle Al in Oceanside, California. Al had divorced his wife, and his kids went to live with relatives. He bought a three-family house in the beachside community and fixed it up. The top floor was rented out to tenants. The girls and Babe lived in the middle apartment, and Al lived in the ground-level apartment, a sort of bachelor pad, now that he was single again. He put in a circular staircase from his apartment up to Babe's, giving them a duplex. At the time, Babe had one of her infrequent jobs, as a secretary to the pastor at a Catholic church in Oceanside. On Sundays, Babe would dress Dolly and Generosa up in pretty dresses and black patent leather shoes and take them to Mass.

Al hired Beryl,* an English housekeeper, who often acted as babysitter for Dolly and her sister. Generosa really liked Beryl, who was very nice to her, and she was particularly charmed by Beryl's British accent. Generosa began to realize that she liked the housekeeper better than her own mother.

After a year or so, Babe started spending more time away on flings and the girls were left with Beryl and their uncle Al or others.

That was when it happened. It involved a man that Generosa trusted as she did any other adult, as if he were the father she had never known. When he asked her to rub his shoulders and neck with her little hands, she did it. He thanked her and told her that she was a good girl and that it felt good. Sometimes he rubbed her shoulders and that felt good, too. Slowly, he would have her rub another part of his body a bit more each time they were alone. Then he would rub another part of her body. One time, he had her touch a part of him she had never seen before and something strange happened. It made her feel funny and bad but he told her that she had done a very good thing—but that it was a secret. Then he touched her somewhere he had never touched her before and she was scared. When it was over, he told her that what they had done was their special secret, just between them. He warned her that if she told anyone, like her mother, they would be very angry and would not believe her. Everyone would think she was bad. Someone might even come and take her away from her mother.

Generosa was terrified. For the first time in her life she turned inward, to a place deep inside where bad things happened. She wanted to bury the bad things there and leave. Suddenly, everything she had been taught was wrong. Not all adults were her friends. Anyone could betray her, hurt her, make her feel afraid and lonely and bad about herself.

Generosa said nothing and everything went on as if nothing had happened. Maybe it would never, ever happen again.

But by the time she had almost forgotten about it, it did happen again. It always started with rubbing shoulders when they were alone. She was powerless to stop the descent into that deep place for bad things.

In church one Sunday, Generosa knelt on the padded kneeler, her head barely reaching the top of the wooden pew in front of her. As the organ music played, she looked up at the stained glass windows with the colorful images of Jesus. Generosa put her little hands together and prayed to God. She prayed for the bad thing to stop.

Later, she prayed at home, but it happened again. And again. God did not answer her prayers. Why? Because she was bad? Was God really there? If he was, why didn't he help her? Why didn't her mother protect her? Generosa told no one about the sexual abuse.

One Halloween, Al arranged for Beryl and her friend to stay with Generosa and Dolly at the house while he and Babe were away. Later, Al discovered that the two English girls had been bringing sailors and others back to the house and having raucous, boozy parties while the kids were there, so he fired Beryl.

In 1963, Al married his second wife, Marge, and moved into a beachfront home in an exclusive enclave called Emerald Bay in Laguna Beach. He set Babe and her daughters up in a beachfront cottage in Oceanside.

Two years later, while in the shower, Babe felt a lump in her breast, but she ignored it, hoping it would go away. Not only did it not go away, it got bigger. Babe was embarrassed about the location of the lump and did not mention it to anyone. She did nothing, although she was frightened. Cancer, which had killed quite a few of her relatives, was a plague in her family but still she denied that anything was wrong and went to more parties, more dancing, more drinking. For some time, the lump seemed to stop growing and it didn't hurt, and Babe hoped that it was nothing, despite the fact that occasionally she was very tired and felt strange things happening inside her body. In 1967, she was so weak and dizzy that she couldn't stand up and couldn't breathe. She finally went to a doctor.

It was far too late. Babe's denial had killed her.

The breast cancer had spread through her abdomen and into her ovaries and into her brain through the bloodstream and lymphatic system. Babe's daughters were told that their mother was ill but the true nature of her affliction was kept from them. Generosa prayed in church for her mother. As the organ played the holy music, she asked God to make her mother better. But the more she prayed, the sicker her mother got.

As Christmas approached, her mother worsened and had to take medicine that made her sleepy. It also made her act crazy, as if she didn't know what was going on. A doctor had given Babe morphine for the pain and it had worked for a while. But the pain kept getting worse and she kept increasing the dose to keep ahead of the agony, gradually descending into an opium stupor in front of her girls. They didn't have money for gifts for Christmas, so Generosa, who had learned to sew from her mother, kept busy designing and stitching pillow covers in the shape of cute beagles for her relatives. As she slowly, carefully pushed the needle and thread through the material, Generosa concentrated on the work, not on her mother sitting on the couch. She took comfort from the fact that she could take cloth and thread and scissors and create something that was pretty and looked like a real puppy. Generosa had made it, and even though she had to give it away, it would always belong to her.

The disease attacked Babe's brain, slowly destroying it, a little bit each day. As she lost weight, her eyes sunk in their sockets, her cheeks hollowed, and her body wasted away like that of a concentration camp victim. Generosa's mother's pretty, soft face hardened into a death mask.

Generosa wondered whether she would get cancer when

she grew up, and if it would kill her. She vowed that she would never suffer such a slow death.

Babe was losing the battle and was taken to St. Joseph's Hospital, in Orange, where she had emergency surgery to remove part of her brain. Dolly and Generosa were too young to be allowed to visit. Within a few weeks, Babe was dead. When their uncle Al and his new wife, Marge, told them that their mother had gone to heaven, Generosa and her sister cried. Generosa was just ten years old when they buried her mother. The girls went to live with Uncle Al and Aunt Marge, who was a lawyer, and his kids in Emerald Bay, an exclusive community on the coast just north of Laguna Beach. With its beautiful homes, palm trees, and magnificent views of the Pacific, it was quite different from the places where Generosa had lived before. But the home was not huge and accommodations were crowded.

After her mother's death, Generosa was looking through family photos with Dolly, when her sister showed her a picture she had never seen before, a shot of a handsome, blond sailor in a strange uniform. Dolly explained that the man was Generosa's biological father—not the man she had been told was her father, the man in an institution, whose last name she bore—Clarence Rand. On the back of the photograph was written the name Generoso. She had been named Generosa after the sailor, Dolly explained. Her father had not been married to their mother. It was a family secret.

The revelation hit Generosa like a bolt of lightning. That was when Generosa's vague feelings about her mother began to take shape. She remembered her mother yelling and screaming at her a lot. Not only did Generosa feel her mother had abandoned her by dying but she had lied to her. She believed that her mother had resented her from birth because she was illegitimate, because her mother saw in her eyes the sailor who had left her. In Generosa's eyes, her mother did not want her. Her mother had been weak and had failed to protect her. Generosa resolved to be different. She would be strong. She would have lots of money. Also, Generosa vowed that should she ever have children, she would be a better mother. She would never lie and would always protect them. Now that she was free of her, Generosa decided that her mother's death was actually a good thing. Later in her life, she would tell people it was the best thing that had ever happened to her.

It was the answer to her prayers.

2

TED: HOMETOWN HERO, 1949

Ted was born at Allegheny General Hospital on the North Side of Pittsburgh, Pennsylvania, on a hot, hazy August day in 1949. Steel executive Bob Ammon beamed when the doctor told him that his wife, Bettylee, had just given birth to their second child.

"You have a new son," the doctor informed Bob.

Bob's twenty-one-month-old daughter, Sandi, was the apple of his eye, but when he heard that he had a son he was overjoyed and couldn't get the proud grin off his face. He immediately ran out and bought a bright red suit for his son, who would be named Robert Theodore Ammon, although most people would call him Teddy. Bob brought the little outfit back to the maternity ward, where his son in the scarlet suit was conspicuous among the other newborns in their pale swaddling clothes. From day one, Ted Ammon stood out.

Teddy Boy, as he was called by his mother, joined his older sister, Sandi, not quite two years older, and completed the Ammon family. He enjoyed a happy, active Beaver Cleaver childhood in suburban 1950s America, a location so distant from the present that it might have been another planet. His dad worked as a manager for the Shenango Steel Works, churning out metal to drive the United States manufacturing economy in the days when there was no such thing as a Japanese-made car on the American market.

Teddy was competitive by nature. His first words were "Me too." Followed shortly thereafter by "Me first!"

Bettylee was a driven, intelligent, perceptive woman and she helped develop those qualities in her son. She especially encouraged his competitive spirit. Ted had a sharp mind and was a quick study.

"Teddy Boy, you can do anything you set your mind to," his mother often told him. She meant it and Teddy believed it.

When Ted was in the eighth grade, his father was transferred to East Aurora, New York, to run an entire steel plant. East Aurora was a small town twenty-five miles from Buffalo. Ted's father wanted him to follow in his footsteps in the steel industry. Otherwise, Ted was expected to join another major corporation, sign on as a company man, and start his slow, steady rise to the upper middle. By the time such expectations were voiced, Ted had other ideas.

Ted came home from school, did his homework, and joined the family at the table for dinner every night at six-thirty. His father was the coach of Ted's Little League baseball team and sometimes acted as umpire, calling the plays. Muscular, lanky Ted was already well on his way to his full six-four adult height. He also raced on the swimming team. In the summers, the family divided their time between their New Jersey shore house and Ames, Iowa, where Ted and Sandi and their cousins spent idyllic times in the country on their grandparents' farm.

Ted seemed to have an almost photographic memory. He and Sandi took separate piano lessons from the same music teacher, and Ted could sight read a new piece once and have it memorized. Then he would go out to play while Sandi had to stay at the keys. They both loved music, and Ted discovered Dave Brubeck and other musicians. Jazz became a lifelong love. The Beatles arrived when Ted was fifteen and he and Sandi loved their music, which scandalized their conservative father.

In high school, Ted was on the football and swimming

teams and was a popular student with lots of friends. He had one pretty girlfriend after another. By this time Ted had become the handyman of the house, figuring out how things worked and making repairs, to the delight of his mother and the relief of his father. He took pride in mastering a task without instruction, simply by evaluation and logic. Instruction manuals were for other people, not because Ted was a snob but because he didn't have the time and because it was more fun that way. That was how he learned. Once he went after a problem he went at it with everything he had, even if it seemed impossible. Sometimes, impossible was a challenge.

Ted was a torpedo in the water, which was why he was chosen as the anchorman on the swim team. In the final, big meet during Ted's senior year against their big rival, Sweet Home High School, Ted's team was more than a lap behind in the freestyle relay race in the indoor pool. It seemed impossible. The race, the meet, and the championship seemed lost when Ted was tagged by his last teammate and knifed into the water. But Ted immediately began to gain on the lead swimmer. As the home crowd went wild, Ted clawed his way closer and closer to the competition.

"Ted! Ted! Ted!"

Even the swimmers under the water could hear the echoing chants and stomping feet urging the underdog on. The rhythmic roar synchronized with Ted's furious, flailing arms, propelling him faster and faster.

"Ted! Ted! Ted!"

The lead swimmer could not believe his eyes as he saw Ted pull even with him and then pass him—just in time to slap the side of the pool and win the race, the meet, and the championship. Ted's team and the ecstatic crowd surged poolside and lifted the soaking-wet hero onto their shoulders and carried him off.

On that day, Ted was golden, with a perfect mind in a perfect body. He felt he could never fail at anything. It was proof that, if he worked hard enough, he could achieve the impossible, no matter what the odds.

3

DANNY: THE BOXER, 1973

Danny and his younger brother, Jimbo, along with two other boys, were playing a charming practical joke known as the Flaming Sack of Shit. The boys had pulled it on several other tenants in their Flushing, Queens, apartment building. Now it was Jimbo's turn to lay the trap.

It was a simple trick, one played by mischievous grammar school boys, when they were being boys. First, in the days before pooper-scooper laws, the boys had to scoop up dog poop from the gutter into a brown paper bag. Then they twisted the top to make a wick. Next, they would sneak up to the front door of a neighbor they knew was home, place the package on the welcome mat, light the wick, ring the bell, and run like hell. Then the unsuspecting homeowner would open the door, look down and see the burning bag, and stomp on it to put it out—thereby getting a foot full of hot excrement.

But Jimbo wasn't as fast as Danny and he got caught. When their father, Bob, got home, he was not pleased. He pulled his belt off and asked his sons how many licks they thought they deserved for their stunt.

"Five," said Jimbo.

"Daniel?" asked their dad.

"Two," Danny replied.

He figured that he had not been caught, Jimbo had, and he had not been the one to actually light the bag, at least that time. Danny's first plea bargain was very unsuccessful. "Being that Jimbo is being honest, you'll get five and he'll get two," their father informed him.

Bob Pelosi was a banker, a former U.S. Marine and decorated Korean War veteran. He had been wounded in action in the freezing foxholes of that war and left many friends behind in the hard soil of the peninsula. His horrific war experiences left him changed forever. When startled, or awakened suddenly, he would sometimes instinctively lash out with his fists, at attackers long gone.

His son Danny was a cute, high-strung boy with long blond hair, a Cub Scout in the local Flushing troop. Danny was one of six kids. Barbara was the eldest, followed by Bobby and sister Janet, who was called "J.J." Danny was the fourth child, trailed by Jimbo and Joan. Danny called Jimbo his "bigger little brother" because he was taller. They were best friends and played stickball in the street and stoopball and handball. They were both New York Mets fans and wanted to play shortstop or centerfield for the Amazin' Mets when they grew up.

Their parents—handsome and athletic Bob and the beautiful, blond Janet—worked hard to save money to get the family out of the city and into the suburbs on Long Island, a better environment to raise their children. When Danny was eleven and in the sixth grade, the family moved to Center Moriches in Suffolk County, on eastern Long Island.

Actually, more than half the people who call themselves New Yorkers live on Long Island, but no one referring to Long Island means Brooklyn or Queens. Suburban Nassau County and rural Suffolk stretch from the Queens border one hundred miles east, into the Atlantic Ocean, before tapering off into two narrow peninsulas, the North Fork and the South Fork. The elite Hamptons are on the South Fork. Center Moriches is on the south shore: the archetypal Middle America suburbia, which extends inland from the sandy beaches to the glacial ridge that runs down the island's spine.

Danny's father had emerged from a blue collar background to become vice president of a bank. At night, he came home to his wife and children in their home near the Great South Bay, with its ever-changing view of the wide water and sky. Right down the street was a park and a beach.

On the first day of sixth grade in his new school, Danny got into a fight with another boy and was disrespectful to a teacher. He received a spanking from his father. He settled down a bit and joined Little League baseball. But when he misbehaved again at school, a teacher rapped his knuckles with a yardstick. Danny went home and told his dad. Bob was not happy that a teacher had administered corporal punishment to Danny. He went to school with Danny to see the teacher. In the classroom, he picked up the yardstick.

"Is this what you hit my son with?" Bob asked.

"Yes."

He whacked the teacher's hand.

"How does that feel? The only one who hits my son is me!"

One night when he was thirteen, Danny and his buddies raided his parents' liquor cabinet and got bombed on all the different liquors. Danny got sick as a dog and swore he would never drink again. He earned a spanking for it and was also punished for sneaking out on his motorbike and on his father's boat. As a teenager, he always seemed to think that his plans for getting away with things were foolproof, but he almost always got caught.

After one of his daughters was accosted and almost raped, Bob Pelosi taught all his kids to defend themselves. In 1978, Danny was just four-foot-ten, just as he had been in grade school. He was being bullied, so his father gave him some lessons in hand-to-hand combat from his Marine days. He showed Danny how to kill a man in five seconds, by grabbing him around the throat from behind and putting pressure on the back. He also showed him the proper place to strike someone on the bridge of the nose, so that it would break, and how to break a jaw with one punch. Danny went to school on Monday morning and went looking for the biggest kid he could find. He attacked him and broke his nose. Danny's father was upset to learn that Danny was in trouble again and that the defensive skills he had taught him had been used aggressively. Danny got another spanking. Some in the family thought that Bob was justified in the occasional spankings he gave his kids, but Danny resented them. He would later claim to have learned to be aggressive from his dad.

"So, you're a tough guy?" Bob Pelosi asked Danny after the incident. "Maybe you can make a career out of it and make some money."

He signed Danny up for boxing lessons. He assumed that Danny would get his fill of violence by being knocked around in the ring. But Danny was the one who did the knocking around. He could take a hit and keep on swinging. He had a lot of rage. He went through one sparring partner after another. Danny got into it, learning combinations, footwork, and timing. He was a natural. Soon, his new goal was not to play baseball but to go to the Golden Gloves and then to the Olympics as a boxer and grab the gold.

Danny grew from a short wimp into a tough-guy ladies' man. He started to hang out with a bad crowd in high school. Strangely, he chose to begin speaking in a crude, uneducated way, unlike his parents. His teeth were crooked and he seemed to chew his words and spit them out. He was hanging out with rough kids from blue collar backgrounds and using their profanity-laced dese-dem-dose brand of speech. He felt that he had to be strong and tough because his father wanted him to be that way—so he could protect the family.

He and his friends got into trouble for stealing a case of beer, the first of many scrapes with the law. Danny's parents were appalled at his arrest but they hired a lawyer and stood by him, as they would in the future.

When Danny was seventeen, his parents began having marital problems that would eventually end in divorce years later, a traumatic event for the entire family. His father later married a colleague at the bank, another vice president named Dorothy. Danny was deeply affected by the split and seemed rudderless. He began to act out. He had a chip on his shoulder but took pride in the fact that he could handle himself:

"I don't take no shit from nobody."

Danny's official quote for his high school yearbook was, "Let each become all that he is capable of being."

In February 1980, Danny got kicked out of high school for trespassing on school grounds.

Like a character in a bad Hollywood teen movie, Danny tried to take five girls to the prom, by picking them up separately, dropping them off, making an excuse, and picking up another in his father's new Cadillac. Danny was trying to have his prom cake and eat it too, and was doing well—until a car accident interfered with his plans.

The next morning, after Danny did not come home, Bob Pelosi found his new car and Danny at a repair shop. The hood was bent over the smashed windshield and there was a girl sprawled across the backseat.

"Wait! I can explain!" Danny yelped, running from his father, dodging around the vehicle until his old man gave up.

"Listen, Jocko, you can run but you can't hide. You gotta come home sooner or later," Bob told him.

Danny met his future wife, Tamara, who called herself Tami, at a graduation party in the summer after senior year. Tami was an active student, a member of the volleyball team, the Leaders Club, and the prom committee. She didn't particularly like Danny. For her yearbook quote, Tami chose, "A friend is someone who understands your past, believes in your future and accepts you today just the way you are." Tami was at the party with her boyfriend Ralph,* who was six-foot-one. They were having an argument and Ralph slapped Tami across the face in front of everyone. Danny's father had always taught him that hitting a woman was a terrible thing and Danny intervened.

"Hey, try me, asshole," he said, slapping Ralph.

They had words and went outside, where Danny dropped the bigger teen with a three-punch combo—a quick left and a right to the body and then an uppercut.

"Ralph, from now on, she's dating me," Danny told him; then, turning to Tami: "Hey, from now on, you're dating me."

"No, no, no," Tami protested.

But the next day he kissed her and she agreed.

Danny was arrested again, this time for assault. He got twenty days in jail, on the Suffolk Honor Farm in Yaphank. He would later drop out of boxing competition, making the unlikely claim that his arrest had ended his career in the ring. He was never a contender. His father told him that he hoped his jail term would teach him a lesson.

When he got out of the honor farm a month later, Danny was picked up at the front gate by Tami's father and grandfather. Tami was pregnant.

"You're gonna do the right thing by my granddaughter, right?"

"Right," said Danny.

In March 1982, Danny and Tami got married. Danny got a heart-shaped tattoo on his left bicep, to commemorate the occasion:

"Tami."

4

VALLEY OF HEART'S DELIGHT

Generosa, the orphaned baby of the family, formed a special relationship with her aunt Marge, but the other kids at Uncle Al's house were somewhat resentful. Marge wished that Generosa could stay but there was not enough room, and the friction and jealousy among the kids was building. The smallest thing would set her off and she would lash out viciously. She seemed secretive, devious, manipulative, an outsider. She was just nasty and she was going to get what she wanted and get it her way or not at all. Generosa's cousin, Al Jr., who was two years older, thought that Generosa was scary and learned to stay out of her way.

Dolly had become a problem teen and was sent to Santa Clara to live with her and Generosa's older half-sister, Terry, along with her husband and their two younger girls.

Marge had a rich friend, Jane Reagan,* who lived in Laguna Beach with her husband and young son and daughter. They also owned a beautiful eight-bedroom home and horse ranch in the scenic Santa Inez Valley. Jane offered to adopt her. Generosa went to live with the Reagans in the lap of luxury. It was every little girl's dream—to live on a ranch and have her own horse to ride every day. Her surroundings were idyllic, with the golden, rolling hills, a swimming pool, and stables. Her new guardians taught her to ride and care for a horse—and to jump, the most exciting thing Generosa had ever done in her life. She got a feeling of joy and power in the saddle, as her stallion obeyed the commands of her hands and feet and she flew over the landscape. It was as if they were one huge majestic thing, hurtling over fences and obstacles in their path, freed and unstoppable. Generosa was good at it, competing in horse shows and winning ribbons. She also began doing well in school and they gave her piano lessons and had her teeth straightened. She was a rich girl, with a loving mother and father, living on an estate and riding her own horse.

Generosa, who had a tendency to be chubby, was beginning to mature into a woman. She was pretty, like her mother, with lustrous, wavy, natural blond hair, high cheekbones, and fine features. Her perfect smile was lovely but would vanish with the onset of one of her increasingly frequent temper tantrums. Her facial features would undergo an alarming, almost frightening transformation. Generosa had changed from a sweet child into a sometimes moody, rebellious adolescent and no one knew the reason why.

In late 1967, the Reagans called Generosa's half-sister Terry and explained that Generosa was causing problems in the household with the other children. She was very demanding, never satisfied with anything, no matter how good it was, they said. She measured love by the yardstick of material possessions. The Reagans were worn out. Generosa was rejected again. Terry, who knew what it was like to be abandoned, agreed to take Generosa.

In January 1968, the Reagans had Generosa flown by private plane up to Santa Clara, near San Jose, California, to a spot called the Valley of Heart's Delight, because of the beautiful bounty of endless fruit orchards. The orchards were steadily being replaced by houses and the computer industry later rechristened the area Silicon Valley. Generosa joined her sister Dolly at the home of Terry and Dick, a high school English teacher, and their daughters Amy and Julie. The comfortable four-bedroom, two-bath house, in the middle of an orchard, was big enough to give Generosa her own room but she was not happy to be there. She was seething with anger and resentment. There were no stables, no horses, no swimming pool, no estate with riding trails. It had all been snatched away.

Generosa unpacked, taking out her most prized possession, a leather bridle worn by the horse that she would never ride again. She hung her bridle in the place of honor, on the wall, announcing who she was, where she came from, and where she was going. When Generosa left the room, little Julie, all of four years old, peeked in and saw the weathered leather loops, the chewed bit. Her eyes widened in awe. A real bridle from a real horse. To her, the metal fittings sparkled with stars. She wondered what it was like to ride your very own pony. She was drawn to the magical bridle and tiptoed in. She reached out and reverently touched it, sniffed the musky animal aroma that clung to it. Generosa's screams snapped her out of her reverie.

"That's mine! Don't ever touch it!" Generosa screeched, hitting Julie. "Get out of my room! You don't belong in here!"

After a few months, Generosa calmed down, but her attitude and hair-trigger temper never went away. She was also becoming a talented artist.

As soon as she turned eighteen, Dolly left and got an apartment in San Jose with friends. Terry, who knew that Dolly also had suffered an abusive childhood, understood her need for independence, but worried what would happen to her. On her own, Dolly soon got into a fast crowd that was into drugs and sex.

Terry, who had been sexually abused by a family member as a child, was one of several in the clan who suffered from bipolar disorder. In 1970, she descended suddenly into a dark place, a depression that she could not shake. The deeper Terry sank, the more difficult Generosa became, almost as if she sensed her weakness. Every request was met with an argument. She often reminded Terry that she was her sister, not

her mother, which doubly hurt Terry, considering that she
had invited Generosa into her home rather than abandon her.
Terry and Dick thought that she was becoming a bad influ-
ence on the other girls, who saw her getting away with things
they could not. Although it was a tough decision for them,
Terry's illness made it necessary. In June, Dick explained to
Generosa that Terry was not well and could not handle her.
The situation was not working out. Generosa's heart sank.
She had heard speeches like it before and knew what was
coming. She was right. She had to go the next month.

"Well, whatever happens, I love you and we'll just have
to do what we can do," Dick said.

"I understand that," Generosa said. "I love you."

Generosa cried over the rejection by her fourth family.
She had been pushed away by her mother, her uncle, the
Reagans, and now by Terry and Dick. No one wanted her.
Each time she was kicked out, there were fewer tears and
more anger. Her trust was burning away into wrath.

Generosa was sent back briefly to her uncle Al's home in
Emerald Bay. They did not know what to do with the rebellious thirteen-year-old, and appealed to another side of the
family to take her in. They called Fran Thomas, who had
two teenage daughters, and asked her to take Generosa—just
for the summer vacation.

Fran and her husband, Les, agreed. Her honey-colored
hair in pigtails, Generosa arrived at Fran's home in Los Angeles in July 1970. They were distantly related by marriage
but they were strangers. Fran's daughter Carol was eighteen,
Mary Beth had just turned sixteen, and Generosa was four-
teen. Nobody asked her about the death of her mother or
about the hard times she'd had or even why her sister had
sent her away, particularly since she was there only for the
summer. But the problems soon began. Generosa moved into
Mary Beth's bedroom. Suddenly, Mary Beth had lost half of
her room. Both Mary Beth and Generosa felt put out at the
accommodations.

Sometimes Generosa would just vanish. Someone would eventually ask, "Where's Generosa?" and a search would begin. Several times they found her sitting alone in the car, in the garage, looking frightened. They thought it odd, but they did not know about Generosa's deep, secret place inside her.

Fran soon discovered that Generosa was not there just for a vacation. She was there because no one else wanted her. She had worn out her welcome everywhere else. She discussed it with her husband, Les, and they made some inquiries and then sat down with their daughters to discuss it.

"Generosa needs a home," Fran explained. "What do you girls think?"

They liked Generosa but had a few questions. It was a big adjustment for everyone. Mary Beth and Carol agreed to welcome Generosa into their family and she was called in to the family conference. Fran told Generosa that they wanted to invite her to become part of their family. She told her that they were lucky enough to have talked the nuns at St. Mary's Academy, where Mary Beth and Carol were students, into accepting her in September.

Generosa's reaction stunned them. St. Mary's wasn't good enough for her and she wasn't particularly interested in anything Catholic, it seemed. She had most recently been Protestant and for years had lived like a rich girl and now she demanded her due.

"I want to go to a boarding school where they have horses," she declared.

Fran told her that she would go to St. Mary's or leave.

Generosa donned the St. Mary's uniform under protest and the family settled into a routine of school and work.

They soon discovered that Generosa hated anything around her that she thought was ugly and tried to make it beautiful. One day, Mary Beth came home to find her bedroom dresser painted orange by the artistic Generosa. The sliding closet door now featured a gigantic orange-and-blue butterfly. She began turning out paintings with her own unique spectrum. One work featured a strange, blue sun radiating orange rays on a fantasy landscape.

As time went on, Fran and others in the family suspected
that Generosa, whose moods blew suddenly hot and cold,
suffered from manic-depression. She was a very intelligent
and creative girl but she did not want to be at St. Mary's and
didn't care who knew it. She did nothing horrible but the
nuns were not interested in smart alecks. By Christmas, it
had reached a crisis. Fran was called to St. Mary's and the
nuns gave her the bad news: "We don't want her back."

"What's the matter?"

"Well, her mouth, her attitude. We took her in on your
girls' reputation and she's not like them."

Fran was embarrassed and outraged. She had begged the
nuns to find a place for Generosa and now she implored
them to give her a chance to straighten the girl out. They
didn't say no but they obviously thought it was a waste of
time. At home, there was a showdown at the kitchen table
and Fran confronted Generosa and told her that she had to
decide if she wanted to be part of their family.

"Generosa, you've got a wall that you've built to protect
yourself. You sit behind the wall and you tell me that I don't
love you and that everybody else doesn't love you. You have
to take that wall down yourself, brick by brick," said Fran.
"I'm going to ask you a question, young lady, and you're the
only one who can answer it. I will not put up with this shit. I
will not have you put out of school."

She asked Generosa if she was willing to change and
warned her that she had to shape up or ship out. Again.

"I will make two phone calls. The first will be to your uncle but he won't take you. The second call will be to find you
a foster home."

Generosa was quiet but didn't cry. She had no more tears.
She looked at Fran and thought before answering.

"Well, I know what I have to do."

She was subdued, and slowly, surely, she changed her attitude and did well in school. After she straightened out,

Generosa joined the tennis team and she and Mary Beth played together. Generosa spent as much time as she could on her art. Like many teenage girls, she began to develop a picture in her mind of the ideal husband: rich, handsome, and supportive. Her favorite television show was a new one, *The Mary Tyler Moore Show,* which opened with the young Mary arriving in the big city to make a new start and make her mark, throwing her cap in the air as someone sang, "You're gonna make it after all."

The next year, in 1971, Fran got a call from Generosa's uncle Al. He told her that her sister Dolly had been killed in a car crash. Dolly was a passenger in the car when another vehicle broadsided it. Generosa had been close with Dolly and cried for her dead sister. It seemed she did have more tears, after all.

They had started out as strangers but Generosa, Mary Beth, and Carol quickly became sisters. She began calling Fran "Mom." Generosa did not date in high school but went everywhere with Mary Beth and her boyfriend Steve. One day, Steve let Generosa, who wasn't yet sixteen, drive his car in an empty parking lot and she came alive. She floored it and sped around and around. Generosa loved driving fast. It made her happy. On her sixteenth birthday, her uncle Al gave her a red 1966 Mustang. It was her first car and she loved it. She drove fast, with the windows open, her blond hair blowing in the California breeze, and the stereo loudly playing Jimi Hendrix.

Generosa stayed with Fran and her family until 1975, when she started her freshmen year at the University of California at Irvine. There was more room at Uncle Al's home in Emerald Bay after Al Jr. went off to college, so she moved in and began bicycling to college every day, a trip of almost fifteen miles. She took sculpture but concentrated on painting classes. She developed a controlled, minimalist abstract style popular at the time. She also became involved with photography and showed some artistic talent there as well. Generosa had an eye, a genuine talent for art and design. She jogged on the beach and felt that she was on her own and independent, although her uncle was paying the bills.

In 1977, Generosa's uncle Al Legaye legally adopted her. It was a big secret, and Al Jr. was blown away when he found out about it. He was not the only one in the family to wonder about the change. Al told his wife, Marge, that he wanted to make Generosa feel like she had a family, that she belonged. When Al's other kids found out about the adoption, they were unhappy and resented it, childhood rivalries surfacing once more. Generosa did not take the Legaye name. She assumed that her uncle and aunt had adopted her together. But Marge was actually against it—because there seemed no reason for it and she felt that it would just cause bitterness in the family. Later, when Generosa found out that Marge had not joined Al in the adoption, she stopped talking to her.

The following year, Generosa began to work with her uncle in his office furniture leasing business. Despite her artistic temperament, she became increasingly interested in family finances and money in general. She asked her uncle for money for various reasons and he told her that the family trust fund had been used up years before. She had great difficulty trusting anybody and did not believe him. She felt she had been cheated out of her inheritance, her mother's share of the family farm. She decided that anything she wanted, she would have to get for herself.

Howard Ashe,* who also lived in Emerald Bay, was introduced to Generosa in 1979 and found her charming, witty, and attractive. He asked her for a date and they drove up to L.A., to the Music Center, to see a musical and go out to dinner. He had barely begun to speak when Generosa interrupted him. She wanted to find out what he intended to do with his life, what his prospects were. And more.

"What does your family do?" she asked.

Howard thought that was strange.

Actually, his family was rather wealthy, but they were not the type to show it. He thought that her prying questions were in poor taste. He began to tell her about his family, but

Generosa continued to probe, asking very specific questions about how much money they made.

Jeez, on a first date, he thought.

What a turnoff. Suddenly he felt as though he were being interviewed for a credit report. Howard was surprised by the driving ambition underneath the artistic veneer, how directed she was. The other artsy types he had met were just the opposite. He never asked her out again.

Generosa graduated from the University of California at Irvine in March 1981 and began making money from her art and design work. She soon announced that she was moving to New York to make it in the art world.

Once in Manhattan, she began systematically cutting herself off from virtually everyone who knew her when. Her sister Terry, who regretted the necessity of turning Generosa out, wrote to her in an effort to apologize and reconnect. Terry's heartfelt letters were returned, unopened. On one, Generosa had hurtfully scrawled, "I don't want to hear from you again."

Several people who knew of Generosa's artistic talent and burning drive to succeed expected her to become rich and famous. They were certain that they would read about her in the newspapers one day.

5

THE RELUCTANT LAWYER

Ted entered the freshman class at Bucknell University in August 1967. The postcard campus was situated on a hill above the Susquehanna River in central Pennsylvania. Ted played lacrosse and pledged to the Phi Gamma Delta fraternity. He started out to be an architect because he wanted to build things. He changed his major five times and finally settled on an unusual double major in arts and in economics, a reflection of his business upbringing and his desire to create. Ted played football and had a lot of fun with new girlfriends and his teammates and frat brothers. Just as in high school, he was hardworking but a bit of a procrastinator and didn't need to work as hard as others to get good grades, because of his innate intelligence and phenomenal memory. He decided to enter the U.S. Air Force to be a pilot and signed up for the Reserve Officer Training Corps. His parents had a fit, but Ted later washed out because he failed his eye exam. He supported the government and was in favor of the Vietnam War on the grounds that it fought communism. On a college campus in the 1960s, it was a decidedly minority and unpopular viewpoint. When Bucknell students demonstrated against the war, Ted grabbed an American flag and took to the street in a spontaneous counterdemonstration with a few other conservative students. His family was amused to suddenly see him on the news that evening, enthusiastically waving Old Glory.

"Look, it's Ted!"

He graduated from college in June 1971, still uncertain about what he was going to do. But about one thing, he was certain. Ted did not want to follow in his father's footsteps. He did not want to be a company man, spending thirty years with the same firm, working his way slowly up the corporate ladder. Ted did not want to go where people knew him or his dad, or to some industrial or business perch for Bucknell alumni. He wanted to do something different. His girlfriend at the time lived in San Francisco and Ted decided he wanted to try the other coast, the path less traveled. He packed all his stuff into his Ford Pinto and drove cross-country. Although the 1970s had begun, it was still the 1960s socially, especially in San Francisco and in California. By this time, Ted, although still patriotic, had changed his view of the Vietnam War. But he was not on a hippie journey of self-exploration to find himself, he was just looking to find his own way in the world. He was not worried about selling out but was simply looking for the right buyer, or, better, for a role as an entrepreneur, which appealed to him a great deal more than being a corporate yesman. His girlfriend's father was a department store executive and he got Ted a job in the shipping and receiving department of a warehouse. The relationship with his girlfriend did not work out but Ted enjoyed being on his own for seven months, working in the real world, while he tried to find his place.

He finally applied to a training program for international banking in San Francisco and was accepted. Ted immersed himself in the Bank of America training program and quickly learned about international finance. One of his fellow trainees was an attractive, sharp young woman named Randee Day and they hit it off immediately. Randee was athletic like Ted, but almost a head shorter, slim and blond. Ted had always been attracted to beautiful, intelligent, competitive women, and their romance developed during their intense training period.

They both graduated from the course and Randee, who
was a year older, got a job right away, in England. Ted followed her there and they set up housekeeping in London.
They married at Christmastime in 1974. Eventually, Ted decided that international banking was interesting but he also
wanted to become a lawyer. The only problem was that he
had not gone to law school. Undaunted, Ted began to study
on his own and hired a tutor. He took the English legal test
and passed. He began working with a British law firm that
specialized in maritime law. He and Randee cultivated a new
circle of English colleagues and friends. One close friend
was Colin Hastings,* an American who worked for Randee.
Colin and his wife became lifelong friends of Ted and
Randee. They went skiing every year in the Austrian alps.

When Randee was transferred to New York, they both returned home. Ted then studied for and took the bar exam in
New York, and also passed that the first time, without the
bother of attending law school. He went to work for a presti-
gious law firm and then for another but soon became bored
with the routine tasks assigned to junior associates at law
firms.

Ted's parents had moved back to Pittsburgh and one
Christmas Ted brought his bride home for the holidays. He
introduced Randee to his parents and his sister Sandi and her
husband, Bob Williams, a tall doctor from Alabama with a
laconic Southern drawl and a dry sense of humor. Ted and
Sandi teamed up against Randee and Bob in a game of Monopoly. It quickly became intense, with Randee and Ted
competing fiercely to rule the board. Ted loved games and
he loved winning but he lost that day.

In 1978, Ted and his family were shaken by the death of
his father. Ted was in the middle of a big case when he got
the news but he calmly completed his work before yielding
to his emotions.

Both Ted and Randee worked long hours and had to endure time apart because of Randee's travel, which at first
just made their time together more precious and exciting.

But as the years went by, the pace did not slow, and they had too little time to work on their relationship. They drifted apart, but still Ted was devastated when Randee told him that she wanted to call it quits. He wanted to work it out but she was adamant and eventually they agreed to a legal separation and went their own ways. Randee had chosen her profession and was busily engaged in it, but Ted was still unsure whether he wanted to continue to be a lawyer. He had to go by the book—the law—the instruction manual for lawyers. There was little room for creative thought or solutions. It was boring. He was also in a hurry. He wanted to make a lot of money, so it was logical to try to make it as quickly as possible.

In 1983, Ted and Randee got a divorce but they were still cordial. Their marriage wasn't a disaster, it had just never developed. They vowed always to remain friends.

6

REHAB

Danny got a job at a local gas station. He and Tami used their wedding money to transform her parents' cellar into an apartment. Danny's next job was as a laborer with the masonry firm that employed Tami's father. The pay was $240 a week.

In August 1981, Danny got busted again, for unauthorized use of a motor vehicle. Bob Pelosi got a call, late at night, to go and bail his son out. Whenever Danny got arrested, he called his dad, who got him out of jail by paying for a lawyer and bail.

On July 14, 1982, Danny was sent to work at a commercial work site in Farmingdale. While he was swinging a sledgehammer above a false ceiling, the ceiling beam gave way. He crashed through and fell nine feet to the floor below, in a downpour of wood, ceiling tiles, fenders, and auto parts. The next thing Danny knew, he was dazed, on his back, and on the floor. The following day, he went to a hospital, where he found he had a concussion and cuts and bruises. X-rays revealed a herniated disk in his lumbar area. Once he was home from the hospital, he took prescribed Valium for the pain, and it worked, at first. But soon he had to take more and more pills to get the same relief because he was building up a tolerance. He started out by taking two pills every four hours and ended up going through bottles of the stuff. He was hooked. When he couldn't get enough to kill the pain, he drank on top of it. He was laid up in bed for three months, on his stomach. Every time he lifted his head it throbbed so much, it felt like it would explode. The only things that dulled the ache were the pills and the booze.

Their first child, Rachelle, was born in September 1982. Danny added her name to the heart-shaped tattoo on his left bicep that already bore his wife's name. With little money coming in, except what food and cash came from Tami's parents and other family, Danny and Tami went on welfare for six months in order to receive Aid to Dependent Children. They were supposed to pay rent but they never did. As his drinking and pill popping increased, Danny got into two more minor car accidents. In the summer of 1983, he was busted for DWI but refused to submit to a blood test to determine whether he was drunk. A judge later suspended his license.

Danny took whatever jobs he could find but his arrest record made it tough to find anything decent. When he didn't have a job, he pulled junk out of nearby woods to sell for scrap metal. He collected cans, copper pipes, car batteries. When he had a few bucks, he would go to used-car auctions and "turn over" cars. He would buy a junker for four hundred dollars, wash it, and then sell it for seven hundred—a substantial profit, but the scale was small, requiring constant turnover to live hand-to-mouth.

In November 1983, Danny left the scene of a two-car accident and was arrested again for drunk driving. He had also been on Valium and marijuana. Two months later, he was involved in a four-car pileup on the Long Island Expressway.

He came home drunk on yet another night and began yelling at Tami. His little daughter began to cry and scream because she was afraid of him. When he realized that, he felt ashamed. He had hit bottom. His entire family confronted him about his addiction and he agreed to try to kick the habit, for them, for his daughter, for himself. He and his wife went for marriage counseling.

Throwing off the yoke of drug addiction is a difficult and dangerous process. But, rather than go to a doctor or a hospital, Danny decided on a do-it-yourself approach. Typically, he chose an instant, head-on, manly plan of attack. He would go cold turkey and sell his Valium prescriptions for cash. He got a pair of handcuffs and chained himself to a column in a friend's basement for three days. It worked, to a point. With his dungeon rack method, Danny had stripped his body of Valium. But he had also ripped off his protective cocoon of numbness and exposed the forgotten lower-back pain that the pills had kept buried for two years. He celebrated with scotch, which again dulled the pain. As with the dope, he soon got into a rut: He would consume copious quantities of booze until he felt nothing and passed out, a pattern he would follow for the next five years. Soon, his family noticed that he had simply replaced drug with drink. Tami confronted him.

"Look, you stop taking Valium, you're drinking like a fish," she said.

The arguments, problems, and debts continued. The couple broke up and Danny moved out, each dated other people for four months. Six months after his basement experience, Danny's family again pressured him to get professional help for his problem and he finally agreed.

In February 1984, Bob Pelosi took his son in for rehabilitation at the C.K. Post Alcoholism Treatment Center in West Brentwood, Long Island, on the grounds of a state mental hospital. Danny had been drinking but he and his father were told that he was not drunk enough. Only acute cases were admitted. It was absurd, but Bob had to take Danny out to a bar to get him really drunk—so that he could give up drinking. When they returned, Danny was sufficiently smashed.

Dr. George Smith* asked him what and how much he drank.

"Beer. A case a day," said Danny.

"For how long?"

A year, year and a half, Danny replied. He listed his history of arrests for drunk driving, assault, and other offenses and said that he was on probation. He blamed his drinking on the accident.

"Have you had hallucinations?" Dr. Smith asked.

"Yes."

"Have you thought about suicide?"

"I thought about hanging myself," Danny said.

After more questions and an exam, Smith decided that Danny could not care for himself and admitted him to the facility. Danny was taken to a room without a lock in the closed facility, where he was given some Valium and told to sleep it off. The professionals concluded that Danny was using alcohol to dull his considerable anger, which he was using to deny the emotions of hurt and self-pity. He was impulsive, had a bad temper and no self-discipline. Within two days, Danny was slacking off and being disobedient. A month after he was admitted, he began having angry outbursts. At the end of the first week in April, Danny went home on a weekend pass and returned a day late. He vanished a second time and admitted on his return that he had sneaked out of the building. He was kicked out of rehab. It was strike two.

Danny went back to his old ways, looking for work, hustling, drinking. Occasionally he went to AA meetings but he even got kicked out of one of those after he began screaming at a guy who was speaking. Danny went to a lawyer to find out if he might still be able to file a lawsuit over his back injury and the lawyer told him yes. In December 1984, Danny and Tami filed a $2.5 million civil lawsuit in Suffolk County Supreme Court against the business on whose work site he had been injured in the fall two years earlier. The court papers said that Danny's back injury was worth $2 million. Danny's sexual services to his wife, the "comfort and happiness in his society and companionship" that she no longer had due to the accident, were valued at $500,000.

The next month, Danny went back to court to plead guilty to his 1983 DWI charge. The judge sentenced him to sixty days in jail. He served forty days of that sentence at the Suffolk County Honor Farm. He didn't have to kick booze because he was able to get it on the sly at the farm.

The following year, in December 1985, Danny was arrested again, this time for possession of burglar's tools and resisting arrest. For a change, Danny's friend was the one driving drunk—but Danny got busted anyway. A cop pulled them over in the small Hamptons village of Quogue at night, gave the driver a drunk test, and arrested him. Danny started mouthing off at the cop, just as another one arrived. He shoved one of the cops and ended up behind bars again.

His second child, Danny Jr., was born in February 1986. The joyous occasion was marred by the fact that Danny had to go on welfare again for several months to secure the benefits for his new baby that he could not provide. Tami, already caring for both kids and running their home, was also going to college. In June, she received her associate degree in early-childhood education. She did an internship at a nursery school and then worked there for a year as a teacher. She also cleaned houses and babysat to make money. Eventually, she went to the New York Institute for Alcoholism and Addiction for one year to become an alcoholism counselor. Tami was now officially qualified to deal with her husband's problems.

In December 1987, Danny was busted again, this time for assault with a weapon—hitting a bartender with a glass of beer during a drunken argument. Again, his father was awakened by a phone call, and again he bailed Danny out and paid for a lawyer.

By 1988, things were beginning to look up. Danny and Tami moved out of her parents' basement and into their own rented home, on the street where Danny had grown up. But in July of that year, Danny was arrested a second time on drunk driving charges. He was driving his younger brother James's truck and told cops that his name was James Pelosi. They soon discovered he was lying. Once more, Bob Pelosi bailed Danny out and paid for the lawyer. Exasperated, he informed Danny that he had spent about forty thousand dollars on bail and lawyers for all of his arrests.

The next year, in February 1989, Danny got a third opportunity to stop drinking, when he pleaded guilty to DWI and the barroom brawl charges. A judge sentenced him to six months in the Alcoholic Rehabilitation Program of Suffolk County, in Yaphank, otherwise known as the Drunk Farm. Unlike other places he had been, there were no open windows to sneak out of for a drink, no hootch for sale by inmates.

Whether he liked it or not, Danny had just given up drinking.

He attended Alcoholics Anonymous sessions behind bars and tried to learn to deal with his anger and rage and stay sober, one day at a time. He exercised and did whatever else he had to do to get through the day.

Danny was released on the Friday before Memorial Day weekend in 1989. He went to an AA meeting the same day he was released. During meetings, he would make the familiar introduction:

"Hi, my name is Danny and I'm an alcoholic."

He went through a lot of the usual torments of recovering alcoholics. He got the shakes. He had nightmares. He fought intense cravings for a drink to stop the pain. Sometimes he got the dry drunks, in which he would wake up sober but feel drunk. These symptoms would come and go for the next two years. Finally, Danny really stopped drinking. He would spend the next nine years sober. His loyal family was overjoyed that at last he had quit drinking and getting arrested. He worked hard, came home at night, and became a better father. It looked as if Danny had straightened up and was flying right. Because he had kicked booze, he was allowed to move back into his in-laws' house, with Tami. He started doing electrical work again although he never got an electrician's license.

In October 1990, Tami's grandfather gave them a generous present of ten thousand dollars in cash to make a down payment on their own home in Manorville, a rural community near Center Moriches. That same year, their son Anthony was born. Danny had his sons' names tattooed onto his right bicep, along with an American eagle.

Throughout all the money hassles, legal problems, and other screw-ups, Danny held out hope that his upcoming civil lawsuit over his 1982 fall would fix it all, would get him out of the hole and become a sizable score—the Big Payout.

PART TWO

Flowers

7

FIRST FIGHT

Generosa Rand was a working artist, a New Yorker for just two years in the spring of 1983. She was a serious painter, sculptor, and photographer and was busy networking in the art and gallery scene, hustling to get shown. None of her works had human beings in them. They were all abstract compositions of form and shadow, line and texture. Generosa loved to go to construction sites with her camera and photograph giant rolls of cable, stacks of pipes, and other building materials. She also liked watching the rough, muscular construction workers, with their rude language and crude sexuality, but she never took their pictures. Her work showed talent and promise but, to pay the bills, she got a New York real estate license and worked for a firm selling and renting high-end real estate. Generosa had reinvented herself in Manhattan, portraying herself as a creative, rich trust-fund brat from sunny California, who was working for a living as a hoot. There was a trust fund, of course, but it had gone bust years earlier. Generosa, through the art crowd, had gotten an entrée into the core of the Big Apple's wealthy circles. Her real estate job also allowed her to enter the universe of the New York elite, for whom real estate was akin to religion. She looked the part of a blond, horsey-set heiress and she certainly knew how to ride well and play tennis. She also knew how to talk, which names to drop, and how to dress, and had a wonderful sense of style and design, an eye for quality and beauty. But part of her haughty, mercurial, artistic temperament was her contempt for the upper classes and their pretensions, or so she said. Generosa told her friends that she was not like those shallow society matrons who defined themselves by their rich husbands and lived vicariously through their spoiled, pampered children. But despite her protestations, Generosa was drawn to money and the lifestyle it could buy, all the fine things she appreciated. Because Generosa's New York friends thought she came from wealth, her bitterness about New York's millionaires did not seem like sour grapes. It seemed like strength of character.

Ted, an up-and-coming lawyer on the rebound from his divorce from Randee, was enjoying his new single life and the money that allowed him to live well. While working at his Manhattan law firm, Ted had dealings with the well-known firm KKR—Kohlberg Kravis Roberts—which had become famous for perfecting the controversial but highly profitable business of LBOs, leveraged buyouts, of big corporations. It seemed to Ted that these guys were on the cutting edge, banking buccaneers who raided the value locked up in fat, undervalued, publicly held corporations and made off with piles of loot. Ted let his friends at KKR know that he was interested. Ted was successful but was still looking for someone to complete his life. He liked being a bachelor but he also wanted a partner and a family. Part of him yearned to come home at six-thirty every night to his wife and kids and sit down for a family dinner, just as his father had done.

Looking for new digs, Ted went through the *New York Times* real estate ads and found a likely place, in the low nineties on the Upper East Side, near the East River. He called the number and reached a woman with a sweet, almost childlike voice and an unusual name, Generosa Rand.

She had an accent but Ted could not quite place it. He made an appointment to see the apartment. But he was unexpectedly busy that day and decided to blow off the real estate woman. He never showed up. The next day, he got an angry call at the office. Generosa laced into him and told him that he was rude. She had waited for him until after dark. How dare he just not show up? she wanted to know. Who did he think he was? Did he think he was the only one who was busy, the only one whose time was valuable? This time, the childlike voice had an edge of steel in it. Generosa was furious and could not stand rich people who thought they could treat others like dirt. It was not your typical, the-customer-is-always-right response. Apparently this Generosa didn't care about kissing up to him to make a sale. Ted felt a bit guilty, having his chivalry challenged, and he was intrigued by the tough saleslady. Maybe it was a smart technique, after all. He apologized and set up another appointment, promising to keep it. It seemed as if they already had a relationship. Ted and Generosa had their first fight before they had their first date.

Ted kept the appointment and was instantly glad he did when he saw Generosa in person. The tough-cookie voice went with a slim, sexy blond young woman. She obviously knew her business, even though the apartment wasn't really right for Ted. He was, instead, interested in her. He asked her out for coffee, saying that he wanted to make up for his behavior, and Generosa agreed. They went out and began to chat, and Ted, now thirty-four, was infatuated with the twenty-seven-year-old Generosa. She obviously liked what she saw too. At first, they talked about finding a place for Ted, to their mutual advantage. Soon, they dropped the pretense of business and began dating regularly. They had a lot of fun together and Ted was proud to show her off. Ted was a lawyer but he also loved art and architecture. He appreciated her art and photography and her keen sense of style and beauty. They also shared a love of the finer things in life and dissatisfaction with their current jobs. Both had larger ambitions. If anything, Generosa was even more decisive and ambitious than Ted. They were driven, brilliant, creative people and the sparks flew. Their affair burned hot and fast and they were soon in bed together. Within a month they were living together.

Ted was ready for the relationship and enthralled with Generosa but not ready to get serious. He had just been dumped and was not even close to thinking about remarrying. Generosa, although fun to be with, was serious about everything. He told her that he was considering the possibility of quitting his law firm. He had had an offer from a well-known powerhouse firm that specialized in the incredibly lucrative field of corporate takeovers. Generosa encouraged him to make the move.

Ted called his sister Sandi one night and said he had some news: "Sis, I've met somebody," Ted said, with a tremble in his voice. Obviously, he thought she was somebody special.

"I really like this lady. Come up for Memorial Day, and if I'm still dating her, you'll like her."

Sandi and her husband Bob met Generosa and both liked her, although it was immediately apparent that hard-charging Generosa and laid-back Bob were from entirely different planets. Generosa was fun loving, witty, and bright. She was ambitious and competitive, like Randee, but also had a creative, artistic side. She was perfect for Ted. By the time Ted and Generosa visited Sandi and Bob and their two daughters, Wendy and Cheri, for Christmas 1983 at their home in Huntsville, Alabama, Ted and Generosa's relationship had become serious. When everyone was opening presents, Ted, with a sly smile, produced a small cube of black velvet and presented it to Generosa. Everyone gasped, believing that Ted was popping the question. But when she opened it, the jeweler's box contained a set of earrings. Everyone said they were lovely but it was a bit of a letdown for everyone, especially Generosa.

"Earrings?" said Sandi, when she met her mother in the kitchen. "What the heck are earrings?"

To Bob, it was obvious that Generosa was trying to catch

Ted, but his brother-in-law was a smart fish that had been landed before and thrown back in the pond. Ted was not about to bite on any hook, if he could help it.

Generosa was hurt, and after the holidays she told Ted that she was serious about him and about marriage and would not be trifled with. They discussed it and it came to a head in February 1984.

"Either we get married or I'm leaving," Generosa demanded.

Ted was not ready to get married and he said so. This time, Generosa's hard-sell sales technique backfired. They broke up. Generosa told her girlfriend Ronnie what had happened, how Ted had been such a cold bastard. Ronnie knew that Generosa was particularly stung by betrayal, something that had plagued her all her life.

Ted called Sandi to say that he had broken up with Generosa. Then, a distraught Generosa called.

"I never want to speak to him again," Generosa told Sandi, in a fury. "I am deeply hurt about how he did it."

There was tremendous anger in her voice. She felt betrayed and used. Sandi was very sympathetic but she was in an awkward position. Generosa wanted to remain friends. Ted later told Sandi that he had spoken to Generosa and asked Sandi not to contact Generosa and to wait until she heard from her.

"Don't call her, she'll call you," Ted told his sister.

Sandi liked Generosa but Ted was her brother. When Sandi did not call her back to commiserate, Generosa's temper flared again. Now she felt betrayed by Sandi and vowed never to speak to her again.

In June 1984, Ted left his law firm and was recruited by Kohlberg Kravis Roberts. This was the new direction Ted had been looking for and he dived into the world of LBOs and corporate takeovers with gusto. He worked long hours but found time to date a series of women. Generosa told Ronnie that she was very upset about it. Months later, Ronnie was chatting with another girlfriend when a familiar name came up.

"I've got to get going, I've got a date with Ted tonight," the girlfriend told Ronnie.

She described how tall, dark, and handsome Ted was, how much she liked him.

"Ted who?" Ronnie asked.

"Ted Ammon."

"Ted Ammon?" Ronnie was stunned.

She told her girlfriend about Generosa's experience with Ted, that she felt Ted had been leading her on. She persuaded her to drop Ted, who was surprised at the unexplained rejection. Ronnie never told Generosa. She knew it would hurt and humiliate her and she would just be furious at her girlfriend, whom she also knew—and maybe even at Ronnie. Generosa was a strong, opinionated woman with a bad temper but Ronnie valued her friendship.

On a rainy, breezy afternoon in October of that year, Ted and Generosa were in between paramours and pretty much off each other's minds when they almost literally bumped into each other in the cavernous Metropolitan Museum of Art, on Fifth Avenue. It was a startling coincidence, an opportunity for Generosa to vent her rage, but she did not. Instead, they were genuinely surprised and secretly pleased that fate had arranged what their pride would not have allowed. They chatted and agreed to go out for coffee. It took only a few breaths for the heat of their love to reignite, but Generosa made it clear that she had not changed. It would soon become clear that Ted had. He liked the way Generosa was never in doubt, the way she set goals and efficiently organized everything toward that end. She knew what she wanted and she went after it with all of her considerable energy. She was determined to make things better, to carve out the best life possible, a life surrounded by beauty. Soon after the brief encounter, Ted called Sandi.

"Sis, I'm in trouble."

"What's up?" she asked.

"Well, Generosa and I have started dating again."

"Oh, Ted, that's great news!"

"Well, I'm in trouble because she wants a ring this time."

"Well, it's about time," Sandi chided.

"Generosa has given me an ultimatum, that we're getting back together with a ring on her finger, or we're not getting back together."

Ted agreed to the demand and asked Generosa to marry him. She happily accepted. It was a fulfillment, a milestone for her, her first marriage, a necessary next step in her envisioned life. She went into high gear. Her marriage and her wedding would be perfect, a work of art.

The bride-to-be designed her own ring, a stunning double diamond ring with two huge stones. Generosa also designed the wedding, which was set for February 2, 1986, at an Episcopal church on Fifth Avenue, followed by a beautiful sitdown dinner, all artfully and expensively arranged, down to the last detail.

Generosa had begun carving out her perfect life.

8

WEDDING

Generosa was ecstatic planning her wedding. The step-by-step creation of the unique artwork that would be her nuptials engaged her mind and her artistic sensibility. The closer the wedding got, the more the details of guest list, hotel rooms, veil, gown, and menus arose; the more intense the bride-to-be became, her understandable enthusiasm building to a fever pitch and beyond.

She had already systematically cut herself off from most of her relatives from her California past, but after they became engaged, Generosa and Ted flew out to the coast, and she introduced him to her uncle Al, her adoptive father, in Emerald Bay. To Ted, it seemed as if he were marrying a trust-fund girl from a rich family, which is the way they wanted it to appear. Generosa's cousin, Al Jr., was there and met Ted for the first time, as well. He felt that his father and Generosa were hoodwinking Ted into believing that Generosa was to the manner born. Her uncle Al was impressed with Ted and bragged to anyone who would listen that Generosa was about to marry Ted Ammon, from KKR in New York, a handsome prince of the banking profession, a world-beater.

But before the wedding, Generosa broke off all contact with her uncle Al and mysteriously never spoke to him again. He told the family that he had no clue why she had suddenly cut him off. He said he had sent her an art book and never heard from her again.

"I guess I sent her the wrong book," he said, shrugging.

Ted sent a KKR corporate jet to California to pick up Generosa's aunt Marge, who had divorced her uncle Al, and whisked her in style to New York for the big event. Al Jr., a banker, and his wife, Generosa's best friend Sally, were also invited to the wedding. They were the only other ones "who knew her when" who had been invited. Generosa asked Sally to be her matron of honor. Generosa later became enraged when Al Jr. called her and told her that his wife, Sally, was having a difficult pregnancy and could not travel by jet, in a pressurized cabin, to New York. It meant that they would have to drive and she would miss the wedding rehearsal. Generosa angered her cousin when she made it clear that she felt her wedding was more important than a risk to their unborn child. She also scolded them when they balked at renting a tuxedo for their three-year-old son, an unacceptable lapse, the bride felt. Sally decided to stay away from her former girlfriend's wedding. Nothing had changed, Al Jr. thought. Generosa was still nasty and out for herself. She was going to get it her way, or not at all.

Al Jr. flew alone to LaGuardia Airport the night before the ceremony. Ted picked him up and drove him to the New York Athletic Club, where he would stay. They stopped off at Ted's office at KKR, a huge space with a million-dollar view of the skyline, and an executive dining room where the meals were prepared by the company's gourmet chef. He and Al Jr. talked about business and Ted told him not to be impressed by the world-class surroundings.

"Al, the deals you do are like the deals I do but there's just a change in the decimal point."

Yeah, right. Al chuckled. Ted liked money but he liked the art of the game more, Al Jr. realized. He liked Ted a lot more than he liked his cousin. Al Jr. understood Generosa's social-climbing attitude—because his goal had once been to be a millionaire by the age of twenty-one, and if anyone got in his way, he would run over them, just like Generosa. It was not an uncommon attitude in their family. They talked about Generosa and he warned Ted about her temper, that she would be hard to handle.

"You've got a big job, man."

Ted laughed.

Al Jr. felt that he had to warn Ted about his bride.

"Does Generosa know how much you make?" he asked.

"Here's the deal," Ted replied. "When it comes time to file my income tax return, all the pages are covered and she just signs it."

Al Jr. walked into the wedding rehearsal that night and came face-to-face with Generosa. When she looked at him, she was startled by how much he resembled his father, her uncle Al, when she was a little girl. It was almost like look- ing at the past. She did not kiss him on the cheek or say hello or apologize for her behavior. She was cold, filled with righ- teous indignation.

"You and Sally have shown me disrespect!" Generosa screamed at him. "I'm a New York socialite now and you can't disrespect me!"

Al Jr. was blown away. He couldn't believe his ears. She was nuts. He had had it.

"I will show you disrespect when I leave this room," he shot back. "I will leave the door open."

He turned and stormed out the door. He got a cab back to the Athletic Club, packed, and went back to the airport and got on the first flight home.

The wedding went on without him, a lovely affair, with a bride and groom who were obviously deeply in love and sin- cere that their love, as put in their wedding vows, would last "as long as they both shall live."

On the flight home, Al Jr. fumed about Generosa. The re- hearsal, the tuxedo, all of it was just an excuse for Gen- erosa's mysterious agenda. For some unknown reason, he decided, she wanted to close off her life before Ted by getting rid of everyone who had known her then. Unlike Ted, she obviously was a snob, who felt she was better than her own family. He knew that she had had a horrible childhood but that was no excuse for her behavior. Al Jr. didn't know her real reasons but he no longer cared. It would be a cold day in hell before he ever spoke to her again. He felt bad for Ted, though. He was a nice guy who had no idea what he was getting into.

9

LIFE OF ART

Ted and Generosa were a matched set, an intense, Type-A
Power Couple in Manhattan. After the wedding they
moved into a town house at Fifth Avenue and Seventy-fifth
Street. They began their married life as two of the most privileged people on the planet, on the Upper East Side of Manhattan; he the dashing, corporation-gobbling LBO pirate, she
the blond, blue-eyed trophy wife, gracious society hostess,
and equestrienne, but also an artist with attitude. Ted was
happy to have his new wife order their lives, down to the last
napkin ring, and he actually liked and encouraged her sarcastic, thumb-your-nose attitude. He found it amusing, except
when she occasionally turned it on him. She protested, to
anyone who cared to listen, that despite their upscale lifestyle
and her expensive tastes, she was not one of those shallow,
pampered, pretentious, rich society wives, one of that crowd
who cared only about money and position. She saw herself as
a maverick and despised such people. She was an artist with
vision. The couple threw lavish parties and were open to
meeting new people, which was a good thing, since Generosa
developed an unfortunate habit of blowing up friendships at
the first whiff of suspected betrayal.

Ted was now wealthy enough to have a limo and a driver

named Milton. Generosa hired a woman housekeeper and a personal assistant–butler named Steven, along with Steven's companion, Bruce, who became the cook.

Steven, the forty-five-year-old butler, was thin and balding and looked a bit like comic Bob Newhart. His companion, Bruce, was an excellent chef and enjoyed his own cooking so much that he was quite hefty. He was shorter, with dark hair and a bushy mustache that reminded some people of Gene Shalit.

Ted insisted on healthful organic meals and snacks and banned junk food from the house. Steven was into astrology, psychics, and the occult and inculcated Generosa in fashionably arcane superstitions. Bruce the cook claimed to be a spiritual medium, able to communicate with the dead. After their cat died, Bruce said he had contacted the feline spirit in the other world and talked to his dear, departed pet.

After having her astrological chart done, Generosa was unhappy with being an Aries, the sign of the Ram. She disliked the image of an insensitive battering ram, a personality with tremendous ambition and drive and difficulty dealing with others. The description fit her like a glove but conflicted with her preferred persona of an artist. She fudged her birthday to claim a Pisces cusp, because she liked the qualities of that sign more: a sensitive, perceptive, artistic type, with a tendency to create and live in ideal fantasy worlds.

"Well, I was born on March twenty-second, but I'm really a Pisces," Generosa claimed.

Generosa, the struggling artist, ran the household and the retinue of servants. Of course, no one called them servants. They were referred to as "staff." Generosa's staff did all of the domestic tasks, freeing her to pursue her art and photography career. She threw herself energetically into decorating and furnishing and redoing the place. Refurbishing was her favorite thing, even more so than her art. She was a pro, but when she was finished, there was a letdown after showing it

off, a bored funk, a depression. She seemed happiest when
in process, when she had a decorating project, transforming
ugliness into beauty; but she was vaguely ill at ease with
simply enjoying her creations.

They soon moved to another town house, a five-story
sandstone structure at 19 East Ninety-second Street, just east
of Central Park, in the Carnegie Hill historic district, which
was around the corner from Andrew Carnegie's old mansion
on Fifth Avenue. Ted and Generosa's town house had three
windows on each level of the façade. In front, a black
wrought-iron fence framed a set of stairs to the basement-
level entrance. Generosa happily had everything ripped
apart and reconstructed according to her specifications. She
discovered that she truly loved remodeling and adding designer touches, such as built-in bookcases in the living
room. She filled them with big books about art, architecture,
and photography and shocking and controversial works,
along with lots of hardcover literature and popular fiction.
Generosa painted a large, blue, architectural mural in the
foyer that featured an acropolis-like temple. The window behind the comfortable kitchen dinette looked out on a court-
yard. The windowsill featured four small, spherical trees and
two foot-long, black-and-white cow statues. Generosa had
sculpted, in cement, a life-sized version of the tuxedo cow,
which she placed on the roof, to graze. It was one of the rare
living creatures that appeared in her art. "Elsie" was part of
the family. Generosa's friend Ronnie, among others, thought
the giant cow sculpture was stupid but kept her opinion to
herself. Generosa had also started collecting art and her
taste was often unusual. Peter Cohen, an artist friend, made
interesting "sculptures" out of huge, tangled mangrove-tree
roots from Florida. Cut off just above the roots, they hung au
naturel from the living room ceiling, creating a bizarre,
gnarly morass growing down from above, the trunk seeming
to disappear into the ceiling. It certainly was different, sort
of like living in Peter Pan's tree house, except that, unlike

Peter Pan, Generosa had paid five figures for her tree. When Sandi and Bob visited the new place, they were immediately struck by the huge root system looming above their heads. Bob, perplexed, turned to his hostess.

"Generosa, is that a tree root hanging from your ceiling?" Bob asked, his amusement barely disguised.

"Yes, Bob. Isn't that great?" she gushed, immune to Bob's playfully wry tone.

She explained that she knew the artist. But as far as Bob could tell, God was the artist. Generosa described the harvesting procedure and how the artist got them up to New York without harming the gargantuan taproot.

"Isn't it great art?" she asked, in all seriousness.

"Well, I'll be," Bob mustered politely.

Later, Bob chuckled to Sandi that the seller of the swamp root in Florida "was laughing all the way to the bank." Sandi wasn't quite so critical and, in fact, with each visit the mammoth mangrove root grew on her, until she could appreciate the artistic beauty of the form.

Generosa also created her own wall sculptures from string and paper, one running the length of their town house. Another was a kitchen wall "installation" with hundreds of randomly spaced "found objects," like pushpins and soda can pop-tops and other junk, pinned to the wall. Ted loved Generosa's art but many friends secretly thought it was ridiculous. Privately, Generosa admitted that she had "lost my role as a struggling artist" because of her privileged position, but she made more art than ever.

Ted and Generosa became friends with new neighbors Jurate Gazikas, a former journalist with the defunct *Washington Star,* and her husband, Roger Altman, a financier who would later become assistant treasury secretary during the Clinton administration.

Generosa immediately set out to improve her new environment, which was the best the city had to offer but wasn't quite perfect enough for her. The park was at the end of the block; which made it a glaring omission that there was no green on the block. Generosa researched it and discovered that it would take at least three years for New York City to get around to beautifying the block for free, so she simply wrote a check and had a private landscaper plant more than a dozen specimen trees up and down the street. Next, she went after a store on the corner of Madison Avenue that left its unsightly garbage piled out on the curb, attracting rats. It drove her nuts.

"It's ugly. I can't stand it," she told Jurate.

Generosa was disgusted and outraged and she swung into action. She made calls and applied pressure, forcing the store to comply with her wishes and build an enclosure to secure the trash. When they had a similar problem with the one apartment house on the block and the landlord balked at the expense of building a separate, curbside enclosure for his tenants' garbage, Generosa called her carpenters. The workmen descended on the hated spot and constructed the refuse compartments in a single day. She never tried to collect from the landlord and she never asked anyone on the block for a dime. Generosa was also very active in a neighborhood battle to prevent the construction of a building extension that would have risen 180 feet into the air, towering over the town houses and shadowing the block. She whipped up local support and marshaled forces and petitioned until they were able to cut the height of the proposed project in half. She was a perfect community advocate: She had lots of money and time on her hands and was filled with righteous indignation and manic energy that drove her night and day. The problem was that she lost control of her emotions in the heat of anger. Her face would get red and her voice would get louder and her language more extreme. The difference between Ted and Generosa was that he was graceful under pressure, while she usually lost it. Ted was very indulgent with her and never said an unkind word or put her down. He was proud of her passionate community efforts. When the

Jewish Museum on the corner of Fifth Avenue hung out a large banner announcing an exhibition, it was like a red flag in front of a bull. Generosa launched a passionate campaign to ban the banner.

"That cheap, disgusting banner!" she fumed. "It's an absolute rag! We've got to get it off!"

Everyone on the block appreciated Generosa's efforts but many questioned the new cause and a few began to wonder if she wasn't a bit off. Jurate liked her new friend and admired her spirit, taste, and sense of style, but she had heard the unkind talk and was also worried that Generosa was so extreme. She never knew what mood she would find Generosa in and she began to suspect that her friend was bipolar. During one private chat, Jurate hinted at her concern and Generosa responded with a startling self-appraisal.

"I *know* how I am, and there's a reason for it," she said, fixing Jurate with a penetrating gaze. "It's because of what happened to me when I was young."

Her dire tone made it clear that she didn't want to discuss it further. Jurate respected Generosa's privacy and didn't press the matter but correctly assumed the worst.

When Generosa got bored with her completed town house and ran out of community battles on her beautified block, she found a home in the green hills north of the city, in the small colonial town of Bedford, located between two scenic New York City reservoirs. It had become a summer spot for the wealthy. Generosa immediately had the home gutted and began another rehab project, hiring contractors and directing them every day until her exact ideas were created in wood and plaster. Then she decorated and filled it with furniture. It was an impressive job, except for the bottom line. Generosa was an incredible refurbisher, as long as money was no object. She demanded only the best, and if something was not done exactly right, she would insist on tearing it out and doing it over. The contractors made a lot of money and Generosa had her show home for summering, riding, and entertaining. Generosa did not just trot around in Central Park. She had her own horses and was a competitive amateur jumper in horse shows up and down the East Coast, from New Hampshire to Florida. It was hardly a safe sport, and she risked injury by galloping around a course and jumping over fences and obstacles, clinging to the back of a thundering, chuffing animal. But it made her feel alive and she reveled in it, as she had when she was a girl. She had, as they say, a good seat, and she could take a short jumper course in less than twenty-three seconds. She excelled and won trophies, and the cash that went with them, but had there been no one to compete against, she would have raced herself.

It was the roaring eighties. Ronald Reagan was in the White House, business was unchained and unregulated. Then a recession struck. The largest transfer of private wealth in the history of the republic was in progress. America was also making the transition from becoming the planet's largest creditor to becoming the world's major debtor. While the corporate pirates looted value locked up in companies with LBOs and got rich, Uncle Sam went from banker to borrower.

At Kohlberg Kravis Roberts—KKR—Ted was a tireless worker with a creative approach to the complicated dealings involved in takeover bids. Ted was no longer bored. He worked furiously, to the full extent of his powers, on major deals like the takeover of Storer Communications, which netted KKR hundreds of millions of dollars. And that was just one deal.

Leveraged buyouts were a creation of the "me decade" of the 1980s. LBOs are very strange events and are still controversial. First, a group of raiders would locate a fat target, a corporation whose stock and assets were, for some reason, undervalued, according to the stock price. It was best to win the cooperation of the concern's board members in advance, for an uncontested buyout. That way, a bidding war between two or more suitors—which would eat up the fat profits—could be avoided. Next, the raiders would quickly secure massive financing from one or more big banks to fund their buyout offer to the stockholders of the corporation, who could be expected to agree to sell their shares for a windfall profit. The raiders inflated their offers with controversial "junk bonds," which made the takeovers possible. Then the raiders would run the company, selling off assets, divisions, or property, and consolidating operations to achieve massive profits. That often meant wholesale layoffs of loyal workers who had been doing a good job for a profitable firm. At the end of the process, everyone who owned stock made a nice profit, the bankers made a bigger profit, and the raiders garnered the lion's share of the liquidated assets, sometimes obscene amounts of cash—all for wringing money out of someone else's company with other people's money and shaky bonds. Everybody was happy—except the workers who got fired. The ethics and morality of corporate takeovers became a national debate, from the financial pages to Hollywood, which turned out movies like *Wall Street* and *Other People's Money*. In *Wall Street,* the part of the slick, charming, reptilian takeover king, Gordon Gekko, was played by Michael Douglas, who declared, "Greed is good! Greed is right! Greed Works!..." and went on to proclaim that greed would save the USA. echoing the actual words of financier Ivan Boesky: "Greed is all right . . . greed is healthy. You can be greedy and still feel good about yourself."

KKR's best-known figure was Ted's boss, Henry Kravis, a dark-haired diminutive dynamo who had made a fortune from hostile takeovers and lived the kind of Manhattan lifestyle usually reserved for royalty. Kravis had married a tall, gorgeous brunette model named Carolyne Roehm and they were constantly in the gossip columns and society news, especially after making a gigantic donation to the Metropolitan Museum of Art.

Business was booming and Ted labored on several huge

takeovers, including the $2.5 billion deal for Storer Communications, a Miami broadcasting and cable television concern. The profits for KKR when the deal was done in 1985 were immense, and Ted got a slice.

Before Storer, Ted was involved in the $1.25 billion deal to take over World Color Press, the largest printer of magazines in America, whose titles included *Time* magazine, *TV Guide, Cosmopolitan, Sports Illustrated,* and a thousand others. The firm had some two dozen printing plants in the United States and Canada, as well as other interests in Europe and Hong Kong. The company operated on long-term contracts and made money even during bust times. That made it attractive to the buyout boys. KKR did very well on the deal, and so did Ted.

He was creative, even artistic, in his own way, in business. His work challenged him to come up with new solutions and he loved brainstorming, trying to figure a way to solve a problem without an instruction manual. One of Ted's associates calculated that Ted would erupt with about 700 new ideas, 697 of which were ridiculous. But three of those ideas were amazing, and the key was figuring out which three. Once that was done, Ted got his reward. Fine wines and food and travel were all great, but he loved the finesse of the deal, the accomplishment, more than anything else. Even when the pressure was intense and deadlines loomed, Ted loved it.

When the stock market dropped 508 points, on October 19, 1987, Black Monday, leveraged buyouts seemed to some big players not just a fad but a better way to make money, even in a disastrous market.

The biggest transaction that Ted worked on was KKR's $25 billion takeover of RJR Nabisco, the conglomerate of the Reynolds tobacco company and Nabisco, the cookie and snack giant, in the autumn of 1988. Ted Ammon, already a multimillionaire by the time he was thirty-six, was one of the sharp associates who figured out how to overcome the financial and technical obstacles involved in the complicated deal. The head of RJR Nabisco had already chosen another financial group to arrange a friendly takeover of his company, but KKR jumped in, arranged for the unprecedented financing from several banks, and made their own bid to the stockholders, setting off a bidding war for RJR that pulled in a third group of suitors. When counterbids required KKR to either put in a final bid or drop out, Kravis said that he had had it, that he and his team were all heading off for Thanksgiving vacations to recover from the failed bid. Most of the team went to sunny climes but Kravis and his model wife headed to Vail, Colorado, to hobnob with celebrities at the trendy ski resort. Actually, it was a ploy to throw the competition off guard during the holiday. At the same time, Ted and Generosa flew down to the tropical Casa de Campo resort in the Dominican Republic, where he met his family for the holiday. He swam and sailed and dined with his loved ones, including his sister Sandi and her husband, Bob, and told them nothing about the KKR secret bid. He and everyone else at KKR had been sworn to secrecy.

After the holiday, their highest bid took everyone by surprise and they made financial history. But once all the publicity died down, their final share price, jacked up by the auction, was too much. They had spent their profits. They still got large fees from the transaction but nobody became insanely rich from it, despite the public perception that they had. The whole affair was later chronicled in a best-selling book titled *Barbarians at the Gate,* by Bryan Burrough and John Helyar. Ted was mentioned several times in the book and could be seen in the background in photos of the takeover ceremony. The book was later made into an HBO TV movie starring James Garner.

It seemed now that Ted was unstoppable. And the same manic determination that drove his business dealings was evident in every part of his hard-charging life.

On a ski trip to the Swiss Alps with pal Colin Hastings, Ted plowed into the thick European powder with gusto, with the fervor of an Olympic slopesman. But even here Ted refused to take instruction or go by the book. He would schuss fearlessly down a white trail, hit a jump, and do what he called "a helicopter turn," ending up face-first when he hit the deep snow. Ted also loved going off the trail into the deep drift, a bad combination.

One time it almost went too far. Colin was following Ted into a ravine when he heard Ted yell as he fell down in the deep stuff. Then Colin turned and fell himself. They were splayed in separate spots in ten feet of loose snow, and neither could see or hear the other in the V-shaped ravine. They were well off the piste, with no ski patrol in sight. This was a situation that could well become dangerous. Colin tried to right himself, struggling and digging at the snow and becoming wet and cold and, increasingly, tired. Then his cell phone inside his ski jacket rang. Startled, he groped for it and dug it out.

"Hello?"

"Colin?" Ted asked from his hole in the snow yards away. "What does the manual say?"

They both laughed. Without a manual, Ted directed Colin up and out of the ravine and they laughed about it over a drink in front of the fire back at the lodge. It was vintage Ted: rescuing himself from a situation he had created himself with his outer-limits behavior.

But at work, Ted's boredom began creeping up. Even though he was at the top of his profession and his personal millions were piling up, he had the feeling that he was in a rut, golden though it may have been. It was beginning to seem like he was going by the book, one that he had not written. And he was working for bosses. They were bosses who treated him well and valued him highly, but part of him still itched to accomplish things on his own and dreaded the trap of becoming a lifelong company man. Most would have killed for what Ted had, but he wanted to be his own boss, which was not possible at KKR, at least not for some time. Life was short. He would strike out on his own when the time was right, something that no one else at KKR had ever done. Ted evaluated companies as possible KKR takeover targets every day, and he began also to look for himself. He had no idea what he was going to do, but he already had his eyes peeled for the next opportunity, the next trail umarked by other skis.

10

THE STONE FLOWER

Generosa heard the doorbell of the town house and thought, They're early this afternoon. She hadn't expected the delivery of groceries for another half hour. Pleasantly surprised, she corralled the two barking dogs, Xerox, the chocolate Labrador and Kodak, the English setter, in the kitchen and went down to the front door, which opened a half a floor below the sidewalk of East Ninety-second Street. The dogs had prompted Generosa to hire another servant for her staff—that only–in–New York type of employee, a dog walker. But the staff had left for the day and Ted was not yet home. Generosa was alone, so, of course, she looked through the peephole in the door. Because it was below street level and was screened by a black wrought-iron fence, the entrance was not fully visible from the sidewalk, which was uncrowded. She saw two deliverymen.

Generosa had ordered food and supplies for an army; she always ordered more than she needed. As soon as she snapped the deadbolt and opened the door, they rushed in. It wasn't the food delivery. Two husky men, now wearing ski masks, shoved her inside and manhandled her to the floor. She tried to scream, but the sweaty pair covered her mouth with duct tape. They took her directly to the basement and went right to the door to the utility room. The men knew exactly where they were going. In the utility room, they taped her to a chair, bound her hands and feet with the sticky stuff, and blindfolded her.

She was totally helpless, sure that they meant to rape and kill her. Her heart raced and she struggled to breathe through her nose. Then her blindfold got dark. They had turned off the light. She heard the door shut.

Generosa was terrified. At first, she was not sure if one was still in the room, watching her. It sounded like two of them going upstairs, obviously looking for something. Why? Who were they? She struggled against her bonds but they would not yield. She could see only darkness. She panicked and experienced a kind of flashback to the helpless victim she had been as a child, when the man who molested her did things she did not like. She sobbed and twisted in her dark prison, the adult plunged suddenly back into that deep, secret place inside where the helpless child hid from harm.

The crooks quickly went through the place, snapping up Generosa's jewelry from the safe behind the bed in the master bedroom. They were pros. No muss, no fuss, in and out fast. They took only the high-end stuff, including her double diamond ring with a yellow and a white diamond of two and a half karats each.

After they had left, Ted came home to an empty house and called for Generosa, who usually met him at the door. The dogs were still barking in the kitchen but their mistress was nowhere to be seen. When there was no answer, he looked through the house, a bit annoyed, but he neglected to check the basement, except to shout down the stairs:

"Generosa?"

There was no answer, but hearing her name brought Generosa back. She tried to scream but little noise escaped. Upstairs, Ted made a few calls, in a vain attempt to find her. When he learned that she had last been seen at home, waiting for groceries and for him, he searched the town house again, in earnest, from top to bottom. He went into the basement and called for her again but he did not open the utility

room door. It did not occur to him that she could be tied to a
chair in the darkness there. Eventually, he discovered that
the safe had been cleaned out. After two hours, he finally
found her tied to the chair, in a state of feral panic, and she
blurted out her story, sobbing. Ted called the police, who
took a statement from Generosa. She was unable to provide
detailed descriptions of the intruders, but she thought that
she had seen them before. The police did not make any arrests, which only fueled her paranoia. The men had known
exactly where the safe was, the layout of the house. What
else did they know? Generosa was traumatized and Ted was
compelled to turn the town house into a fortress, with un-
pickable locks, TV surveillance cameras, including one on
the front door, and a state-of-the-art alarm system. They
changed their phone number and Ted hired armed guards.

The ordeal deeply affected Generosa, who feared that the
men would return. It was months before she would be left
alone, and the ordeal seemed to change her. Fear was always in
the back or the front of her mind. A wrong-number phone call
or a strange person at the door or on the street might set her off
on a fear flashback. She talked to Ted about her terrors and
about her past. He was very understanding and sympathetic
and went out of his way to make her happy and put her at ease,
which went a long way toward helping her recover. She had a
duplicate engagement ring made but, of course, it was not the
original token of love and devotion that he had given her. It
was a copy. Ted thought that the effects of the event would fade
with time, but they never did completely. The couple resumed
their life and their routines, but from that day on, Generosa
was more suspicious of others, paranoid, always looking for a
downside. She became increasingly aggressive, which was not
quite the same thing as living without fear. Her increased fear
contrasted even more with Ted's natural fearlessness.

While Ted was busy building his career, Generosa kept
busy running the household, planning social events, horseback riding, and pursuing her photography, although she
also took great interest in Ted's business. He bought her a

huge loft in Soho so that she could pursue art with a passion, with the best equipment and supplies money could buy. Her studio, at 383 West Broadway, was an incredible duplex with garret skylights. One friend compared the studio to Marie Antoinette's rustic little mill on the grounds of Versailles Palace: the rich man's wife, playing at being the struggling artist on the proceeds of big business.

Ted loved her art and was a big supporter but Generosa did not want to be seen as his trophy wife—she wanted to be recognized on her own as an artist and used her maiden name, Generosa Rand, for her art. With money no longer an object, Generosa was free to indulge her most extravagant concepts. She shrink-wrapped a Chrysler K-car in plastic, a conceptual statement that was seen as not very original. She had several shows but the art world took little notice, although Ted was proud when the Sony Corporation bought one of Generosa's copper wire sculptures for its office building, her first big sale. She lived and worked in both worlds, the downtown avant-garde artist during the day, the rich, uptown socialite at night. Generosa always made sure that she was home and available for Ted whenever he needed her. Everything she and her staff did was geared toward making a perfect environment for him. They had dinner together most nights, and Generosa would send the staff home so they would be alone at the end of the day.

Ted worked hard and played hard, jogging, cycling, sailing, and skiing like an athlete. In the summers, he and Generosa, another fitness junkie who worked out every day, would go with a group of friends to ride bicycles in the South of France, pedaling about the countryside, chowing down on provincial food and great wines at inns at night.

Ted and Generosa also visited Sandi and Bob several times in Alabama. One night in Huntsville, they were all out to dinner at a restaurant frequented for years by Sandi and Bob. The owner, chatting with his seated guests, placed his hands on Generosa's shoulders and gave her a brief, friendly massage as he spoke. Generosa stiffened at the stranger's touch, her eyes wide. The blood drained from her face, which assumed a look of horror. When the restaurateur departed, Generosa freaked out.

"That was just terrible!" she blurted, startling the others, who asked what she was talking about.

"He should never have touched me or anybody else!" Generosa shouted.

Sandi, trying to make light of it, said, "It's not a big deal."

"It *is* a big deal! Nobody should ever do that!" she spat.

No one other than Ted knew about the massages she had been given as a child and what they had led to. At a loss as to why Generosa had overreacted, the other diners changed the subject and forgot about the odd incident.

Now that Ted was subsidizing her art career, Generosa hired another member of the "staff" in 1990, Phyllis Hellman,* to do all the menial tasks that were now beneath her, something most artists were unable to do until after they had made it. Generosa had an art "opening" of flat works, mostly geometric designs that failed to set any fires in the art world. But Generosa was not deterred and continued doing her thing and hanging out with an avant-garde crowd downtown. Mostly, Phyllis worked on Generosa's photography, which was the younger woman's area of expertise. Generosa would wander around at industrial or construction sites, snapping photos of inanimate compositions that interested her. Phyllis would then develop the black-and-white photos and print them in the darkroom.

Generosa demanded a lot from Phyllis but she also gave a lot and held herself to the same high standards. Phyllis never saw Generosa angry but she did see her frustrated, sometimes at her own inability to perform a very difficult task. Phyllis admired the strength of the self-made woman and they became friends. When Phyllis met Ted, she was very impressed with him and with their relationship. Over time, Ted would become her favorite person in the world. Phyllis and Generosa were both private people, outsiders, but they opened up to each other and talked about their lives while they worked. The curvy and svelte Generosa talked about being an overweight child, about being made fun of because of that. She spoke of the pain of betrayal, of the feeling that she was abandoned by her mother, that she had never received the care and love of a mother.

"My mother resented me because I was an illegitimate child," said Generosa. "You don't have the right to inflict your pain on your children."

As they became closer, the older, wiser Generosa helped bring Phyllis out of her shell. They discovered that they had never known their fathers and both had left California to escape their pasts. One day, while Phyllis was talking about her childhood trauma, the women realized that they had a terrible secret in common. When Phyllis confided that she had been sexually molested by her uncle when she was a child, a somber Generosa told her:

"The same thing happened to me. I was afraid to tell anybody."

They both had experienced what they each thought was a private, unique experience; the retreat to a place deep inside themselves where bad things happened. Generosa said that the ordeal made her scared of men and made it difficult for her to trust anyone. As a result, she always felt that "most people were just out to get something from you," a fear that had been reinforced recently, when people befriended her just to get close to Ted, hoping to get money from him for some deal.

Phyllis told her boss about the trouble she was having with her boyfriend, who had turned out to be twisted and violent and was stalking her.

"Phyllis, you really need to be careful of who you get involved with," Generosa counseled.

When Generosa found out that Phyllis was staying in an abusive relationship because she did not have the money to escape, Generosa gave her eight thousand dollars to enable her to pay off her debts so that she could sell her house and move on. Phyllis, who felt as if Generosa had saved her life,

later discovered that she was not the only person her friend
had helped. Generosa told Phyllis about her pain over her inability to have children. Ted wanted children more than she
did, so Generosa had stopped birth control and begun trying
to get pregnant. But it was harder than they had expected.
Soon, however, Generosa got pregnant. Several months
later, she was already planning for the new arrival.

Ted was in the middle of a meeting at KKR when he got an
urgent phone call. Generosa had been rushed to the hospital
after experiencing abdominal cramps and bleeding. There
was a problem with the baby. Ted dropped everything and
rushed to the emergency room. The doctors told them that
Generosa had an ectopic, or tubal, pregnancy, a strange condition in which the fetus affixes itself in the wrong area and
actually becomes a parasite, endangering the mother. The
pregnancy had to be terminated.

It is very painful to discover that you may never have your
own biological child. Couples feel damaged, incomplete, in-
ferior. Generosa was shaken. She and the life she was fash-
ioning for Ted and herself were no longer perfect. Ted was
everything to Generosa and she wanted to give him children,
as much as he wanted to be a father. They consulted fertility
specialists and even attempted the stressful and difficult process of artificial insemination, a roller coaster of hope and
dejection. After more than a year of trying, they reached a
point where they had to decide between abandoning their
hopes for a child and opting for adoption. It was a painful
subject to discuss, even with close friends and family. Because of the anguish, Generosa was ready to forget children
and she was already crusting over her pain with attitude.
When people inquired, some got different answers than others. When Jurate, a mother herself, asked what was new on
the baby front, her friend's answer gave her a chill:

"I don't want to get pregnant," Generosa declared flip-
pantly. "I wouldn't be able to ride."

• • •

In the former Soviet republic of Ukraine, a pair of fraternal twins with milky skin and hair the color of corn silk were born on the Ides of March, 1990. Their biological mother found herself in circumstances quite different from those enjoyed by Ted and Generosa, and she was not able to care for her children. The beautiful, blond, blue-eyed boy and girl, Gregory Ruslan and Alexa Svetlana, were placed in a state orphanage, a stark building that had a number instead of a name. Like many other foundlings who did not receive the latest inoculations and medical care, they were at risk for diseases that many Americans thought were extinct. Officials there hoped to keep the brother and sister together and wanted to put them up for adoption by a wealthy foreign couple. As they grew, the brother and sister learned Russian and clung to each other, waiting for a family. Although the orphanage was poor, the underpaid staff did their best to care for the children and make the institution a home. Some told bedtime stories to the children, Ukrainian and Russian folk tales about Baba Yaga the witch, and others. Even before they could understand the words, the twins heard stories such as "The Tale of the Stone Flower," a parable from the Ural Mountains about artistic obsession with perfection.

It was the story of Danila, a sculptor, and a magical lifelike flower carved out of stone. Danila labored to chisel a perfect blossom out of green stone, one that seemed alive, that exactly imitated the delicate flesh of the flower. He completed an excellent image of a flower, but once he had finished, he was very sad because it was not good enough. He smashed it to bits with a hammer. Danila cared more about making a perfect stone flower than he did about his fiancée or his friends. He left his beloved young lady behind and journeyed to the mountains, where he entered a fabulous, glittering cavern of jewels. It was the home of a goddess, who showed him perfect, magical stone flowers more lifelike than anything carved by men. He begged her to show him how to carve the petals out of rock, and she led him to a huge block of uncut malachite and told him that this was his stone flower. He protested that he had hoped the goddess would show him how to sculpt it, but she laughed and told him that he had to listen to the stone. She explained that he could not force the stone to become what he wanted. When, in time, he learned to listen to the wishes of the stone, Danila created the cold stone flower. When he was reunited with his betrothed, and was happy at last, he realized that the force of life in nature and especially in the flesh-and-blood people who loved him was the most precious creation of all.

The legend ended with a warning: The stone flower was the most beautiful in all the world, but whoever sought it would never find happiness.

11

BIG FLOWER

Ted, like Generosa, was also bruised by their failed efforts to have a family but he was not willing to give up. After all, he was now worth $50 million. But what good was money if it couldn't buy what you wanted, if it couldn't make your dreams come true? The couple agreed to adopt and consulted a Manhattan lawyer who specialized in foreign adoptions, the kind in which the parental rights of the biological mother and father were legally terminated.

In domestic adoptions of Caucasian children, it was a sellers' market and infertile couples often had to agree, in essence, to also adopt the biological mother and make her a part of the family. But foreign adoptions could be arranged so that they were final. Places like Russia and the Ukraine were a source of white children, many of them born to Gypsy families, but there were plenty of concerns for prospective adoptive parents. In the Kiev area, the 1986 Chernobyl nuclear accident threatened each new generation with unknown medical conditions. Also, the former Soviet Union was afflicted with appalling rates of alcoholism, which caused brain-damaging fetal alcohol syndrome in the children of women who drank heavily during pregnancy. And there were the greedy bureaucrats, the "aparatchicks" of the Communist system, with their hands out for bribes along the way.

But Ted and Generosa were at the top of the food chain and were offered only the best. They were shown photographs and documentation on several likely, healthy prospects, including chubby, two-year-old blond twins, Gregory Ruslan and Alexa Svetlana. They had almost been adopted by another Manhattan power couple, who had changed their minds about having twins.

The girl looked like Generosa had when she was small, and though Generosa believed she never had a family, she felt an almost supernatural attraction when she looked at the photo of the adorable brother and sister. It was as if they were her own children, somehow misplaced on another continent.

"That's it!" she cried. "These are the children I want!"

The lawyer made the arrangements and they were soon on their way to Moscow and then to the Ukraine, the first of several trips. They stayed at a local hotel and paid visits to the orphanage. The twins spoke baby Russian and not a word of English, but it didn't matter to Ted and Generosa. They felt a deep ache of love, a physical twinge of bonding from the first encounter. When they went to bring the children home, they were alarmed to find that Alexa was in the hospital. At first, they thought it was hepatitis, but it proved to be tuberculosis. They called Sandi's husband, Bob Williams, in Alabama, for a medical opinion, asking if they should travel with a tubercular child.

"Oh, bring her home," Bob told them, breaking their terror with a laugh. "If you're going to have sick kids, you might as well get started now."

Ted and Generosa were instant parents, a wonderful and terrifying experience. The family spoke different languages but managed to communicate with smiles and hugs. Grego's first English word was *taxi*.

In the spring of 1992, Jurate and Roger Altman were on the curb on East Ninety-second Street, waiting, when Ted and

Generosa arrived home from Kennedy Airport. The new parents were physically exhausted but glowing with ecstasy after the adventure of a lifetime. They were whole again, their perfect lives back on track. For Easter, the newest Ammons went to church with their parents and Aunt Sandi and Uncle Bob, who flew up to meet them. Then, it was time for a chocolate Easter-egg hunt.

The children were Generosa's new and greatest project. She had hired a nanny to take care of the kids, increasing the household staff to five. She had to let her photography assistant, Phyllis, go because she suddenly had no time for art or photography. Phyllis understood and wished Generosa and Ted the best. It was obvious that they were incredibly happy. After their struggle to have kids, and helping to free Phyllis from her problems with her boyfriend, Ted and Generosa deserved their happiness. They were wonderful people.

The kids were beautiful, well behaved, and had a zest for life. They wore the best clothes and attended the finest private schools in Manhattan, where they would be groomed for success. Alexa attended Chapin and Grego went to Saint David's. Grego was very outgoing and close with his sister. He was much like Ted as a child, a real guy's guy. Ted and Generosa were revitalized by their kids and resolved to prepare them to take their proper place in society.

Ted, still at KKR, saw his urge to make changes in his professional life grow stronger. It was great to climb mountains and admire the view, but after a while of looking at the scenery, Ted wanted a different range of mountains to climb when he woke up in the morning. Just as Generosa needed different environments to reclaim and reshape, Ted needed new challenges to avoid the trap of the same old thing, no matter how profitable. He confided his thoughts of striking out on his own to Generosa, who had already suggested it to him. She felt that Ted was doing great things for Henry Kravis and KKR but was not getting his due. She was very supportive, perhaps to a fault.

Ted was offered an incredible position in London but Generosa rejected it because she had no interest in moving there, even though Ted loved that city. Generosa was also opposed to moving to England because the laws would have required them to put their dogs in a pet quarantine facility for six months, which she would not do. It was a case of the tail wagging the dog but Ted did not press the issue.

She told Ted that he was the best thing about KKR and it was time he set up his own shop, in competition with them. She grilled Ted on his ideas and plans and made her own suggestions. More and more, Generosa felt that KKR and in particular Henry Kravis were holding him back, even though Ted was hardly being held down. At first they discussed it at night, after the kids went to bed, but soon Generosa began blabbing openly about how much Ted did for the firm and how little he was appreciated. She also fixated on Kravis's lovely wife, Carolyne Roehm, viewing her as the epitome of the shallow trophy wife of the corporate raider. Generosa was incapable of suffering those whom she decided were fools. When she began openly berating Mr. and Mrs. Kravis at KKR social functions, it became personally embarrassing for Ted, not to mention hurtful for one of his bosses and his wife. To some, it seemed absurd because none of it was true.

Carolyne Roehm, Generosa said at one gathering, was not a person of substance, the implication being that Generosa, the artist, was. Embarrassed, Ted asked her to be quiet, but it was too late. Generosa's nasty words found their way around the firm. A few who had heard Generosa's rant thought it was simply envy of Kravis's larger fortune and his wife's beauty and fame. One listener was also of the opinion that Generosa's art was a great deal less substantial than the kind supported and collected by Kravis and Roehm. Ted had been having second thoughts about leaving his comfortable berth at KKR but Generosa had no such doubts and continued to push Ted into making the break. Perhaps it was simply Generosa's usual habit of burning bridges when she suspected disrespect, but, by sabotaging Ted's relationship with

Kravis, she seemed to be intentionally burning Ted's bridge for him. While he was standing on it.

One afternoon in September 1992, Bob Burton got a call from his business associate and friend Ted Ammon. After the preliminaries and family-health questions, they got down to business.

"I want to come over and talk to you," Ted said.

"Well, what's the subject?" Burton asked.

"No, I just want to talk to you," Ted replied mysteriously, refusing to elaborate.

Burton was suddenly worried. If someone like Ted Ammon suddenly had to talk to him in person, one of two things was going to happen. Number one, he was going to ask him to do something with the stock or, number two, Ted was going to fire him. Since things were going pretty well, getting fired seemed unlikely. Ted arrived soon after, sat down, and began chatting about families and several other things before he got to the real subject.

"I wanted to come over here to personally tell you that I'm leaving the investment banking business and I'm going to be an operator."

Bob couldn't believe his ears. Ted was leaving KKR and was going to run a company.

"You've got to be kidding, Ted. You don't know anything about running a business."

"No, I've made up my mind," Ted said calmly. "I'm going to do it."

There was no discussing it. Ted was already moving on this.

"What kind of business are you going to go in?"

"I'm going to go into the printing business."

Burton had been in the printing business at the Moore Corporation.

"You've lost your mind. There's no way you'll make a nickel in that business if you don't understand it. If I were you, I'd call Henry Kravis right now and ask for my job back."

If Ted had been hoping for a ringing endorsement from Burton, he did not show his disappointment.

"No, that's what I want to do and that's what I'm going to do."

Henry Kravis and others at KKR valued loyalty and were reportedly very upset when Ted told them he was leaving. He was the first to jump ship from what had been a historic and incredibly lucrative voyage. Why would he do that? Did he intend to compete with his old firm? The predominant buzz was that Ted was always a bit flaky and that leaving KKR proved he was nuts. Also, he was investing part of his considerable wealth in high-risk Internet ventures. Some predicted a big fall. But Ted remained on good terms with his alma mater and even threw a plum deal their way, allaying some concerns.

Bob Burton remembered his exchange with Ted later, when his friend made a lot of money for his shareholders and proved him incredibly wrong. With no prior experience, Ted suddenly became a major figure in the business of printing newspaper circulars. It wasn't sexy but it paid, to the tune of $1.9 billion in annual revenues. Ted named his company Big Flower Press. The name came from one of his twins, who, while learning English, pointed at a huge orange sunflower and said, laughing, "Big flower!" It seemed to describe their lives, a large, complex, fragrant blossom, opening into symmetrical perfection in the warming sun.

Ted made a lot of money at Big Flower and his net worth continued to expand with the Internet bubble. He had gotten in on the ground floor of the Internet and telecommunications boom, as Internet stocks soared, often on losing enterprises, in total defiance of logic. Online stocks were suddenly hot, the latest thing. Ted had found the next big thing and surfed the wave, pumping up his $50 million net worth beyond $200 million. At the peak, Ted was worth a princely $400 million. Seven years later, Ted would sell Big Flower for a big profit and set up a boutique firm, Chancery

Lane Capital, to make his own takeover deals, doing what he had done at KKR—but this time he was the boss.

Because he was the boss, flying in his own jet, Ted brought the kids with him on business deals to Europe and elsewhere, combining business with pleasure.

Once in a while, Ted would drop out of sight for a day or two when on a business trip. It drove Generosa crazy that she couldn't reach him. The first time it happened, his office and his wife feared that he had been in an accident or had been kidnapped. But by the time they were ready to call the police, Ted would pop up and call.

"Hi, I'm in Switzerland!"

Or Scotland, or elsewhere, surprised that he was missed. Ted claimed he occasionally needed to get away to think and clear his head. It became part of the Ted legend, his vanishing act.

These were magical days for the family. Ted and Generosa were in love and the kids were growing up. They started with tricycles and later graduated to two-wheel bicycles, following their father on his run through Central Park. With the assistance of her able staff, Generosa had the children and dinner ready every night at six-thirty. The staff were required to make themselves scarce before Milton drove Ted home for the meal and family time, just like Ted remembered from his childhood. After dinner, they taught the twins English. Laughing on the living room rug, Ted and Generosa would lie on their backs, each holding one twin's hands— lifting the giggling kids into the air with their legs, teaching them to "fly," the new parents seeing the world anew through their young eyes.

During the kids' second Christmas holiday in the United States, when they were three and a half, Grego became fascinated with the telephone. He would pick it up and have long conversations with no one, much to the amusement of his parents.

"Don't come, bad man!" he said into the phone, warning an imaginary villain to leave his family alone. "Don't come to my house, bad man."

Generosa's fears after her home-invasion nightmare had not disappeared and they now extended to the newest members of the family. Because of this, Ted was already making plans for a bodyguard for the tots, a sixth household staff member: There was never an actual abduction threat but the twins were guarded as if they were the president's kids. An armed former cop watched over them as they grew. He was a nice gentleman but his being there worried some in the family. Ted, also concerned about the future now that he was a father, prepared a last will and testament that set up trust funds for Grego and Alexa in the event of his death. Ted made a bank the coexecutor of his will, along with Generosa, who would inherit virtually everything if Ted died.

The kids were heirs to millions. They played on their private jetliner and learned to ski and sail at the finest resorts. When the twins were four, Ted and Generosa took them to Disney World, to meet Donald and Mickey in make-believe land. Generosa did not pack lightly. The family brought changes of designer clothes for every conceivable occasion, including sixteen pairs of shoes for Alexa. The twins were no longer orphans in a troubled land, they were a prince and a princess, living happily ever after inside a real fairy tale, in a magic kingdom.

12

GROWING PERFECTION

Generosa used some of Ted's money to set herself up in business as a home remodeler. He encouraged her in her new enterprise, realizing that the more time she spent on her projects, the less time she had to interfere in his affairs. Their summer home in Bedford had not worked out because they were not invited to become part of the social set she criticized and envied.

Ted had been a minor figure in the *Barbarians at the Gate* book and *The Wall Street Journal* had put his departure from KKR on the front page, but he was not known outside the financial community and was not a superstar there, either. More the golden boy. They sold their redone home in Bedford for a nice profit and Generosa set her sights on the Hamptons. She began scouting for a home in the Long Island summer playground for the wealthy and well known. She purchased a house in need of repairs and used some of her contractors from the city and found others on Long Island. Once it was gutted and fixed up according to her exacting instructions and decorated according to her taste, she put it on the market and sold it for a tidy $500,000 profit. Ted was impressed and proud. Obviously his wife had a talent for what she was doing. Her work also resonated with his; buying an undervalued property, tearing down the old, fixing it up, creating new structures and profit. And Generosa had the instincts and the aggression of a takeover artist.

She used profits to buy, in her own name, a former car dealership in East Hampton for $1.75 million. She planned to tear it down and redo it as a large commercial property, designed on the outside like a mansion. On the inside, she was thinking about building space for retail shops, or an upscale Home Depot–type remodeling center for the landed gentry. The problem was that the community and the Village of East Hampton did not agree with her plans. They contacted her and let her know that they wanted her to sell the property to them, to become part of the adjacent Village Green.

She and one of her contractors sat down with the mayor, Paul Rickenbach, in the white, two-story colonial home that had become the Village Hall, to discuss the issue. In a very condescending tone, Generosa quickly made it plain that she was going to do whatever she wanted with her property and no one was going to stop her. She said that she could make a lot more money her way. Rickenbach was shocked at her imperious attitude. She told him she had better taste than the village, which would be better off when she was done. She left no room for negotiation, which was not a smart move, because she needed their approval. As a result, their opposition would block her project for years.

Once she proved herself as a businesswoman, Generosa decided to conquer the Hamptons. She picked East Hampton. Her discriminating eye found a high-end fixer-upper: a white, three-bedroom, 1950s home on a nice piece of property in the exclusive estate section at 59 Middle Lane. The smallish, somewhat worn house rested under a huge, ancient oak. Generosa purchased it from the owner for $2.7 million. A nationally known gardener offered her services to help the Ammons landscape the property. She and Generosa sat down and discussed ideas for landscapes but the woman quickly beat a graceful retreat when Generosa announced that she would plant only yellow flowers out front and only blue ones out back.

The house was a few blocks from the ocean and just one long block from comedian Jerry Seinfeld's $16 million oceanfront estate. There were other rich neighbors, of course, although most were not famous. One mansion down the lane belonged to Barton Kaplan, a flamboyant, gay heir who was somewhat infamous for his sybaritic and expensive parties, which would have scandalized the founders of East Hampton, a group of Puritans who settled in Massachusetts and Connecticut before moving south to the village in 1648.

The colony was first called Maidstone, a name preserved in the exclusive, oceanfront Maidstone Club. In 1798, the good men of East Hampton shaved the hair off a peddler, rode him back into town on a rail, and dunked him in a pond—because he had gone to church with the measles and infected one hundred members of the congregation. The angry peddler got a good lawyer from Manhattan, Aaron Burr, who sued the village and won the princely sum of one thousand dollars. It would not be the last lawsuit in the neighborhood, but the bucolic nature of the village would be preserved by future generations.

Albert Einstein, another past visitor to the East End, fashioned theories to explain the mysteries of the time-space continuum—but they were incomplete. Einstein never discovered that money, multiplied by itself, infinitely, can actually alter time and space and create an alternate dimension of peace and beauty. In East Hampton, riches transport those of means not just to scenic, rural property but back in time to a safe place where there is virtually no crime and some residents do not lock their doors until they leave at the end of the season.

Elsewhere on Long Island, it was 1992, but in East Hampton, the clock had stopped—but with all the modern conveniences. A man's home was his castle, sometimes literally. Folks had enough property to make the neighbors disappear. They owned their own sky. At the beaches, in the village, or out in the lanes, driving, bicycling, jogging; it was

a small town. People said good morning and meant it. Life
was good. For Ted, it was like going back to the 1950s in
East Aurora, but nicer.

Mrs. Ammon did not want just to build her dream house
in the Hamptons and move in. She intended to conceive and
create a perfect, gracious home that would be noticed, envied, and chronicled in magazines. She wanted to give
Martha Stewart a run for her money. She wanted to arrive.
She wanted to be seen as a Renaissance woman, an artist, a
patron of the arts, and the architect, designer, landscaper,
gardener, and contractor from start to finish. Although she
had done some designing, she was neither a landscaper nor a
contractor and she certainly had not been trained or licensed
as an architect. Ted had passed the bar exams in London and
New York without the inconvenience of attending law school
and Generosa was set on acting as an architect without having to become one.

But instead of studying and getting a license, Generosa
got around her problem by luring young architect Jeff Gibbons away from his firm by encouraging him to go out on his
own, with the Ammon residence as his first solo project.
That way, she thought, she could assure full credit for herself for the project. And, as an added bonus, Generosa would
have Jeff's services for less than what his old firm would
have charged. As he embarked on the project, Jeff thought
he was well prepared because he was experienced in his profession and in dealing with difficult clients, not to mention
his life experience. He thought he could handle it.

He also thought that the only sharks in East Hampton
were in the ocean.

Jeff and Generosa sat down to make sketches and discuss
her concept for the home. It was a remodeling job, but the
changes were so great that it would, essentially, become a
new house, inside and out. She wanted the façade to resem-
ble an English country cottage "but in the back, you can
blow it out" to make more room. Generosa and Ted's new

home would be a six-thousand-square-foot residence with a
curved "eyebrow" window in the middle of the front roof,
like a winking, shingled eye. It would be multigabled and the
color scheme inside would be beige, gold, and black. On the
ground floor, it would have two guest bedrooms, four bath-
rooms, a den, a living room with fireplace and flanking
French doors, a dining room with beamed ceiling, a mudroom, a state-of-the-art kitchen, a sunroom with two walls
of glass, and a two-and-a-half-car garage, with space for
Generosa's preferred mode of transportation, her golf cart.
On the second floor, above the guest wing, atop the main
staircase, would be the master suite and bath, closets and
dressing area, and Ted's adjoining study. On the other end of
the second floor would be the children's wing. Alexa and
Grego would have their own playroom. They would have
their own bedrooms, and a double bathroom, next to the
nanny's bedroom and bath. There would also be a basement
with a wine cellar for Ted's collection of world-class wines.
In the rear yard, they would construct an eight-thousand-
square-foot pond, with a bridge over the middle. On the
other side would be more lawn, an in-ground pool, and the
pool cabana.

The closet in the children's playroom would hide a secret
door in the side wall that opened into a hidden "safe room,"
at Generosa's insistence. She was planning the perfect mansion and was adamant that it include a secret security cham-
ber where Generosa, Ted, and the kids could hide if the
home was invaded. It had been more than two years since
Generosa had been manhandled and tied up, but she still felt
that danger was stalking her, even in tranquil East Hampton,
where there hadn't been a murder in two decades. Inside the
safe room, the door would lock to keep out invaders. There
would also be a telephone and a panic alarm hooked in to the
burglar alarm to summon the East Hampton police.

Generosa also wanted five sets of washing machines and
clothes dryers in various spots around the house. That way,

the servants could do all the laundry in a very short space of time and leave, allowing Ted and Generosa time alone. Also, Generosa had a fetish about her underwear. She would not allow anyone else to touch her underthings. One washer-dryer set would be in the master bedroom suite upstairs so that Generosa could do her own washing, drying, and folding of her undergarments.

"I want one in my bathroom so no one has to touch my underwear," she told Jeff.

A model, like a very detailed dollhouse, was made of the home. During one of their planning sessions at her Manhattan town house, Generosa took an Amstel Light beer out of the refrigerator and told Jeff that she was an insomniac. She stayed up late and got a few hours' sleep but awakened at four or five in the morning. As a result, she was tired in the afternoons and always took a nap, after having one bottle of beer. Her staff in the town house, who took care of things like driving and errands and caring for her children, made it possible for her to get her beauty rest. Of course, if she did not take a nap in the afternoon, she might have slept through the night. She told Jeff her guilty secret about the beer but asked him not to tell anyone that she drank alone during the day.

"I don't want anyone to think I'm an alcoholic," she explained.

At first, it was fun, Generosa and Jeff having an adventure together, but she quickly made it clear who was in charge. She immersed herself in the project and became obsessed, as if her life depended on it. She would be up before dawn, churning out notes for Jeff and the contractors in her tiny, tight hand, a mixture of printing and script in which the letters were just an eighth of an inch high. No detail was too small. Anything other than instant compliance with her commands was met with fury. Her pretty blue eyes went cold, her face went red, and her words were infused with a hatred that had to have come from somewhere else, because no one could get that angry over hardware or moldings.

"Are you awake?" she would ask Jeff in phone calls at seven in the morning.

"Yeah."

"You are not!"

Jeff made the mistake of driving with her. Once. Generosa drove very fast and loose and Jeff was alarmed. When he joked about it she smiled and explained that she still had her California driver's license, more than a decade after she had moved east.

"Why?"

"I don't want to take the road test."

The couple he was now working for had piles of money. They had a town house on the Upper East Side, and owned a Learjet, they dressed their kids in Ralph Lauren clothes, helicoptered out to the island, and went to all the finest resorts, but they seemed somewhat apart from the other rich white people in town and out east. Jeff asked an innocuous social question. As she sped down the East River Drive in Manhattan, roiling river on the left, skyscrapers on the right, Generosa explained that, although they were building a home in East Hampton, "Ted and I don't want to get involved in the whole social scene."

You can't get involved because no one wants you, Jeff thought, smiling, nodding his head and keeping his mouth shut. Many others had learned about Generosa's irrational temper long before he did.

"I never want to read my name in the newspapers," she said.

As they apparently became friends, Jeff made the mistake of calling her Jenny, for short. Her response had icicles dripping from it.

"Never call me Jenny. Jenny is the name of a mule."

The foundation was dug, the concrete was poured, and the roof and frame of the expanded house went up. The architect, contractors, vendors, and workers would squint at the baby printing on their daily marching orders from Generosa, as she explained in detail, from the master list on her clipboard, just exactly what they were to accomplish that day, and how they were to do it. Jeff should have been suspicious when Generosa told him that he could not put his JEFFREY P. GIBBONS, ARCHITECT sign out front. She claimed that professional signs were tacky and she wouldn't have any on her property. Jeff was proud of his first independent project but he let it go. His name was on the plans.

As he got to know her, Jeff realized that Generosa's aggression stemmed from her insecurity. She was not a happy person. Perhaps she was incapable of happiness.

"I'm so lucky," Generosa gushed one day at her Manhattan town house. "I have the most wonderful husband in the world."

Jeff wondered if she was trying to convince him or herself. If she was so lucky and so happy, why did she regularly snap at and abuse people who depended on her for their living?

Her tantrums became an almost daily event. One morning, she was in a total snit, pointing to the screws on the light-switch plates and the wall sockets. Jeff looked but saw nothing wrong. They were the right plates and had been installed neatly and properly.

"The screws!" she protested. "They're all crooked!"

Jeff was confused. He did not know what she meant and he said so. Generosa explained that the light-switch plates and wall-socket plates not only had to be perfectly vertical but the visible screws that held them in place had to be aligned vertically and/or horizontally as well—or else. That is, the single groove on a flathead screw had to be oriented either straight up or level, and had to match the others. The X of Phillips-head screws had to be set so that the perpendicular grooves were exactly horizontal and vertical, not akimbo. It was totally inconsequential, meaningless, and utterly unnoticeable to anyone other than Generosa. Jeff could not believe what he was hearing. Talk about having a screw loose. That was when he realized that his mercurial client was not just an exacting bitch. She was crazy.

Generosa's temper had gotten worse. At the first hint, or

imagined hint, of a snub or betrayal, she lost all control in the blink of an eye and went directly to in-your-face, I'm-going-to-get-you rage. There was no reasoning with her, no appeal. Just fuck you forever. Strangely, Generosa's reactive behavior resembled a dynamic of the street, the violent attack that follows a "dis" insult, which instantly transforms a routine exchange into a life-or-death affair of honor. Nothing could have been less appropriate in Generosa's world of Rich White People, masters of the cool attack.

When one contractor admired her strength and power, Generosa told him that she was strong because her mother had been weak.

"My mother died of insanity. I had to struggle to get where I am and I'll be damned if anyone is going to take it away from me."

Her mother had died of cancer, but the contractor did not know that. Generosa's struggle, as far as he could tell, had been how to find a rich guy to marry. Since her last declaration had nothing to do with anything they were discussing, he wondered who she feared was going to take it away from her. He wondered but he said nothing.

Generosa felt that servants had to be put in their place, and that was her job as head of the staff. Ted usually let Generosa berate the servants, while he went to read a book or make a call. Jeff decided that the handsome, six-foot-four Ted, although he projected a persona of calm and reason, enjoyed watching his wife kick ass. He seemed to encourage her. But Generosa's errors or whims would frequently result in something being constructed and then ripped out because she had not realized what it would look like. On a $3 million, three-year project, in which the handmade cabinet hardware alone would cost $110,000, tremendous amounts of money were wasted. She always blamed it on someone else. She tried to envision things, to carve the flower in her head, but her lack of experience was a problem.

One weekend, she had Jeff and Ted lug logs around in the

hot sun for hours, to mark the edges of the proposed pond. After several hours of her changing her mind, with sweat dripping down his face, Ted exploded.

"Jesus Christ, Generosa!"

Once the pond was created, Generosa had an ornamental stone and concrete bridge constructed over it. She insisted that it be paved with sod, a continuation of the lawn, so that she could drive her golf cart over it. Generosa was very pleased with her bridge—until she brought a new friend, who was known as a style maven, over to see the house and grounds. It would be Generosa's dress rehearsal for her Hamptons arrival, and everything went well until the woman squinted at Generosa's big, expensive white bridge.

"How quaint," the woman said, in a patronizing tone. "It almost looks like Disneyland."

That was it for the bridge. Suddenly, Generosa hated it. It was all wrong. She had never wanted it that way. Generosa had them tear it apart and install a simpler, wooden bridge in its place.

In the middle of the house project, Jeff's mother became terminally ill. She had gone into a coma in a hospital in Pennsylvania and Jeff told Generosa that he had to be with his mother. She did not offer any sympathy. When he rushed to his mother's side, Generosa demanded phone numbers from him—not to send flowers but to track him down when she needed him. It was like working for Ebenezer Scrooge. She called him at the hospital, demanding to know when he would be back, as if he could schedule his mother's death in a day planner. He tried to remain calm and explain the situation but she wasn't interested.

"Well, you are going to finish my house, aren't you?"

Jeff was no longer shocked by her behavior. He told her he would complete the project. He later heard from a friend, who had spoken to Generosa, that she was thinking of firing him because his mother's dying was interfering with her completion schedule. The friend told him what Generosa had said:

"Hasn't anyone in his family ever died before?"

In November 1993, Generosa insisted on having the furniture she had picked out delivered to 59 Middle Lane so that she could see what it looked like. It was freezing and the house had a roof but no walls, just large, clear plastic sheeting. An icy breeze blew through the living room. She soldiered on. It was like playing with full-sized furniture in a giant, fabulous dollhouse. Generosa had Ted, Jeff, and a contractor move the furniture one way and then another and then back again. At first, it was absurd but fun, but it quickly became torturous. She made Ted hold a heavy bronze lamp up to simulate a floor lamp in the bedroom, here, there, back again. He let her know when his patience was exhausted.

"Goddammit, Generosa!"

After the movers loaded the furniture back into the truck, they drove it to a storage facility for safekeeping. When the walls and furniture were finally in, the kids were again shown their rooms—and the secret safe room. They were told what it was for and drilled in security procedures. They adopted it as their secret clubhouse and played there with their toys. Alexa brought her teapot and cups and saucers and set up a tea party with Grego and her dolls in their secret room.

Generosa seemed pleased when the landscaping began in the autumn of 1993 and continued in the spring of 1994. It meant that the project was getting closer to completion and that she could be even more hands-on. She was working with two landscape gardeners, who were also charmed by Generosa at first but soon felt her bite.

Generosa wanted golden tulips for a flower bed out front, and, as usual, she had an image chiseled in stone inside her head of what the flowers would look like. She consulted with one landscape gardener, Tim Hatter,* who warned her, "Now, you know tulips look one shade in the morning light and a different shade in the evening light." Generosa said she knew that. She picked the exact shade of yellow she wanted and the gardener planted the six hundred flowers.

They were beautiful. That weekend, he drove up the Ammon driveway and caught sight of a blur of exploding yellow in the newly planted flower bed. It was Generosa, amid a sea of yellow, her yellow hair a mess, ripping out bunches of tulips by the roots, in a frenzy, like a madwoman, and tossing them over her shoulders.

"They're the wrong shade!" she screeched, as she slaughtered the flowers.

One person who heard of the bizarre scene was reminded of the Red Queen in *Alice's Adventures in Wonderland,* who wanted to lop off heads because her roses were the wrong color. But, in real life, it wasn't funny. She ordered Tim to pay for replacements, or she would sue him, mentioning the name of a large Manhattan law firm. After she had uprooted the flower bed, she next attacked the other tulips along the front fence. He would have to pay for those as well, she demanded. He'd warned her, he said, but his protests had fallen on deaf ears. Later she also made him replace, again at his own expense, the trees by the front door because they did not produce the red berries she wanted.

Generosa also hired landscape designer Sarah Donley, who donned a bathing suit and waded into the newly filled pond to plant water lilies and other foliage to make the artificial pond look as if it had been there for a generation. In keeping with her yellow-orange color scheme out front, and blue and white out back, Generosa chose an orange trumpet vine to adorn the front entrance. Out back, they would go with blue hydrangea, lilac, blue vinca, and nasturtium. She lined one side of the long driveway with 150 ferns, at a cost of twenty thousand dollars. She also wanted to do succession plantings, in which the flower beds are composed of different flowers that bloom at different times, so there are always blossoms to please the eye. She wanted instant beauty.

"I always want to have color," Generosa instructed.

She told Sarah that she was an artist and a sculptor and a

designer. As they chatted, and interacted with the other contractors and the workmen, Sarah realized, from Generosa's body language and the things she said, that she did not like men. Sarah wondered why. She had worked for difficult clients before, ones that got off on abusing the help, but Generosa was a new experience for her. When Sarah called to postpone an appointment, her client was furious—even when Sarah explained that her mother was very sick.

"No, you have to come," Generosa told her. "I don't understand what's wrong with you. People are born and people die. My mother abandoned us and I grew up in an orphanage. I struggled to make it to where I am today but I'm all alone and I made it. I won't let anything or anyone get in my way."

She's crazy, Sarah thought. She's definitely crazy.

She had never met anyone so uncaring in her life. Sarah did not know that Generosa was not a self-made woman or that the only time she had been in an orphanage was to adopt Alexa and Grego.

Generosa was like a drill sergeant with the kids and it wasn't just an occasional lighthearted pose. The kids got their marching orders too, and Generosa insisted they hop to it.

"Chop! Chop!" she would bark, hurrying them along.

When Grego was three, he started toddling up the framed staircase, which had no railings or support. He stumbled and Sarah reached out to catch him.

"No!" Generosa yelled, slapping her arm away. "Don't you dare! He has to learn on his own."

She told Sarah that she and Ted didn't want their kids to be wimps, they wanted to toughen them up for life. Sarah thought she was sick. She wondered if the poor kids would be as crazy as their mother. She felt sorry for them. Generosa complained about how bad her mother had been to her. Did she have any clue how she was treating her own kids?

When the Ammons began moving their belongings into the house, Sarah finally got to see some of Generosa's art. It

was absolutely awful. Many were drab, abstract, flat pieces.
But one looked like a huge, white bees' nest. The lady of the
house proudly displayed it over the fireplace in the living
room. Sarah thought that Generosa's art was just like she
was: intense, devoid of feeling, and just plain strange. Where
in somebody's mind does this come from? Sarah wondered.

Her client even drove fast and recklessly in her golf cart.
Sarah had seen her bump into things, so she never parked
her car where Generosa could hit it. Generosa became more
and more difficult and now wanted other flowers ripped out,
such as the Helenium, or "Helen's flower," a yellow peren-
nial out front. Every time there was an argument, she
claimed that it was Sarah's fault the color wasn't right, or
whatever.

"I can't fucking believe that you knew the color I wanted
and you did that—you chose the wrong color!"

Sarah was getting sick of the routine. One more thing and
I quit, she decided.

Generosa showed Sarah the newly installed lawn in the
backyard. Generosa gestured to the sea of perfect green and
said, "I want an island of five hundred lavenders in the middle of the lawn. I just had it sodded."

Sarah gently tried to suggest plants other than lavender
but Generosa would not budge.

"Generosa, it's not going to work. Lavenders can't take
much water."

She explained that the sod needed much more water than
the lavenders. It was one or the other. Either the lawn would
die from lack of water or the lavenders would rot from too
much.

"I want lavenders."

Sarah put in several hundred lavender plants, about two
thousand dollars' worth, and waited. A week later, Generosa
called, madder than a wet hen. The lavenders were dying.
What a surprise.

"I can't believe these fucking plants are dying and you'd

sell something terrible like this to me," Generosa told her, implying that the plants were defective.

Sarah reminded her of her warning: She had told her they would die.

"I don't remember you telling me that," Generosa claimed, obviously lying. She gave up her claim that the plants were bad. "I don't understand why it isn't working."

She demanded that Sarah replace the plants and pay for her pigheaded mistake. Sarah did not do that. Generosa bombarded her answering machine with nasty, obscene complaints and threats that increased in viciousness each time Sarah did not call her back. Finally, Sarah called Ted, making one more try for sanity before she quit.

"Ted, I've been trying my best to work with your wife but I just can't handle her phone calls," Sarah said.

"What do you mean?" Ted asked, knowing full well that Generosa was at it again. Defending his wife, he started to tell Sarah that she was out of line, and she gave up.

"I just have to inform you that I can no longer work for you," she told Ted.

When Ted relayed the news, it hit Generosa like a slap in the face. No one quit on her; she fired them. She went berserk. She contacted the law firm Ted used and told them that she wanted to sue Sarah for messing up her garden, breach of contract, fraud, whatever. Generosa wrote a letter to Sarah, telling her that the law firm was the best in the world. She added that she was sending a copy of her false claims "to every supplier, contractor and worker who has been working with you, so they know I'm not fooling around." She demanded copies of every bill Sarah had ever given her, all her records. The message was clear: I have millions and you don't. Don't fuck with me.

Jeff heard from a vengeful Generosa what she was doing to Sarah.

"I'm going to put her out of business," Generosa vowed.

Jeff realized, with a very uneasy feeling, that once Generosa decided you had betrayed her, you were to be destroyed. And she had Ted's money to do it. He banished any thoughts of quitting.

Generosa's revenge was ugly but no one paid any attention. Sarah later decided to leave the business, in part because of clients like Generosa.

As the house neared completion, Generosa became even more intense. Everything was rush, rush, rush. They wanted the home to be finished so that they could move at the beginning of the 1995 season. Memorial Day is virtually a religious holiday in the Hamptons. Ted took Jeff aside for a confidential chat.

"Jeff, when do you really think the house is going to be done?"

"July."

Ted blanched.

"Well, don't tell her that."

A few days later, Generosa asked Jeff the same question, with Ted standing next to her. Jeff looked at Ted but he was playing dumb. Had Ted told Generosa? Should he lie, as Ted had suggested, or tell the truth? Jeff did his best to skirt around the truth but Generosa didn't like his answers and began screaming and ranting, outraged that the house might not be ready until July. Heads would roll. Ted, too, acted outraged.

"Well, it better not take that long!" Generosa threatened.

Somehow, the house was mostly finished on time. It was beautiful. There was a cedar picket fence on the lane, with an expanse of flat, green lawn beyond, the huge, gabled country cottage rising out of a skirt of yellow flowers, sheltered under a budding oak. Generosa had built her dream house. It was perfect, the home of aristocrats, of a happy family. It looked like a cover of *Architectural Digest*. Out back, the pond and the bridge and the pool were magnificent and inviting. The only odd touch was the life-size black-and-white cement cow that Generosa had brought from the city, it was now grazing near the pool. Jeff was proud of his work and brought his family to see. He later stopped by with a friend, and they were happily chatting with Generosa when Jeff began talking to his friend about designing the home.

"Wait a minute!" Generosa snapped, suddenly frowning, her cheeks red, her eyes glaring. "Seriously, I'm not joking . . . you're not telling people you did my house, are you?"

"Well, who did?" Jeff asked, incredulously.

"I did!" she screamed. "You only copied things out of books!"

She warned him not to claim designership of her house, even though he was the architect and had designed and redesigned it. It was clear to Jeff that she had considered it her plan all along, starting when she would not let him put his sign out front. That was the start of a nasty campaign by Generosa to tell anyone who would listen that she, not Jeff, had designed the home. As his final bills came due, Generosa suddenly told Jeff that she thought he was overcharging her. In fact, she wondered if he had been defrauding her.

Incredible. Squeezing contractors was a sport among the rich, Jeff had discovered. One billionaire was infamous for not paying his bills. Generosa informed Jeff that she would not pay him what she owed. Jeff thought that he could appeal to Ted, but he backed up Generosa and said that they would turn the matter over to their law firm. Jeff knew that he could spend a lot of money fighting, but the large, white-shoe Manhattan law firm would either win or make the fight so long and expensive that he would not come out ahead. Any lawyer he could hire, they could bury in mountains of paper. Jeff lost all respect for Ted. The man he thought might show some decency was just another wealthy land shark. For the first time, Jeff lost his temper and three years of frustration burst forth.

"Good things don't happen to people like you, who treat people this way!" Jeff screamed. "The way you treat people will come back and get you!"

13

MONEY CHANGES

Ted always supported Generosa in her endless battles with architects, landscapers, contractors, designers, merchants, servants, friends, and relatives, including his mother, but he was tiring of it, and particularly of the escalating nastiness of it all. Most of it seemed unnecessary. He loved his wife dearly but was beginning to wonder if the fortune he had earned was helping or harming her. Money seemed to be changing her personality for the worse. It certainly had not bought happiness. He began to see a dynamic evolving in which Generosa would blow up a friendship and Ted would try to work damage control.

"Get rid of them!" she ordered, after deciding that she had had enough of one couple.

He knew what some people were saying, the former friends who would no longer have anything to do with them because of Generosa's behavior. They thought that her charming, artistic eccentricity had evolved into strangeness, her independent assertiveness into arrogant bullying, her wry sense of humor into vicious sarcasm. Her snobbery was also out of hand. Generosa actually refused to speak to one couple because they got a place in the Hamptons north of the highway, as opposed to below Montauk Highway, closer to the ocean, where she and all the fashionable rich people lived. Ted knew that Generosa had been deeply wounded by her failure in the art world and by her inability to give him a biological child, but he had hoped that would fade now that they had adopted their wonderful kids.

Generosa seemed to be less resilient than others, less able to recover from life's shocks. He knew where the hate came from; she had told him what had been done to her as a child. Ted wished that he could do something about it. That was her most painful scar, the one she never wanted to discuss, and who could blame her? The man who had committed the unresolved crime against her three decades earlier was dead. But, for some reason, her untreated childhood trauma seemed to be interfering now, more and more, with how she related to people—even to Ted and to Alexa and Grego.

Sometimes Generosa ducked outside for a secret smoke. Ted, who was a health nut, did not want her to smoke, especially around the kids. She smoked like a fiend, but never inside, otherwise Ted could smell it. She also had secret hankerings for junk food, but Ted did not allow any in his house. His children were to be fed as many natural, organic, nonchemical foods as possible. No fake anything. No canned whipped cream, only Bruce's handmade crème fraîche.

One afternoon, while Ted was away and another couple was over for lunch, Alexa grabbed a chocolate chip cookie, despite being told by her mother not to have any before lunch. Generosa flew into a rage, grabbed Alexa and the bag of cookies, and began shoving them into her daughter's mouth. As she force-fed Alexa, she screamed at her and asked sarcastically if she wanted more. The startled guests stopped the force-feeding and wondered what was troubling their hostess, why she would do such a sadistic thing to her daughter.

The only thing that made Generosa happy was redoing, redesigning, tearing down and building up, creating her ideal of beauty, her stone flower, but that was coming to an end in East Hampton. Ted didn't want to live a life of permanent reconstruction and change, but he was a bit apprehensive about the depression that would follow once the beach house was done. Why couldn't she be happy? When Generosa's mood shifted, he felt like he was walking on eggshells. He had gently suggested a psychiatrist but Generosa was not interested. As far as she was concerned, she had dealt with her childhood by cutting herself off from it and she was just fine. It was everyone else who had problems. It was not that Generosa was incapable of trusting or becoming close with others. The others were untrustworthy and had betrayed her. She had also begun turning her famous temper on Ted, who kept his cool, even when she screamed and lectured him in front of others, which was deeply embarrassing to him.

Pamela Winston,* one of Generosa's closest friends, was one of the first to be invited to the newly completed beach house. She thanked Generosa for the invitation but was sad to say that she had already made other arrangements for that part of the summer. Generosa, without any evidence at all, decided it was a snub. She cursed and vilified her shocked and confused friend, cutting her off. She never spoke to her again. A year later, they met by chance at a charity benefit where there were scores of society matrons in designer outfits, sipping cocktails and chatting. Generosa looked well and fit and was happily conversing with someone. Pamela decided to approach her former friend, hoping that, with the passage of time, Generosa had come to her senses. She hoped that she would want to salvage their friendship and reconcile. And what better place than such a low-key, relaxing event?

Generosa saw her coming.

"Get away from me!" Generosa shrieked, shattering the mood of the event and dumbfounding those around her. "You get away from me!"

Embarrassed and concerned by the bizarre overreaction, Pamela beat a hasty retreat. She had the same thought that several others had already entertained about the mercurial Mrs. Ammon: She was crazy.

Generosa was the ultimate control freak; she took no chances and planned everything. She did not want to leave anything to chance, especially the future. When Ted's skiing buddy Colin Hastings and his wife visited the beautiful new home in East Hampton, he was impressed with the accomplishment: She had created the ideal environment for her family. She was Superwoman, but she carried her own Kryptonite with her in her head. Her inability to completely control Ted was a source of great frustration for her.

Sitting by the pool on a lovely summer day, Generosa surveyed her domain.

"You know, it can't get better than this," she told Colin, who agreed.

But, strangely, the lady of the house was not making a statement of happiness but one of resigned foreboding. She could never top what she had done and things would never be better. She began to talk about how exasperated she was that she could not control all aspects of Ted's business and private lives.

"It's very important that Ted never leave me," she said.

Colin was taken aback. It was a bolt out of the blue. He was sure that Ted loved her very much. What was she talking about?

"I'm going to make sure Ted will never leave me," she volunteered.

She explained that, since she had picked out the décor and furnishings in Ted's world, she had built the "New Ted" and owned him for life.

"If something were to happen, all the friends go with the guy," Generosa declared. "Well, who are you going to choose?" she demanded.

"Generosa, we're friends with both of you," he said.

As Ted had feared, Generosa began to meddle more and more in his business, an unwelcome assistance. One day it all came to a head when Ted was on the phone with his sister Sandi.

"I see Generosa's working for you now," Sandi said.

"What?" Ted asked, confused.

"She's on your phone directory."

"What?"

After Sandi spilled the beans, Ted hung up, picked up his cell phone, and dialed his office number. He listened to the names: "For Ted Ammon, press one, for Mark Angelson, press two. . . ." When he thought the recorded greeting was over, he was infuriated to hear this:

"For Generosa Ammon, press nine. . . ."

He slammed down the receiver. His wife had set up her own voice mail, as if she were part of the firm—without his permission. God knows what she was up to. The normally cool Ted blew his stack, took Generosa off the phone tree, and laid down the law at home.

It barely slowed her down. She began telling people that she made all of Ted's important decisions. Those who knew it wasn't true had another reason to question her mental health. Before dawn every day, Generosa was up alone in the house, drinking strong coffee and busily composing notes for her staff and for Ted, creating the day. Her meticulous, personalized lists, copied from her master, were run off on her computer and detailed what everyone would do and when. She essentially ran a small business: Milton the driver, the bodyguard, Steven the butler, Bruce the cook, the housekeeper of the month, the dog walker, and the current nanny. They, and the kids, had to accept her notes with a smile and hop to it.

Ted was another story. Generosa would grill him about his deals and offer her advice. Every morning, she handed him a note listing what he should do that day, whom he should call, whom he should meet. It started out as simple reminders but it soon progressed to the point where she was interfering with his business. Ted already had a very efficient executive assistant, Kathy Powell, and did not need another. The more vague he became about events at work, the more Generosa called Kathy for details. By 1996, it was becoming embarrassing.

To let off some steam, Ted called Sandi and vented.

"Sis, I'm miserable. I'm thinking about leaving Generosa."

He poured out his frustrations. His wife's radical mood swings were wreaking havoc in his life and everyone else's. When he sat down at the breakfast table, he never knew whether he would be saying good morning to Dr. Jekyll or Mrs. Hyde. And she refused to see a shrink, though she obviously needed help.

"Ted, you've got to make it work for the children," Sandi said.

"If I see one more goddamned list, I'm walking out!"

Sandi counseled a soft-soap approach.

"Ted, when she gives you your list, just say, 'Thank you, sweetheart,' and tear up the list when you get to the office."

"I can't," said Ted.

Generosa, he explained, questioned him on each and every point at night and peppered him with phone calls during the day.

"It's driving me crazy," he said, sighing.

Generosa called Sandi and complained that Ted was becoming cold and distant, cutting himself off from her and caring only about money. Sandi knew that Ted worked long hours and traveled for business and perhaps wasn't as affectionate as he once had been. Generosa felt that she had been the perfect wife, but their problems were cooling their physical relationship.

Later, Ted's mother, Bettylee, listened to the problem and decided that it stemmed mostly from Generosa's upbringing.

"Generosa just doesn't understand how families work," Bettylee said, meaning that it was not Generosa's fault that she had never had a mother and father and did not know that people could fight and make up and still love each other.

With Generosa, it was all or nothing. Actually, it was

worse than that. Generosa did not trust families. The ones who were closest to her had the capacity to hurt her most. On a basic level, she was jealous of any affection Ted lavished on anyone else, including his mother and Sandi.

Generosa made sure that the children, now six, were in bed by seven-thirty on school nights, which gave Ted only half an hour after dinner to talk and play with them. It was quality but not quantity time. The rest of the evening, Generosa reserved for her and Ted alone. He tried to extend the twins' bedtime so that they could have more time together every day but Generosa would not hear of it, saying that they needed their rest. He tried coming home earlier but the kids would be in the bath, right on schedule, according to Generosa's lists. Ted was beginning to suspect that she was becoming jealous even of their closeness to him.

Ted, always popular with the ladies, began to flirt with other women and wondered what it would be like to divorce Generosa. He suggested marriage counseling and they went for some sessions, stopped, and later tried it again, without lasting success. Generosa demanded increasingly elaborate demonstrations of his love but nothing seemed to convince her for long.

At a parent-teacher event at school one evening, Ted was chatting with a mother about their kids and the school. Generosa watched them for a while and then walked over and in a loud voice ordered her to stop flirting with Ted. Everyone in the room heard her. It was embarrassing to Ted and the woman, as well as to those who overheard. It was so out of place, so devoid of class, that some assumed it was just a joke. Generosa was wrong. Ted was not having an affair with the attractive mother. But Generosa was a very perceptive woman. She had the right church, but the wrong pew.

Mary Belknap,* five years younger than Generosa, was an investment banker at a firm that did business with Ted. She looked like Hollywood's idea of an investment banker: bright, blond, and beautiful. Mary, who lived with a man, became social friends with Ted and Generosa. But Generosa's mood turned black when Mary came to a black tie dinner at the Ammon town house in a bewitching designer outfit, including a translucent blouse that revealed her perfect breasts. Generosa was pretty, but Mary was gorgeous, the most alluring woman in the room. Generosa watched her husband's eyes while he looked at Mary. She hated what she saw. Ted, that son of a bitch, and the other men were drooling over her like dogs.

The nerve of the woman to come into my house dressed like that, Generosa thought, her temper barely under control. She's nothing but a whore.

She was jealous of the way Ted spoke to Mary and she knew that they spent time together at work. Perhaps that was one reason why Ted was trying to shut her out of his business life. He would hardly be the first of his successful colleagues to have a fling with a younger woman. It was not unusual for a rich financier to dump his first spouse and shack up with a young trophy wife.

By the summer of 1998, their relationship was strained to the breaking point. Generosa was very suspicious when Ted was not home and she suspected him of infidelity. Her devoted butler, Steven, who dabbled in the occult, took her to a psychic. Generosa asked the fortune-teller if her husband was cheating on her. He was, the psychic told her.

Ted denied it and Generosa couldn't prove it, but the psychic was correct.

Fighting with Generosa was becoming a full-time job for Ted. When he'd retreat to his Chancery Lane Capital office on East Fifty-fourth Street, she'd call him there and yell at him on the telephone. Ted would hold the phone away from his ear and others in the room could hear her clearly— screaming at the top of her lungs.

One such harangue was particularly ominous. Generosa did not say—as many people do in the heat of emotion— that she would kill Ted. Strangely, she said she would hire someone to do it.

"I'll have you killed," she vowed.

She seemed serious. Ted hung up the phone and walked outside his office to where his associate, Larry Field,* was sitting. He had heard Ted's side of the argument. Ted told Larry that Generosa had threatened to hire a hit man to murder him.

"She threatened to have me done away with. I'm dealing with a nut. I'm dealing with someone who's out of her mind," Ted told Larry, shaking his head and chuckling nervously.

"Well, threats can be made in moments of anger," Larry offered.

Ted shrugged.

"This woman is crazy," he insisted.

His nervousness wasn't just from embarrassment. Ted did not know what to do. He didn't want to inflict a divorce on the kids, but he couldn't deal with Generosa's obsessive meddling. Still, if he left her, Ted knew that things would get worse—for him and the kids, who had begun to notice the cracks in the marriage. More and more, Ted would pull his disappearing acts, flying to England or Europe on business and vanishing for a few days. Frantic to track him down, Generosa pestered Ted's assistant, Kathy, who had come to detest her boss's wife.

Generosa's assistant, Phyllis, also noticed changes in her former boss. Strangely, Generosa had become one of the women she herself hated: a shallow, snobby, society wife. Phyllis couldn't imagine Ted forcing Generosa to repress her personality. Why had she? Phyllis felt she had lost a friend and a mentor. Phyllis wondered how it had happened. Generosa was not one of those people. Why did she act like one?

In 1998, Ted's mother, Bettylee, died, devastating him. Her memorial service was in the small Protestant church he had attended as a child. Returning to his childhood home for the funeral was the kind of somber occasion that could cause a man like Ted to reflect on his mortality and the brevity of life. As he looked at his mother's casket, Ted thought about her life and his—where he had been, where he was, and where he wanted to go. And with whom.

His mother was a wonderful woman who had told him that he could do anything he set his mind to. But Ted's first marriage had failed, and now his second was faltering. Why was he such a success at work yet such a failure at home?

His mother was later cremated, according to her wishes. "I don't need to take up space when I'm gone," she had told him with a smile.

After the simple and moving Christian service, Ted turned to Sandi and told her that he too, preferred cremation to burial.

"That's what I would like to have too," he said.

14

THE BIG PAYOUT

Danny Pelosi and his wife, Tami, did not have a mansion with servants and contractors to fight with. They had bills they could not pay and fought with each other. Generosa's hardware bill was more than twice what Danny earned in his best year. Even sober, he repeatedly cheated on Tami; and their marriage was falling apart.

Danny's civil trial over his work accident began on Monday, March 28, 1994, in a courtroom in Riverhead. Preparing for the trial, Danny's lawyers had told him that he could win a million-dollar settlement for his injury and his pain and suffering.

Danny was called to the stand on the fourth day of the trial by his lawyer, Bart Rebore. On direct questioning by Rebore, Danny told the jurors that when he got hurt, he "was just a yo-yo kid, trying to make a living, trying to get by, going to the job that paid me the most money."

He gave his version of the accident but did not finish his testimony and was set to return to the stand the next day. On Thursday, Tami couldn't drive Danny to court, so he took a chance and drove himself with a suspended license. As usual, Danny got caught. He drove into the lot at supreme court in Riverhead, parked, and emerged from his van. Bart

Rebore, who had also just parked his car, was dumbfounded and furious.

"Are you out of your mind?" he screamed at Danny.

As Rebore yelled at Danny, they both turned and realized that they had an audience: a few of the jurors on the case. They too, had noticed Danny driving the van and were watching the lawyer lace into his client.

Back on the stand, Danny was cross-examined by attorney Donald Deegan, the lawyer for the owner of the building. Again, Danny went over the details of his fall through the ceiling and the accident scene in great detail. When he was asked about his early arrests, he at first pleaded a faulty memory.

"I don't know. You're going back to stuff I did when I was a kid."

Deegan then grilled Danny about his three DWI arrests, his speeding ticket, his unreported accident, and his license suspensions.

"And your license is suspended right now, isn't it, sir?"

"Yes, sir," Danny answered.

"Mr. Pelosi, is it not a fact that, when your license is suspended, you're not supposed to drive? Isn't that correct?"

"Yes, sir."

"And that's exactly what you were doing Thursday morning when you came to court? You were driving your van, weren't you?"

"Yes, sir."

"While you were driving without a license. Isn't that so?"

"That's when my attorney asked me if I was out of my mind, yes, sir."

"Mr. Pelosi, you said to this court, and to the jury, that, back at the time of this accident in 1982, you were just 'a yo-yo kid' who followed orders, correct, sir?"

"Yes, sir."

"How old are you now?" Deegan asked.

"Thirty."

"And you're still not following orders, though, are you?"

Danny did not answer the question.

Deegan painted Danny as a drunken liar and drug addict, a scary malingerer and probably a con artist who was trying to make money by switching professions from laborer to the more profitable career of a fall-down artist who faked accidents. Deegan sarcastically referred to the 1988 incident, saying that when Danny had been cut off by a drunken driver, he proved himself "Mister Maturity and Mister Discretion" by bailing out of his car, ready for a fistfight.

At the end of the trial, the jury retired to consider its verdict, for which Danny and Tami had waited and hoped for twelve years. After the jurors reached a verdict, the jury foreman said that the building owner and his tenant, the owner of the auto body shop, had violated state labor laws by failing to keep Danny safe while he worked. They let Danny's former employer, the masonry company, off the hook. But they also said Danny's negligence caused the accident. Danny's hopes for a good verdict and a big cash settlement seemed to be fading. The clerk read the last question, number ten: "What was the percentage of fault of the auto body shop?"

"Sixty percent," answered the jury foreman.

The clerk then asked what percentage of blame they had set for Danny.

"Forty percent," the foreman replied.

The only good news was that the jury had ascribed more blame to the auto body people than to Danny. It could have been worse.

"Members of the jury," said the clerk, "please listen as your verdict is—"

"I'm sorry, I'm sorry, excuse me," sputtered the foreman.

"Wait a minute—" interrupted the judge.

"I made an error," the embarrassed foreman explained. It was forty percent for the auto body shop "and sixty percent for the plaintiff."

The jury had decided that Danny was more to blame for his accident than those who ran the shop where it happened.

"Sixty for the plaintiff?" the judge asked, making sure.

"Yes," confirmed the foreman.

But there was good news. The jury found that the defendants in Danny's two other lawsuits, against the auto body shop and the landlord, were one hundred percent liable. Danny could still get a big payout, which would be determined during the second part of the trial, the penalty phase.

15

A DOLLAR AND A DREAM

Jim Pelosi was sworn in as a New York City cop in 1995. The family was very proud of him. He applied for and was granted the badge number of his great-uncle, who had been killed in the line of duty during the Roaring Twenties.

In June, Danny's wife, Tami, was also making progress and would be receiving her B.A. in human services. But that same year, Danny and Tami had to file for Chapter 7 bankruptcy. Before the penalty phase, though, Danny had to meet with a psychiatrist—something the defense had demanded.

In March 1995, he and his lawyer, Bart Rebore, arrived at Dr. Michael Melamed's Glen Cove office for the session. As he often did, Danny made a bad impression, speaking animatedly in his thick blue-collar New York accent, in which the word *this* came out as "dis" and the phrase *that belongs to her* emerged as "dat bulongs ta huh."

Immediately, Danny seized the floor and, with a smile, told Melamed what he wanted to know. The doctor hardly needed to ask any questions, and Melamed was struck with Danny's arrogance and macho bravado. He paced around the room, at one point, telling Melamed that he needed a few more wall outlets, trying to hustle the doc up for some electrical business. Danny was obviously trim and healthy and not in pain from his accident thirteen years ago.

Rebore tried to slow his client down by telling him: "Dan, it sounds like you're trying to sell yourself to the doctor."

Danny ignored his lawyer and continued babbling, next describing how smart he was: "I ain't stupid. I can learn real fast. When I went to take the test for electrician, I could not understand the questions," said Danny, gesturing with his hands. "You gotta go to school for it, I was told, but I don't really need to do that, because I know what equipment to install, just from my education and experience."

Polishing his tough-guy credentials, Danny told Melamed about his arrests, his accident, about drug and alcohol flashbacks, and that he took Valium. Though Danny was the son of bankers, his exaggerated accent was almost a caricature of an uneducated blue-collar laborer. It seemed to Melamed that Danny described his illegal activities with particular zest and enthusiasm, as if he were proud of them as accomplishments.

Melamed wasn't so sure it was the fall that had made a mess of Danny. Was this guy really trying to tell him that he consumed more than 100 milligrams of Valium a day, in addition to painkillers with codeine, and didn't feel tired?

Danny said he had tried to quit drinking about twenty times, without success.

But tough guy or not, falling off the ladder broke him like a twig, Danny seemed to be saying.

"I didn't feel like a man after the accident," Danny said. "It was difficult to stand up for myself and provide for my family."

Anyone who ingested such copious quantities of drugs could not feel strong. It was just biologically impossible. Melamed couldn't maintain his professional posture and made a comment: "I'm surprised you're still alive at all, using so many sedatives and drinking so much on a daily basis, let alone stand up and feel like a man," said Melamed, "because I have seen people stop breathing from less than that."

Danny blamed all his problems on the accident. He described twenty separations from his wife, cheating on Tami over and over and going through family counseling and individual therapy, but he "continued to drink, drug and lie my ass off."

Tami, said Danny, was good to him and remained supportive despite his character defects.

"What do you think your character defects are?" the psychiatrist asked.

"Anger and rage and the need to take out my rage on other people," said Danny, who called himself "sadistic" because he got enjoyment out of other people's pain and suffering.

Melamed moved on to some tests, handing Danny a pen and paper and asking him to draw two figures, a man and a woman. Danny went to work earnestly and soon produced a childlike effort, a male figure with a very big, wide head without a neck. It had very large staring eyes without pupils and raised eyebrows. The mouth was wide, grinning, and toothless. On top of the head was hair and a cap. To most, the inelegant rendering betrayed simply a lack of artistic talent. But to those in Melamed's profession, it was a trove of dark symbols. Melamed thought that the overall picture of the male figure indicated a sense of fear, futility, paranoia, and inadequacy. He saw the strange eyes as an indication that Danny viewed the world as a dangerous and threatening place. The baseball cap on the head was not an indication that Danny liked baseball but that he was immature and was trying to mask his sexuality.

The large-busted female figure Danny inked also had a big head, with giant eyes and an open, grinning, toothless mouth that looked like it might bite. The overall impression was that of a threatening malelike female figure. The fact that he drew the female in pants with her hands in her pockets showed an evasiveness and unwillingness to deal with situations, which was typical of psychopaths, Melamed believed.

The doctor later composed an eleven-page psychiatric-examination report, in which he diagnosed Danny as suffering from four problems: "Mixed substance abuse, including sedatives, hypnotics, narcotics, hallucinogens, marijuana, alcohol, in remission. Mixed personality disorder with traits indicated above. Strong antisocial traits . . . accident on the job with lumbo-sacral sprain, currently in remission. Ongoing marital stress based on the first two diagnoses above."

Later, at home, Danny read a copy of Melamed's report, which his lawyer had given him, and could not believe what it said.

"I'm not sure of my sexuality because I drew a hat?" he said.

His wife, Tami, entered the room.

"Hey, Tam, guess what? I'm gay!" Danny announced, laughing.

He handed her the report and called Rebore. When the lawyer answered, Danny made another joke.

"Hey, Bart, you want to meet me in the bathroom? What is this? You know, that guy's a real jerkoff. He's out to screw me," Danny said. "Can we get a real psychiatrist to do an evaluation on me?"

The second trial took place in a different Riverhead courtroom, with a different judge, Suffolk County Supreme Court Justice Alan Oshrin. Jury selection began on March 20, 1995. Danny was the first to take the stand and was directly questioned by Bart Rebore.

Danny once again related in great detail his accident and his painful injuries and getting hooked on Valium. But Danny insisted that he "drank like every other normal person drinks."

He admitted that he developed financial and marital problems. He began to abuse alcohol and went into counseling. Later, he said, he stopped drinking, went to AA meetings, and started his own business, although he still had back pain from the accident.

On cross-examination, Deegan asked Danny about his drug use.

"I tried everything," Danny said.

"Cocaine?"

"Everything."

"Hallucinogenics?"

"Everything."

"Smack?"

"I tried everything."

He admitted that he bought drugs from dealers and stole drugs and that he had sold his Valium prescription "to support my family," but denied that he sold drugs to buy alcohol and other drugs. He said that he had sold the prescription to buy food. He admitted that he had driven while drunk. When questioned about accepting cash payment to avoid taxes, he took the Fifth Amendment against self-incrimination.

Throughout the trial, Danny moved his upper body stiffly, like he was uncomfortable. Travis, another opposing attorney, protested Danny's "gyrations in front of the jury. I think they are very prejudicial." Obviously, the lawyer was implying that Danny's movements were staged for the jury. More weirdness followed. Asked about his work history and sensitive about Melamed's report, he made a nonsensical joke on the stand:

"I'm not a faggot. I ain't no queer. Of course I intend to work."

Nobody laughed.

During a break, Danny's lawyer told him that there were two gays on the jury and that his "faggot" remark had not been a good idea.

After Danny finished, he was excused and stepped down from the stand. During his testimony, he had admitted to multiple crimes and to being a liar, and he had taken the Fifth Amendment. Danny thought he had done great but his time on the stand was a disaster.

It was then time for their opponent's case and Deegan called the psychiatrist, Dr. Michael Melamed, as their star witness. Under direct questioning by Donald Deegan, lawyer for defendants Granite Cement & Brick Masons Inc., Melamed described his evaluation of Danny. He displayed and described Danny's drawing, which he claimed was chock-full of symbolism that revealed the demons hidden in Danny's psyche. He said that Danny's male figure betrayed a rigid, self-protective posture that bespoke his insecurity and confusion about his identity. The crude hat represented an assertion of Danny's sexuality. But the eyes Danny had scribbled seemed to fascinate Michael, who was convinced they indicated "overemphasized hostility of the world as a threatening place. The piercing eyes indicated the watching out for threats and dangers from others." He said the female drawing was very masculine with a "very threatening mouth. You could expect to be bitten or yelled at through a mouth like this. The eyes— piercing, piercing, piercing, angry paranoid eyes. I can go on and on about it but basically, it just showed a sense of confusion over sexuality, definitely a sense of paranoia, insecurity, defensiveness and instability."

More than one observer in the courtroom, other than Danny, was of the opinion that psychoanalyzing someone on the basis of their art talent was a stretch.

Melamed scoffed at Danny's claim that all of his problems were caused by his accident. Stormy relationships would be the lot of a sociopath like Danny, said Michael. "In all intimate relationships there would be a need for crisis, for problems, for a person like that." Frequent fights, confrontations, and occasional violent episodes could be expected, he said. The antisocial behavior was not the result of alcohol and drugs but was the result of a lifelong antisocial character disorder. When asked by Deegan if character disorders could be cured, Melamed responded:

"Well, let's put it this way: If it were the case, we would have fixed personality disorders surgically and I would have no job."

Sociopaths like Danny, he said, often brag that they can

do everything, anything they decide to do, but actually cannot do much.

On cross, Rebore asked Melamed if Danny had done anything antisocial during his interview and the psychiatrist explained that antisocial personalities, like psychopaths, "are usually very likable on the surface. Actually, such individuals, as we know very well from, even, movies: they deceive you by how superficially pleasant and nice they are . . . don't they say, 'Don't turn your back on a person like that'?"

"So, if I'm friendly to somebody, that means I'm antisocial?"

Deegan objected but the judge allowed him to answer.

"The answer is no," said Melamed.

After some more sparring, Rebore seized on the psychiatrist's definition of antisocial behavior, which was broad enough to cover the entire human race. "Okay, so that everybody who exceeds the fifty-five miles per hour speed limit is antisocial, in your view?"

"In that moment, yes," said Melamed.

"Okay, have you ever exceeded the fifty-five miles per hour speed limit?"

"This morning," Melamed said, with a chuckle.

"Okay, so you're antisocial?"

"Not in the total context of my personality."

"Okay."

When Rebore again tried to paint Danny as the hardworking father looking for work, sticking with his wife while they were in debt, Melamed countered that it was Tami who maintained the relationship, not Danny.

Rebore tried to ridicule the psychiatrist's report that said because Danny had drawn a baseball cap on the male figure, it meant that he was trying to mask his sexuality.

"So this basically just reflects the inner workings of the mind, rather than Mister Pelosi's intention to draw a child or Joe DiMaggio or anybody else with a baseball cap?" Rebore asked.

Melamed, looking at the drawing, admitted that maybe

the lawyer was right: "It does look like a child and maybe this is the frightened child that's still there."

"The frightened child in us all, Doctor?"

"That's still there."

Danny had high hopes that a positive verdict and a large settlement would fix everything in his life. His lawyers claimed that he would lose more than a million dollars in earnings over the rest of his life, and the pain and suffering in such cases often amounted to millions more. Danny did not have to be there during the whole trial but he lounged in the last row of the courtroom, his feet up on the seat in front of him, his hands laced behind his head, and glared at the jury. Some of the women jurors cast nervous glances his way and he continued to stare at them. They were frightened by his eyes. They decided that he was trying to intimidate them.

After closing statements, the jurors began deliberating. Deegan told the judge that some jurors had fears about Danny. The judge said that an alternate juror had told him that other jurors on the panel "were completely intimidated by Mister Pelosi. They said he sat in the back of the courtroom staring at them. And juror number two expressed some concern for his safety, saying that if he didn't come in with a substantial fact verdict—"

"That somehow or another," Deegan interrupted, "Mr. Pelosi could find out where they lived and that maybe some unfortunate things may happen to them. And during the course of the discussion, apparently, some of the jurors seem to have expressed the same opinion." The court clerk granted a jury request that they be escorted by a court officer to their cars after they had rendered a verdict.

The judge said that if there was a verdict in favor of Danny, he would question the jurors to make sure that they had not awarded him money out of fear.

The jury filed back into the courtroom.

Danny, dressed in a suit and tie, was very nervous. His

heart was beating so hard, his tie was fluttering up and down
on his chest.

"When the jury comes back and they answer yes to the
first question, you rang the bell," Rebore said to Danny, pre-
dicting victory.

On question one—whether Danny had suffered a substantial injury in the accident—the jury agreed that the answer was yes, prompting a moment of hope at Danny's table.

Holy shit, Danny thought, I got it made.

But their hopes were dashed when the foreman read the
answer to question number two—how much money to award
Danny for his injury. The verdict sheet had two lines to fill in
with dollar amounts, and the clerk first asked the foreman
how much they had awarded Danny for "pain and suffering
to the date of your verdict."

"Zero," replied the jury foreman.

There was a faint gasp in the courtroom.

Danny's heart seemed to stop. He turned to his lawyer in
confusion.

"What happened?"

"Loss of earnings for the years 1992 and 1993?"

"Zero," the foreman answered.

Danny didn't get even a dollar, much less his dream settlement. It was over. His big, expected windfall was gone
with the wind, even though the jury thought that he was truly
injured.

The written verdict sheet was rather unusual. The two zeros were not simply penned in; instead, they were over-
scored half a dozen times, as if each member of the jury had
delighted in individually writing his or her own zero on top
of the other jurors' zeros, to emphasize their decision. Their
message was clear: They did not believe a word Danny said,
apparently even when he was telling the truth. Danny felt
that the jury had requested escorts after their verdict because
they knew they were going to ruin his life. His lawyers appealed the verdict but it was a waste of time.

• • •

Despite his problems, Danny remained on the wagon for three more years. In April 1998, he went back to criminal court and pleaded guilty to drunk driving. He got six months in jail and five years' probation. When he got out, he had to report weekly to his probation officer and was required to remain sober and drug free. That same year, he landed a good wiring subcontract out east. The contractor who gave him the work insisted that they go to a bar at two in the afternoon to seal the deal. He would not take no for an answer.

"If you don't drink with me, I ain't giving you that cash deposit," the contractor said.

"Line 'em up," Danny replied.

After nine years on the wagon, Danny got drunk and kept on drinking. He had two shots of tequila and a Budweiser to toast the deal and he got his deposit check. Driving home at eleven o'clock that night, he was pulled over by police for drunk driving. Because he had been drinking, Danny panicked and ran toward his house, just down the block. When he came to his senses, he dropped to his knees and pleaded with the cops:

"I'm the brother of an officer!"

Bob Pelosi got another late-night call from his son, who was behind bars yet again.

The next year, Danny's debts were mounting. He didn't have a dollar to his name that wasn't spoken for.

Early one morning, Danny and his coworkers were on their way into Manhattan on another job when they stopped at a 7-Eleven to buy buttered rolls, egg sandwiches, and strong coffee in styrofoam cups. Some of the guys bought lotto tickets, hoping to hit it big. The machine bore the New York Lotto slogan: "All it takes is a dollar and a dream!"

Danny now had a different dream. As they crossed the East River on the Fifty-ninth Street Bridge, Danny took in the Manhattan skyline and looked up at the luxury condo towers. While they were gulping fast food on their way to work, the rich people above them were eating nice breakfasts off expensive china, drinking fresh-squeezed orange juice out of crystal glasses, and enjoying the view.

Danny began to fantasize about landing a rich woman. After all, he cheated all the time with other women but got nothing out of it. As he voiced his wish, it sounded less like a workingman's daydream and more like a vow:

"There's a woman in here who's payin' those big rents, who's single," he told his pals. "And she's gonna be gorgeous and I'm gonna find her."

16

COVERWOOD

Ted was known for his creative solutions to complex financial conundrums. Now he had a much more complex—and dangerous—conundrum in his wife. He loved her but by now was involved with Mary Belknap, which Generosa may have suspected but did not know for certain.

If he divorced Generosa, she would go ballistic and, if possible, become nuttier than she was already. He did not want to subject the kids to a divorce, especially a nasty one.

When the Internet and the telecommunications bubble burst, when the stock market finally realized the new electronic emperor had no clothes, the stocks tanked. It was a setback for Ted, whose $400 million net worth began to shrink rapidly.

By 1998, Ted knew that Generosa would tie him up and probably leave him with less than half his dwindling wealth. Under New York divorce law, Ted would also have to pay all of the living expenses for Generosa and the kids. In the end, it would leave him with significantly less personal capital. Adding urgency to the puzzle was the fact that Mary had just told Ted that she was pregnant. How long would it be before she started to show and the gossips got wind of it and assumed Ted was the father? How much longer after that would the news take to reach Generosa?

Of course, there was no real, comprehensive solution to the problem. No matter which way Ted twisted and turned, it would never come to pass without rage and pain and expense. But one day that year, Ted hit on what he thought was the best possible answer, a half solution. After having fought a move there years earlier, Generosa had been hinting about moving to London. Ted could move to London with her and the kids and set up business there, as he had wanted to do years earlier. Mary would stay in New York and Ted could commute, using business as his excuse. From Generosa's side of the Atlantic, everything would seem perfect—as long as she could not see what Ted was doing in New York, as long as there was an ocean between them. Of course, the plan would involve deception and subterfuge, things that Ted did not like, but he felt it was the best way, for the moment. He was hardly the first husband to take the easy, self-serving path that allowed him to have his cake and eat it too. At least, until he was ready.

The first deception was soft-selling the idea to Generosa. He was able to rationalize his behavior because he had not definitely decided on divorce. Why hurt Generosa unnecessarily? Why upset the kids? The marriage could work. Maybe, after a while, he would get Mary out of his system.

He told Generosa that they would buy a luxury flat in London and find a beautiful home in the countryside. It wouldn't be like the Hamptons, with a social scene to be left out of. It would just be Generosa and Ted and the kids. She would get a new staff, and, of course, she could gut and redo and furnish and landscape both properties; whatever she wanted, whatever it cost.

It was like giving candy to a baby.

She jumped at the chance to start afresh. That's what Generosa did: new starts. Ted knew that refurbishing a London condo and a big country home—the bigger the better—would keep her happy and busy and out of his hair for at least a year. Her only objection was that they couldn't immediately bring their new dog, Buddy, because English law required that animals be quarantined for six months as a precaution against rabies. Ted suggested that that was the tail wagging the dog but Generosa was adamant. She said that she and the children could not survive without Buddy for six months and the poor dog should not be in a cage for that long, so she made Ted promise to take care of him. It was a deal breaker.

Ted had no idea how he would do it, but he knew how to deal with deal breakers—promise anything to cut the deal and then worry about it later, after the paperwork was signed. Once they were committed, Ted would either find a way to avoid quarantine or he would not. He told Generosa that they would send Buddy there six months earlier, or find some way around it. Generosa agreed and, suddenly, she was happy again. They made plans to fly to England to start looking at real estate and get things squared away for the move.

The Ammons chose a London flat in an elegant Victorian-era hotel called The Cadogan on Sloane Street in fashionable Knightsbridge. The ornate, six-story brick and sandstone building faced the trees, green lawn, and rose garden of Cadogan Square Park. The hotel was once the home of American actress Lillie Langtry, who threw Gilded Age parties for her social set, including Oscar Wilde and King Edward VII. In 1895, Wilde, drunk on white wine and soda, was arrested in room 118 for gross indecency.

For their country home, the Ammons chose Coverwood House, a huge, baronial stone manor on seventeen acres of landscaped grounds, set in the green, rolling hills of Surrey, thirty-five miles from their pied-à-terre in London. It was a gothic eleven-thousand-square-foot mansion with ten bedrooms, a living room, a dining hall, a library, an office, and an art studio. Outside, the terraced property was graced by a koi pond, a greenhouse, stables for the horses, and two tennis courts. But once Ted had put a down payment on the estate, he had second thoughts. He decided not to accept the position with an international investment bank in London. Too late: Generosa was now set on living in England. They decided to stay.

After researching the choices, they decided that Alexa and Grego would attend the Cranleigh School, an upper-crust English boarding school founded in 1865 for the privileged children of the rich and aristocratic. The students wore uniforms, including blazers emblazoned with school crests and school ties. The dining hall, with its arched wooden beams, hanging chandeliers, and great stone fireplace, looked like the Hollywood version of an English boarding school, as depicted in the *Harry Potter* movies. The school was only ten minutes from Coverwood by car but the twins would board at the school during the week and return home only on weekends, holidays, and summer vacations. Of course, it was close enough for Ted and Generosa to visit to watch their children's sporting events, such as tennis and cricket. Alexa was developing into a fine horsewoman, like her mother, who encouraged and helped her.

Surprisingly, for a pair of American kids, they took to their new school with gusto. They made new friends and thrived. One of the reasons they were happy there was that living at school was less stressful than being with their parents.

They lived the lives of landed gentry. Generosa had her horses transported to England and ensconced in the Coverwood stables. Always a solid rider and jumper, she participated in several fox hunts. Ted went fishing and hunting in Scotland for recreation or popped over to the Alps for world-class skiing.

Generosa transported part of her staff, Steven and Bruce, to England. She did a magnificent job of decorating her new treasures, especially Coverwood. Her favorite place was still the beach house in East Hampton but she had created her Gracious Home, the seat of American aristocrats. She was happier than she had been in some time, especially because she believed that now that she had built yet another perfect place for Ted, a place where they could be in their own kingdom, all their problems would melt away. She already felt more at ease in her own skin and confident that everything would work out.

Her friend Jurate, her former Manhattan neighbor, visited Coverwood and was awed by the estate, but more so by what Generosa had done to it. It was the work of a top flight pro. Her taste was exquisite and eclectic. Jurate admired a costly antique sculpture next to a lovely ceramic work she could not identify.

"Oh, I got that at the Pottery Barn," Generosa said, laughing.

It all worked. It was like walking through a magazine spread. Ted went out for a bike ride and the ladies had English tea in the new kitchen. There, Generosa confided that the real reason for the move was to save her marriage. It was five miles to the nearest pub and almost two hours by car to London. Generosa seemed content, at last, but Ted was obviously not happy, Jurate felt. She wished Generosa well with her plan to preserve her relationship with Ted and then the hostess changed the subject, regaling her guest with the tale of her first fox hunt.

Generosa came up with a fantastic way to celebrate Ted's upcoming fiftieth birthday and also their new, renewed relationship after twelve years of marriage. They would fly to the Caribbean with nine other couples. She chose Necker Island in the British Virgin Islands, an exclusive, private island owned by Sir Richard Branson. They would take over the entire island for a week as pampered castaways in the Caribbean. Robinson Crusoe with room service, gourmet feasts, superlative wines, Jacuzzis, swimming pools, massages, and anything else they could think of. At $15,000 a couple, it would cost Ted $150,000 for his week-long birthday celebration. Generosa micromanaged every detail: who had which room, and all the activities.

The palm and cactus emerald isle, set in a turquoise sea and rimmed with coral reefs, was one of the most exquisite

places in the world, with Balinese pagoda pavilions set on
green and rocky headlands overlooking Drake's Channel or
placid Virgin Gorda Sound. For seven days, Ted, Generosa,
Sandi, Jurate, her husband Roger, Colin Hastings and his
wife, Sally, and a dozen other friends walked in beauty.
They also swam in the crystal waters, waterskied, wind-
surfed, snorkeled among rainbows of fish and coral, sailed
astride briny tradewinds, and lounged on sugar sand
beaches. Ted and Generosa shared a magnificent, romantic
Balinese suite overlooking sea and sky but the trip was turning into a disaster for them. Every day was a vacation and
every night was a party, but the week did not rekindle the
beauty they had once had.

Sandi was alone because her husband could not get away
from the hospital. She knew of the stress in her brother's
marriage, but when she saw Ted and Generosa playing and
laughing and dining, she thought that they were over their
rough patch. But before the week was out, Jurate pointed out
to Sandi that Ted and Generosa, although cordial and happy
on the surface, were not as close as they once had been.
Sandi watched them and realized that it was true. The couple
who couldn't keep their hands off each other seemed never
to touch and Ted was often not at her side. Jurate could see
that Generosa was still in love with Ted but the marriage was
obviously on the rocks. As Sally Hastings and Ted strolled
on a deserted beach, Ted talked about his wife.

"I hope Generosa understands that she has a lot to live for,"
said Ted. "This doesn't have to be the end of everything."

The culmination of the week was the last glittering celebration on the night before departure, a costume party. Sandi
came as Carmen Miranda, complete with towering fruit hat.
Generosa was a pirate's wench. Ted, of course, was a pirate,
although the full, ruffled sleeves of the costume Generosa
brought for him made him look less like a buccaneer than a
Latino musician at the Copacabana in 1955.

After the vacation, Generosa reminded Ted of his promise and insisted that he smuggle Buddy into England, the last

component of the perfect, pastoral life Generosa was creating for her family. Ted discovered that there was no legal way to get the dog in and said it was not possible. But Generosa asked around and discovered that there was a pet underground that smuggled pets into merry olde England for their rich owners. She got a name and a phone number and set up the caper. All Ted had to do was fly Buddy to Paris and meet the smugglers in northern France with a bag of cash, she told him. Ted tried reason, suggesting that they do it according to the law, but Generosa would not hear of it. Ted finally gave in.

Buddy did three times what most people would never do. He made three expensive trips on the Concorde supersonic jetliner to Paris, one round trip and one one-way. On each flight, he was the only pet, because the SST had room for only one animal per flight. In August 1999, Ted and Buddy winged to Paris aboard the Concorde. Once in France, Ted purchased a beret, to blend in, picked up a luxury car, and drove with Buddy to the rendezvous in northern France. He waited with Buddy and his bag of money for hours but the smugglers never appeared. Ted called a frustrated Generosa, who was unable to explain why the conspiracy had collapsed. They had agreed on a phone code, in which Buddy was "the package" and the smugglers were "the deliverymen." It was pretty silly, the millionaire and the socialite playing spy. Ted had no choice. He had to return to Paris and fly back to the States with Buddy. He drove back to the City of Light the next day and spent his fiftieth birthday alone, except for the unsmuggled Buddy at his feet, sipping fine Bordeaux wine and enjoying delicious French cuisine in the sunshine at a fashionable outdoor café on the Champs-Élysées.

When he and Buddy got home to New York, Generosa told him that her pet connection had fallen through. She told Ted to smuggle Buddy in by himself. Again, he resisted. He had agreed to hand off to the professional dog runners but was not particularly interested in going into that line of work. When he told Sandi and his friends about Generosa's international pet intrigue, they told him that he was crazy to give in to his wife's nutty scheme, especially since he was the one who was going to do it. They could imagine the headlines: BANKER NABBED AS SMUGGLER.

Generosa threw a tantrum. She was hysterical, irrational. Sandi tried to persuade Ted to bring the dog to her home in Alabama, where Buddy would have a lovely home and room to run. But Ted, who decided he probably wouldn't get the death penalty if he was caught, finally caved in to Generosa's demand.

Those who knew of the Buddy Affair, now numbering in the dozens, told him he was a fool to risk jail for the family dog. Part of Ted always felt that he could really do anything, that nothing really bad would ever befall him, but his friends and family would be on tenterhooks until the scheme was over. Once more, Ted and Buddy boarded the Concorde at Kennedy Airport and broke the sound barrier en route to Paris. In France, Ted drove a Porsche convertible north through the French countryside. He made a stop to give an animal tranquilizer to Buddy, who soon went into a deep sleep on the black-carpeted floor of the car, in front of the passenger seat. Ted placed a heavy black blanket over the dog. But would the experienced customs inspectors instantly spot such a flimsy trick? Ted put on his shades, fired up the Porsche, and nosed it toward the town of Sangatte. There, he drove to the entrance of the Chunnel, the thirty-one-mile train tunnel underneath the English Channel that had been completed just five years earlier. Ted got in line, paid his fare, and drove his sports car into one of the special train cars that held two levels of vehicles for the forty-five-minute trip to England. His big worry was that the drug would wear off and Buddy would wake up and announce his presence. When they arrived at Folkstone, England, Ted drove the car off the carrier and got in line for immigration and customs inspection. He glanced nervously at the blanket next to him. It was still. He handed his passport to the agent and explained that he was returning to his home in London. After quick processing and only a cursory look, he was waved on through.

He had done it. He arrived at Coverwood an hour later, to a hero's welcome from his wife and children. Buddy roused himself and was overjoyed to see the rest of the family. Generosa and the kids did not carry him on their shoulders but the moment felt like that. They were a complete, happy family. Veiled phone calls were made to the United States, happily assuring relieved friends and family from Manhattan to Alabama that "the package has arrived" and all was well. Ted had committed the perfect crime.

Because Ted did not move his business to London, he had to spend a lot of time in New York. Of course, he secretly spent every spare moment there with Mary Belknap. He joined the board supervising Jazz at Lincoln Center and later became chairman, working closely with its artistic director, trumpeter Wynton Marsalis. Generosa was upset that Ted spent so much time away and tried to persuade him to retire, which he had no intention of doing. She did not know that one of the big attractions in Manhattan was Ted's mistress, or that she had given birth to a son. Ted told his wife that he was staying at a particular hotel, and he was, but he was usually elsewhere. Generosa could usually reach Ted by cell phone, so she did not become suspicious.

The incessant shuttling between England and America, even in the swift luxury of the Concorde, was beginning to wear Ted down. The jet lag disrupted his sleep cycle, and he began to take sleeping pills. He began doing deals in Europe, including arranging the $16 billion takeover of British Telecom.

Generosa hired new staff in England. For her housekeeper, she took a plump matron who wore wire-rimmed glasses and pulled her graying dark brown hair in a bun. Her name was Kathryn Mayne, and she called herself Kaye. She and

Generosa hit it off right away. At fifty-three, Kaye was only
ten years older than her new employer, but she quickly assumed a motherly attitude toward her. Kaye reminded Generosa a bit of the English housekeeper and babysitter she
had known as a child in California.

Kaye was born Cathryn Carr in Manchester, England.
Her mother was an Englishwoman and her father was a
Cherokee Indian serving in the U.S. military. When his hitch
was up, they returned to a reservation in the United States,
where Kaye was raised as a Native American. She did not attend school until after she left the reservation at age nine and
returned to England with her mother, whom she shocked by
becoming pregnant at sixteen by her childhood sweetheart.
She was married in 1963, becoming Kaye Mayne, and gave
birth to a daughter and a son before the marriage ended.

As a struggling single mother, she got a job in the interior
design section of a department store. The sexy young divorcee from the north moved into higher circles in London,
where she socialized with wealthy Arabs and bragged about
securing lucrative decorating jobs with some of them, including billionaire Adnan Khashoggi's wife. She met and
married her second husband, but that marriage also found-
ered. She was now a grandmother. Kaye had fought to maintain a good environment for her children. That brought her
into conflict with gangs of punks who hung out near her
London home. She would constantly shoo them away, and
they would curse her out. Her home was burglarized, despite
her four dogs, whom she walked along the bank of the
Thames. When the shiftless youths refused to stop haunting
her house, she turned her garden hose on them and threw
eggs at them. They cursed more and nicknamed her "the
Witch."

Generosa was impressed by Kaye's intelligence and calm
strength and felt that they both had struggled in life. They each
had a somewhat skeptical attitude toward men and an interest
in spirituality. As housekeeper during the renovations, Kaye

kept an eye on the builders when Generosa wasn't around. She also helped with the kids when they were home from school.

When Kaye mopped floors and toilets and did the laundry, she was often so unobtrusive as to blend into the furniture. But the soft-spoken servant was very ambitious and had plans far above her current station. She intended to make the most of her new job. Her goal was to become one of the family, and Kaye would soon become a powerful figure in the lives of Generosa, Ted, and their kids.

With a new staff and the kids in boarding school, Generosa used the studio at Coverwood to get back into her art and photography. Perhaps sophisticated Europeans would appreciate her better than her countrymen had.

Sophia Marco,* a friend of Generosa's, was waiting in the first-class British Airways Concorde Lounge at Kennedy Airport when Ted Ammon walked in. After a kiss on the cheek, they discovered that they were booked on the same flight to London. Sophia began asking after Generosa and Ted told her that things were great and related the latest news. What a wonderful coincidence, Sophia said. She suggested that they spend the whole flight catching up. Once in London, perhaps they could all get together. Ted was very agreeable, until Sophia mentioned what she had learned from the mother of one of her friends in Manhattan.

"I hear you're looking at a new house on Ninety-first Street."

Ted was taken aback, his friendly smile gone. He'd been buying that house for himself and his mistress, and now a friend of Generosa's had found out about it. He hemmed and hawed furiously, but then tried a different tack.

"Well, Generosa doesn't need to know about this," Ted told Sophia.

Sophia was surprised but not shocked. Before she could say anything, Ted went to the airline agent and changed his flight to a regular jet, which would arrive much later than the

Concorde. Ted hurriedly left to go to another gate. So much for catching up. Sophia was convinced from Ted's strange reaction that he was up to hanky-panky, although she did not have proof. It was no bombshell that a rich, handsome ladies' man like Ted might cheat. Sophia always felt that Generosa was odd and Ted was amoral.

In any event, when she arrived in London, she did not call Generosa and tell her that her husband was secretly buying a place in Manhattan. But when she got back to New York, she did mention it discreetly to a few others. Slowly, especially after Mary had her baby boy, tongues wagged and the word got around.

In August 2000, Generosa's suspicions were suddenly rekindled when she heard that Ted had had lunch with his ex-wife several times at the Savoy Hotel in London. Randee Day was having problems in her divorce from her second husband, Ted explained, and needed a shoulder to cry on. Actually, Ted gave Randee a million-dollar loan to keep her solvent during her difficult divorce. Generosa resented it and feared that Ted was having a fling with his ex. He denied it and said that they were simply friends. Generosa, of course, could not conceive of being friends with anyone after a breakup.

Generosa made calls to friends back in New York. She asked about Randee but heard that her real problem had a different name. Ted had been seen with Mary Belknap around town. There was talk, but no one was willing to say that Ted had a relationship with the woman. She had had a baby the previous year and no one could tell Generosa who the father was. Was it Ted?

This was enough for Generosa to seek confirmation elsewhere. She got a screwdriver and pried open the locked desk in Ted's study. She found a bill from a London attorney for a consultation. A quick check by phone revealed that the firm specialized in divorces. Ted had consulted an English divorce lawyer. Her stomach sank.

"That son of a bitch!"

She also found paperwork indicating that Ted was buying a co-op in Manhattan, on Fifth Avenue, that she knew nothing about. Why does he need that? she wondered. Why didn't he tell me about it? She called Ted and confronted him with her discoveries but he still calmly denied everything. He flew back to discuss it in person. In an emotional scene at Coverwood, Ted admitted that he had consulted a divorce lawyer but claimed that he had done nothing wrong and didn't want a divorce. He denied having an affair with Randee but did not deny his relationship with Mary. Ted's cool manner infuriated his wife. He said that he was confused and asked Generosa for time. She didn't believe a word of it. Ted had been fucking that whore, she thought, probably giving her a child, and everyone in New York knew. They were laughing at her.

After the shock and the hurt and the tears, came the anger. It flowed out of her like lava. Generosa went to London and consulted a divorce lawyer herself. She also hired a private detective. The attorney explained that she was in a much worse position under English law. She felt that it was anything but a coincidence. Though it had been her idea to move to England, she was convinced that Ted had somehow maneuvered her into a spot where he could screw her out of a lot of money and property. If he wanted time, Generosa would not give it to him. She made immediate plans to move herself, the kids, Steven the butler, Bruce the cook, and Buddy back to New York. As soon as she got there, she would file for divorce in a Manhattan court. She would also hire a private detective there to get the goods on him.

Ted would pay.

"I have a beautiful home, I have these beautiful children, I gave the dinner parties," Generosa vented to her friend Jurate when she returned to Manhattan. "I created this incredible life for him. . . ."

She could not fathom how she could have carved the

ideal life and still have it shatter. It had all been for nothing, all the work in Manhattan, Bedford, East Hampton, and England, the slaving to create perfect places of beauty for Ted. Perfect was not good enough. Like so many before him, Ted had deceived her. Disloyalty, real or imagined, had always triggered rage in Generosa, and the closer the disloyal person had been to her, the greater the fury. Lesser betrayals had evoked maniacal hatred. Ted was her greatest love, her salvation. It was the biggest betrayal of her life. Worse, Generosa had been unable to give Ted a biological child, but she was convinced that he had one with Mary. It was the twist of the knife in her back.

Her emotional pain was a physical thing; unbearable, unrelenting. She wanted Ted to feel pain like she was feeling pain. Generosa vowed to destroy Ted, to take the only things he cared about, his children and his money. She wanted to scream. She wanted to die. She wanted him dead.

17

A BOTTLE OF SCORPIONS

Generosa filed for divorce in August 2000 and demanded a new residence in New York. These were the opening shots in the conflict. She got a mortgage on an eight-story town house at 10 East Eighty-seventh Street, near the park. Of course, she decided to gut it and redo it and informed Ted she needed a million dollars for renovations. Generosa decided that her new theme for the decor would be the Jetsons, the futuristic cartoon family from the 1960s who lived in an apartment floating in the sky. She would transform the town house into the Jetsons' pad. It was not the last spacey idea she would have.

Because they could not live there during the reconstruction, she and the twins moved into the luxurious Stanhope hotel on Fifth Avenue. Alexa went back to the Chapin School and Grego went back to St. David's, the exclusive private schools that they did not like. They missed England.

Ted stayed at another hotel until he got his new place, and sometimes he flew over to Coverwood on weekends. On one trip, when he went to the basement for a bottle of fine Bordeaux, he found that Kaye, on her mistress's instructions, had closed up his wine cellar with a padlock to which he did not have the key. Generosa wanted to preserve the marital assets, including those that Ted wanted to drink. He got into an argument with Kaye but she would not open the lock. He fired her, which enraged Generosa. Kaye called her mistress in New York and Generosa assured her that she would take care of her. She wanted Kaye to come to New York to be nanny to the twins. Kaye didn't want to leave England but agreed to be flown to the States to discuss it.

The struggle for custody of the friends began immediately. Generosa would not speak to anyone who even talked to Ted. One saddened couple heard Ted's side of the breakup over lunch and then approached Generosa on the street, to offer their support. Generosa, who had heard about the lunch, would not say one word to them. Instead, she literally spat on them. They were horrified. Her eyes were wild as she stormed off. Was she on drugs, or simply off her rocker?

"Everyone's siding with Ted because he's got all the money," Generosa growled to her friend Ronnie, who ran a dog grooming business. "Fuck them all! I don't need anybody!"

Generosa knew Ted was a procrastinator and wondered if he had changed his will yet—the one that left everything to her.

She told several friends that they had to "choose sides" between her and Ted and there was no going back. Her edict also extended to pets. Ted's pets were now hated. She warned Ronnie that she had to choose between grooming her dog, Buddy, and Ted's new dog, Sophie.

"You make your choice right now!" Generosa demanded in Ronnie's shop. "There's no in-between! You groom Sophie one more time and that's it!"

"Okay, I'm with you. I'm on your side," Ronnie assured her.

But Ronnie continued to trim Ted's pets on the sly.

"She's driving me crazy," Ted confided to Ronnie during one secret grooming session.

"She's off the wall, Ted," Ronnie replied.

Aside from profanity-laced tirades or bitter asides in Manhattan family court, Generosa would not speak to Ted for the next year. She talked Ted down to the kids constantly, trying to turn them against their father. At first, the kids defended their father, but Generosa's screaming rages made it clear that they were not to express any kind of positive feelings for him. Her campaign was successful, and the kids became increasingly estranged from Ted.

Generosa complained constantly, to whoever would listen, cursing out Ted for whatever his latest sin was. One day it was that he'd refused to let her take the helicopter to the beach house and she'd had to drive there like a normal person. The next time it was for removing things from the beach house.

Things got even more out of control when a wealthy woman friend who had been through a divorce told Generosa that as soon as possible she should establish a higher standard of living. Eventually, a judge would determine what she was accustomed to and decide how much Ted would have to pay to keep her at that level. Generosa, who had already wasted large amounts of money, began a campaign of spending that would rise to absurd heights. As she began gleefully to spend Ted's money, she realized that she liked it. It felt good to hurt Ted. It galled him to see money thrown away.

When it was Ted's turn to go out to the beach house in August 2000, he invited his friend Colin Hastings and his kids, Chip and Patricia, who were looking forward to playing with their friends Alexa and Grego. Arriving for the weekend, Ted noticed that Generosa had opened a $450 bottle of wine, had one glass of it in a tumbler, and then left the rest to oxidize on the kitchen counter. More waste, he pointed out to Colin. Or was she doing it to bug him?

It was a beautiful but very windy day, and Ted, who had more guts than experience, insisted they go sailing. He loved sailing close to the wind and considered the almost gale-force winds a challenge. They went to a nearby bay and launched two fifteen-foot sailboats from the beach. Colin

and the boys were in one and Ted and the girls were in the
other. As they set out across the bay, Colin, the better sailor,
heeled way over. Grego and Chip loved it. They hiked over
the side and dipped their butts into the rushing water, laughing. Ted, of course, had to do the same, as the girls tried to
imitate the boys. But Ted did not react quickly enough to a
sudden gust and over they went. The boat flipped in a big
splash and turtled, its eighteen-foot mast jammed solid into
the mud of the bay bottom. The girls hung on to the hull
while Ted tried to free the mast spar. When he couldn't do it
alone, Colin sailed close aboard, turned his boat into the
wind to stop, and luffed his sails. Colin, still holding on to
his boat, jumped out to help Ted. His fourteen-year-old son,
Chip, took the tiller with instructions to hold it steady. The
wet girls climbed aboard Colin's boat with the boys. As
Colin tried to help, a great gust of wind from a different
quarter filled the sails and all of the kids were suddenly off
at full tilt across the bay, leaving the two fathers with the
flipped craft.

"Ted! My God! The kids!" Colin shouted, too late.

"Grab it!" Ted yelled, helplessly, watching his kids sail
away.

The men redoubled their efforts, now that they had a second emergency. Their kids were alone in a boat for the first
time, and it was out of control, bucking across the choppy
bay like a horse without a rider. They were headed for the far
shore, where they would pile up on the rocks.

The two friends freed the mast, righted the boat in record
time, and jumped back into the cockpit. Colin grabbed the
tiller and they began sailing toward the kids, who were getting closer to the rocks. Colin and Ted shouted instructions
but the four children were too far away to hear. Suddenly, the
kids' boat came about, away from the rocks, and headed
back toward the beach. Chip was handling the tiller and the
mainsheet and Grego was manning the jib. The girls were
helping the boys. Colin tacked toward the beach to intercept
the kids. Both men jumped out to help their children, who

did not know how to beach the boat. Ted held on to the boat he and Colin had been in.

This time, it was Ted who let go, as the mischievous crosswind jibed the sail and grabbed the empty boat. Off it went, back across the bay, sailing itself away on a wild wind, like the Flying Dutchman.

The kids bailed out and went ashore while Ted and Colin jumped in their boat and gave chase. When they came alongside to the empty boat, Ted jumped into the water and scrambled aboard. They sailed back to the beach and called it a day. Everyone was excited, full of adrenaline, and laughing. Ted praised their efforts and told them that they were heroes. Both fathers were very proud of their children, who had come through the adventure with flying colors. It was like old times.

Generosa would soon gear up for her new rehab on East Eighty-seventh Street, but her most important project wasn't building a home, but tearing down Ted. She told anyone who would listen that Ted was a cad, a philanderer, that he had fathered a son with his girlfriend, that he cheated on his taxes, that he was involved in shady business deals, and that he was sexually kinky. Some of the tales had a grain of truth in them and others were just lies or Generosa's paranoid fantasies. But the wilder her stories became, the more the listeners concluded that she was simply a woman scorned, who had, alas, become unbalanced. Although he had lost about half his fortune in the market and Internet crashes, Generosa convinced herself that Ted was hiding huge assets. She suspected him of burying his wealth with friends or in Swiss bank accounts, where she and the courts could not find it. She wondered if he had secreted a stash of cash with his ex-wife, Randee, in Connecticut. Generosa was convinced that he was still worth at least $350 million, despite his losses. She spread the rumor that he had hidden a pirate's chest of $30 million in cash aboard his new $4 million yacht. Of course, there was no yacht and no treasure chest. In fact, if she had settled quickly, Generosa would have made out well, since the financial pie was shrinking faster than it could be sliced up.

Every time Ted and his lawyer thought that they were close to a settlement with Generosa, she would up the ante and demand more. It almost seemed as if she did not want the divorce and custody war to end.

Ted hired a celebrity divorce lawyer, Adria Hillman, who had a phrase for these vicious, scorched-earth divorces: Two Scorpions in a Bottle.

Generosa hired an armed bodyguard for $50,000 a year. Her housekeeper was also paid $50,000 a year. Bruce the chef got the same. His companion, Steven the butler, Generosa's devoted assistant, received a $100,000 salary. In addition, she paid another $50,000 for a driver, $30,000 for a gardener, and $60,000 in maintenance. Coverwood cost at least $100,000 a year to keep up, bottom line. In court, she demanded $180,000 a month just in basic living expenses. And she wanted all of the real estate—Coverwood, the East Hampton beach house, the London apartment, and her new town house on East Eighty-seventh Street.

Many tasks having to do with the twins had already been delegated to the nanny or others, but now Generosa let the nanny become their virtual mother. The nanny or Steven signed any papers that came home from school. Generosa, who went through cycles of manic activity and morose, paranoid slumps, did not answer her phone or read her mail for weeks at a time, allowing Steven to do it all. When she was manic, she raged, cursing Ted in front of the kids. Steven and Bruce got her a statue of Buddha and a mantra to chant to calm down and achieve inner peace. It did not work. Her spirit was filled to bursting with hatred, self-pity, and a gnawing urge for revenge.

She dragged the twins completely into the battle, making certain that they knew they could only be on her side. It would have been irresponsible enough for her to leave the court papers, with their charges of Ted's infidelity, lying around at home, but she did. She not only encouraged the twins to read the divorce papers, she brought them along to her lawyer Ed Meyer's office to listen to all the sordid details. But even that was not enough for Generosa. Increasingly paranoid, she confided in her children that Ted had marked her for death; thus her bodyguard.

"You father wants to kill me," she announced.

The plot, she warned them, was much broader than just her assassination. He was also planning to kill their dog, Buddy, and Steven the butler, and kidnap Grego. She claimed that Ted had detectives spying on them from the top of the Metropolitan Museum of Art, across the street, and that their rooms at the Stanhope hotel were bugged.

It was all madness from a broken mind, but the kids believed their mother. Alexa and Grego were in the middle and they were suffering but their mother refused to take them to a therapist, something she herself would not do until ordered to by the court.

When Judge Marilyn Diamond ordered her to get help for her children, she still delayed, saying that she was too busy to interview shrinks. Once the twins finally began seeing therapists, Generosa—rather, her staff at her direction—often did not bring them to their scheduled appointments. Their home life was so raw and chaotic that their schoolwork also suffered. The formerly good pupils were often unable to do their homework and were unprepared for tests. Their grades fell. Alexa was not offered a place in the following year's class. Grego's teachers reported that he was so terrified of being kidnapped at any moment, he was not paying attention in class. The court appointed a psychologist to interview the children, as well as Ted and Generosa, which was routine. Ted continued to pay all the bills.

Ted tried to sort out his feelings for Mary, which was all but impossible in the middle of the war with Generosa. Mary was everything Generosa was not: controlled, secure, a woman after Ted's own heart. She was also a banker, rich on her own and never needing money. But he was twice burned, and marriage, at that point, was impossible for him to contemplate.

In October 2000, Ted and one of his nieces and her husband went to watch the twins play soccer. At the field, they saw Generosa, who suggested that they "sit down, as a family" and discuss the holiday schedule, with Thanksgiving and Christmas coming up.

"I don't think it's a good idea to have that conversation in front of the children, in case of disagreements," Ted said, as cordially as he could.

He knew that any conversation he had with her would quickly degenerate into an argument, with her screaming and him leaving. Ted asked his niece and nephew if they would like to go out for coffee. Proving his point, Generosa immediately began screaming that he was a bad father and that having a cup of coffee was "clearly more important to you than taking care of your family!"

Heads began to turn at her ranting and Ted retreated to stop the public scene. Later that month, he decided to go to the beach house in East Hampton for a weekend, as he had been doing occasionally since he returned to New York. Generosa had warned him that she owned the beach house—even though his money had built it. She spent almost no time there off-season but had warned Ted not to set foot in it or bring his exercise equipment or clothes there. He ignored her. She had a proprietary Ayn Rand–type feeling for the estate. An artist owned her creations and could dispose of them however she saw fit. Of course, she also claimed that she had created Ted.

In the second week of October, when Ted picked up the children and brought them to the court-ordered psychologist's office for interviews, Grego mentioned to him that they might go out to the beach house for the weekend. Ted told his son that he had already made plans to go to East Hampton and was driving out that night, a Thursday, and would be there for the weekend. Ted had his assistant, Kathy, call Generosa's butler and assistant, Steven, to say he'd be using the house. Steven passed the message on to Generosa, who called Ted the next day in East Hampton and informed him that they were coming out late Saturday and he had "better not be there" when they arrived.

"You know I had made plans to be here for the weekend. I'm here," Ted replied.

By 10:45 that night, no one had arrived, so Ted went to bed.

Generosa suspected that he was shacked up with a paramour and thought she saw an opportunity for a commando mission to shake him up and get proof for her divorce case, or blackmail material. It would not help her case simply to prove that Ted had a girlfriend. But what if it wasn't a woman? She bundled the kids in the car, along with Steven and Buddy, the dog. First, she stopped at a friend's home in Manhattan and borrowed the key for their home in East Hampton, just a few minutes away from Generosa's beach house. She then drove from the city to Middle Lane, where she slipped into the driveway of the home she loved, which Ted was defiling with his presence. Generosa left the car running.

They quietly filed around to the rear patio, where they all sneaked into the mansion through the pet door just before 11:30. The burglar alarm did not sound because the pet door was not wired. In any case, Ted had not bothered to set it. The tired kids sat in the dark kitchen while Steven and Generosa tiptoed through the living room and up the main staircase, with Buddy trotting along behind. At the top of the stairs, Steven pulled out his camera and got ready. Generosa swung open the bedroom door and flipped on the light.

Steven raised the camera to his eye to catch a shot of Ted in the naked embrace of his lover. Ted was in bed with Sophie, the new puppy he had bought. Sophie roused and yipped. Ted had always loved big, cuddly dogs, who were more likely to lick an intruder than bite. Sophie was anything but a watchdog. Ted woke up and could not believe his eyes. He saw Generosa and the camera in Steven's right hand and realized what they had been up to.

"This is my house!" she screamed. "How dare you be here? You have ruined my weekend! You've ruined the children's weekend. We can't possibly stay!"

Ted shook his head in disbelief at the scene Generosa had engineered. She was yelling at him? He was furious at the intrusion, especially at the camera. Obviously, she was more upset that she hadn't found him with someone. He grumbled and did some cursing of his own. His little puppy hopped off the bed to greet Buddy. They were ready to play. When Generosa saw Ted's hated dog being friendly with Buddy, she kicked the poor puppy, not missing a beat in her loud invective at Ted.

Alexa and Grego sat sullenly in the kitchen, listening to their parents cursing at each other upstairs. Alexa felt weird about what was happening. She understood that her mother was trying to get a picture of her father in bed with his girlfriend, or whomever.

Steven left the bedroom and a disappointed Generosa stalked out, slamming the bedroom door behind her hard enough to rattle the walls. Ted, who usually slept naked, got out of bed, dressed, and walked down to the kitchen. Generosa was telling the yawning kids that they had to leave. Ted noticed that his wife had left the car running, which put the lie to her claim that they had planned to stay for the weekend. It saddened Ted that Alexa and Grego were caught in the middle of what was turning out to be a very nasty divorce. They deserved better. He leaned in the window and spoke directly to the cowed kids.

"I'm very sorry that you had to go through this," Ted told them.

He understood that Generosa was angry and upset about the breakup and he felt sorry for her. But he had no sympathy for what she was doing to the kids.

Generosa roared off, scattering gravel with her tires.

• • •

Like many that fall, Generosa got a chest cold, which quickly turned into serious congestion. It drained her of energy. One morning, while taking a shower, she felt a lump in her left breast. She felt it again. It was definitely a lump. She felt a chill. Then panic. She went to Dr. Mark Borelli,* her family doctor, who told her that she had developed pneumonia and prescribed treatment. The lump in the breast was another issue, he told her. She had to have a mammogram and possibly a sonogram to determine if it was anything to worry about, but she resisted. At home, she called Ted to yell at him. Somehow, it was his fault that she was sick.

"I have pneumonia and a lump in my breast," Generosa told him, and then launched into a tirade about how she needed more money.

Ted didn't believe her. She sounded like she had the flu but he was suspicious that the lump in her breast was only a plea for sympathy, a new way to get money out of him. Ted called Dr. Borelli, who confirmed her story. He told Ted what he had not told Generosa: that he was fairly certain the lump would prove to be cancer. He felt that his patient's husband should know, especially since she seemed resistant. She had to seek immediate testing, treatment, possibly surgery. Ted called Generosa and mentioned that he had spoken to the doctor. He told her to do whatever the doctor ordered but did not intend to tell her that she probably had cancer. He never got the chance. She went bananas. She screamed that he had no right to talk to her doctor, that it was unethical and illegal. She hung up on Ted.

The doctor had violated her most strict edict: He had talked to Ted. She called the doctor and screamed at him for daring to discuss her medical condition with her estranged husband. He tried again to persuade her to proceed with testing but she threatened legal action and hung up.

Generosa had been too young to know the details of how her mother had found a similar lump in her breast in the shower at virtually the same age. She was largely unaware

of how her mother's symptoms went away and later returned
and spread, crawling through her body like silent scorpions.
Even if she had known full well how her mother's fear, igno-
rance, and denial had killed her, she might not have done
anything different in her current mental state. Generosa certainly remembered the brain cancer that came later, the
wasting away, Babe's sunken eyes and cheeks, the drinking,
the morphine, the despair, the delirium. She knew only that
she still felt the way her ten-year-old self had felt thirty
years earlier. She would rather die than get cancer.

Generosa's pneumonia went away after the antibiotics
did their job, and she felt fine.

Stung, Ted stayed out of it, assuming that Generosa
would do the right thing with a different doctor. But she did
not go to another physician. She did nothing at all. When she
would not return her doctor's calls or talk to him, the physician wrote her a registered letter, urging her in strong language to seek treatment for suspected cancer as soon as
possible. When it arrived, Generosa noticed from the return
address that it was from Dr. Borelli, who had spoken to Ted.

She ripped it in half, tossed it into the wastebasket, and
went about her day.

18

TOOL BELT GUY

Danny, before meeting Generosa, took whatever jobs he could get through other contractors, but he was going under. He was drinking and gambling. He had declared bankruptcy and his home was in foreclosure, about to be auctioned off. He couldn't even pay his bills, and had rewired and rigged a bypass on the electric meter at his Manorville home because he could not afford the utility bill.

Dale Cassidy,* a contractor friend, threw Danny work, including a good job for a rich divorcee in the Hamptons. Now Dale told Danny that he wanted to introduce him to another rich woman who was getting divorced. There was a lot of electrical work to be done on her East Eighty-seventh Street town house renovation. They met Generosa at a round corner banquette table in the bar at the Stanhope hotel in Manhattan. Danny was on his best behavior.

Dale introduced him to Generosa.

"Howya doin'?" Danny said.

It was obvious that she was a classy woman, but she carried herself like she was made out of steel. Was she as tough as she acted? As they talked, he realized that Generosa knew a lot about building, rehabbing, and design. Danny turned on his one-hundred-watt charm and Generosa gave him the job. He was happy and hoped that the money would save his bacon.

Danny and some of his buddies got started soon afterward. At first, he thought Generosa was a pain in the ass, but he did everything with a smile. When she didn't like the way something looked, she ordered the workmen to tear it all out and do it over. It wasn't the first time Danny had worked for a rich bitch who didn't know what she wanted and wasted a lot of green doing things over and over.

Fuckin' rich women are crazy, Danny thought. They love spendin' their old man's money.

When Generosa arrived at the town house one morning and found Danny sleeping in his truck, she asked him why. He explained that all the driving back and forth from Suffolk, which took twice as long because of rush hour, exhausted him. It was better to sleep at the job. That way he, and some of the other guys who did it, got a good night's sleep.

"None of my workmen have to sleep in trucks," Generosa declared. "I'll get you rooms at the Stanhope."

That was just fine with Danny. He walked into the Stanhope lobby after work, dressed in blue jeans, work boots, work shirt, and work dirt. The elegant lobby featured a checkerboard marble floor, a crystal chandelier, gilt sconces, and a golden rococo clock atop an inlaid mahogany pedestal. Stepping out of traffic and into the lobby was like entering another dimension. It looked like Buckingham Palace, only smaller. The desk clerk took one look at Danny and his eyebrows jumped up his forehead. Talk about a third-class passenger in a first-class coach.

"May I help you?"

"Yeah, my name is Dan Pelosi, I think you have a room for me?"

The clerk did not bother to look at the reservations computer.

"Allow me to help you find another hotel. One that has

more *affordable* rates," he said, in a distinctly condescending tone.

Generosa stepped off the elevator and Danny told her what had just happened. Generosa unloaded on the clerk. He groveled and apologized profusely and produced Danny's room key.

As Danny worked on the job, he and Generosa became friendly and then flirtatious. Danny always bragged that he could have any woman he wanted. Any woman. And he began to wonder if this was the woman he had been looking for, the answer to his workingman's dream. Danny was not educated much beyond his high school equivalency diploma but he was very sharp, at least when sober. It wasn't long before he knew that Generosa wanted sex and wanted him. He knew she might give him a tumble just to needle her ex, but there was more to it than that. Danny's animal magnetism had attracted the woman of steel. Generosa was on the rebound and very needy.

Generosa met Danny shortly after her spying mission had failed to produce a picture of Ted in flagrante delicto at the beach house. Later, Ted noticed a guy with a tool belt, who said he was an electrician, hanging around with Generosa when he went to pick up the kids. Ted sensed that the guy was a hustler. He thought there was something off about the guy and wondered if he was actually an electrician. Actually, Ted was right. Danny, who told people he was an electrician, had never passed the licensing test and had never entered the apprentice program, although he did good work.

The more time Danny spent at the Stanhope, the more he and Generosa hung out together and talked and drank. Generosa was falling for him like a ton of bricks and he could see it. Of course, Danny was married, but he had never let that stand in his way before. He was receiving Generosa's signals loud and clear. One night, she confided in him:

"I haven't had sex in two years."

The only problem was the job. The crew didn't want to get fired and begged Danny not to shit where they ate. Keep it in your pants and don't fuck the customer, they said. But Generosa might be the one he was looking for, the horny broad with piles of money, his Powerball lotto payoff.

"Promise you won't fire me if we have sex?" Danny asked Generosa, over drinks.

"I promise." Generosa smiled eagerly.

That was good enough for Danny. He stopped playing hard to get. Upstairs in her suite at the Stanhope, they had great sex, and Danny was conscientious and considerate, making sure that his new partner was satisfied. Later, he boasted that he had given Generosa the first orgasm of her life.

"She didn't know what it was," he bragged with a hoarse chuckle. "She thought she should go to the hospital!"

They were from two different worlds, although Generosa was hardly from old money. They had fun showing each other their worlds. One night Generosa took Danny in her chauffeured limo to the 21 Club, where dinner for two, drinks, and a bottle of wine cost more than Danny grossed in his best week. The next night, Danny drove her in his truck to the ESPN Zone sports bar in Times Square, where they watched games and drank beer.

Now that Generosa had a younger, stud-muffin boyfriend, the rough type she used to see at construction sites, she wanted to show him off. In what may have been one of her spacier ideas, she decided to have Danny squire her to the opera, an evening where her tool belt guy could meet the money belt crowd on their home turf. The purpose was to parade him in front of all those couples who had stuck with Ted. She wanted to thumb her nose, and Danny, at them and she knew they would report to Ted. She couldn't take him to the opera in a tool belt, so she bought him a designer tuxedo, Danny's first since the rental he'd worn at his wedding to Tami. Danny had cut off his long hair but he still had a tough-guy haircut, his dark brown hair slicked back like a hood's. Danny was a handsome man and, with a decent haircut, Generosa thought he looked great as they set out for a night at the opera. Danny told her he looked "like a fuckin' idiot in this monkey suit." He had never seen an operatic performance but that was not the only reason why he did not want to go. But it was Generosa's show.

Danny was impressed with the architecture of the palatial, five-arched Metropolitan Opera House at Lincoln Center. As Generosa strolled to her seat on Danny's arm, they ran into several friends who greeted her. She did not introduce him, so the couples looked to him, inquiringly.

"Hi, howaya? I'm Dan Pelosi," he said, pumping hands.

"How you doin'? I'm Dan."

The theater was huge, with rows of boxes flanking the stage and huge crystal chandeliers that dimmed and floated up to the ceiling when it was time for the show to start. Danny thought the opera—the music, the voices, the whole spectacle—was goofy. He couldn't understand the words of the songs because they were not in English, at least he didn't think so.

"What da fuck are dey sayin'?" he asked Generosa.

"Shhhhhhhh. Shut up," she whispered.

At intermission, they left their seats to mingle in the lobby. Danny was tiring of his tight collar and his ill-fitting role in the proceedings and told Generosa as much.

"Yo, this is all about letting your husband know that you're dating a fuckin' young guy but let's not rock the boat here, huh?"

Danny thought it was dumb to rub her old man's face in it.

"When you meet people, just say hello. Nothing else," she instructed him.

She was treating him like an uncouth gigolo. It was not the first time she had corrected him. He was pissed but kept his mouth shut. Back at the Stanhope, she started in again about his accent.

"You have to learn how to say 'Hello' to people—not 'Hi, howaya,'" Generosa lectured, assuming the role of Henry Higgins.

"Look, I speak Brooklyn-ese. That's it—get used to it."

"You have to come across softer to people."

"I come across soft. Look, go with your friends, whenever you want to go to the opera anymore," Danny told her. "I can't do that."

Danny's opera days were over but Generosa was pleased with the evening. She knew the phone lines would be burning tomorrow and Ted would get an earful.

Back in her suite, a nude Generosa slipped under the silk sheets. With a sly smile, she gave Danny an order:

"Go into the bathroom and come out wearing just your tool belt."

"Okay."

Danny went into the bathroom and closed the door. He stripped naked and then put on his leather tool belt, with the hanging hammer, roll of black electrical tape, and other tools. He looked at himself in the mirror, with the equipment swinging and himself dangling down in the middle. He felt a bit silly, like one of the Village People, but the customer was always right. He opened the door and strode out to Generosa, who was waiting in bed.

"If this one works for you, let's do it," Danny said, jiggling his tools.

They did.

When they met, Danny was addicted to alcohol and sex, and Generosa was addicted to money. Rather than help each other kick their respective habits, they each added the other's vice to their own. Generosa, partial to a beer in the afternoon and a little white wine at dinner, soon began getting loaded on whiskey with Danny on a daily basis. With Ted gone, Generosa started smoking like a chimney. Freed from Ted's regimen of health food, she treated herself to junk food. Danny, not surprisingly, became intoxicated with having and spending money. He was rich. It was a great feeling, especially after a lifetime of debt, to pay off his bills and throw cash around. He never wanted to give it up.

One of Generosa's friends warned her that, after their appearance at the opera, others in their circle were gossiping about her and Danny.

"They're jealous because I've got this young, hot boyfriend," she sneered, secretly pleased that the word was out.

At three hundred dollars a night, the rooms at the Stanhope for Danny and his crew were absurd, but they had the advantage of wasting bushels of Ted's money and allowed Generosa and Danny time to be together, while Danny told his wife that he and his crew were being put up by their rich client. He now had an excuse to spend weeknights in the city with her. With all the life-saving money he was suddenly bringing in, Tami was not about to complain.

Ted's money kept paying for Danny's room at the Stanhope, but by this time it was just for show. Danny spent little time in his own room. Accustomed to greasy breakfasts wrapped in wax paper, and cheap coffee in Styrofoam cups, Danny was suddenly one of those people on the Upper East Side eating eggs Benedict on fancy china and sipping fresh-squeezed orange juice out of crystal glasses. He was still working for a living, but he was the boss now, not the employee. This looked like his shot to get off the merry-go-round. Danny had finally latched on to the brass ring.

19

THE STANHOPE

Generosa, sitting in a window booth at the bar at the Stanhope hotel, sucked on a Marlboro Ultra Light 100 and exhaled the blue smoke above the black granite table.

"He's a bastard," she told the cocktail waitress who brought her drink. "I'm going to take him for everything he's worth."

After listening politely for a bit, the waitress nodded and went back to work. She had heard it all before: Generosa cursing out Ted, vowing to destroy him, clean him out. The waitress was not the only employee who thought it unusual for a guest at the sophisticated Stanhope to lay bare her ugly divorce for strangers. She did not know that her customer had few friends left. For someone with such a finely developed sense of taste and decorum, Generosa Ammon was acting very inappropriately, even for herself.

She lifted her Cosmopolitan to her lips and took a gulp. She preferred a rocks glass because she disliked fancy cocktail glasses, which tipped over easily and held less. Before the breakup, before she started drinking more, she had always sipped her one glass of white wine from a tumbler.

She and Danny and her kids and his crew had set up housekeeping at the venerable hotel at the corner of Fifth Avenue and East Eighty-first Street, just six blocks from

Generosa's new town house. The raucous group ate five-hundred-dollar breakfasts every morning and drank and partied loudly in the bar until all hours. They tipped lavishly but they had to, since their four-letter-word conversations clashed with the low-key ambience of the place. Danny drew his friends and family, including his mother and his kids, his nieces and nephews, and others into the new charmed circle at the luxurious Stanhope. One observer later unkindly referred to the nightly gathering as resembling a scene from *The Beverly Hillbillies,* with Suffolk County's working class thrust into tony surroundings, amid bemused sophisticates.

Generosa liked having Danny's crowd around her. He and his friends used the word *fuckin'* in virtually every sentence, hardly the usual chat at the Stanhope bar. At one table, a group might be talking about a Broadway play they had just seen or an exhibition at the Metropolitan Museum of Art, across the street. Some overheard a drunken Danny, decked out in expensive new threads, bragging to Generosa and others about his supposed Mafia connections. Danny had told quite a few people that he knew wiseguys, but many did not believe him. Generosa loved it and couldn't wait to let Ted know.

"He'll shit his pants!" she said, giggling.

Generosa's inhibitions—the few she had—were lowered by her increased drinking. The fact that her choice in men shocked and appalled the people who used to be her friends, and were still Ted's friends, was a lovely bonus.

One night, when she was loaded at the bar, Generosa told a befuddled guest, "I know you're a spy for my husband!"

There were no spies. Nor was this the last time she singled out startled patrons and accused them of being private detectives shadowing her. She was always wrong. Generosa recounted for Danny how she and Steven had failed to catch Ted in bed with someone at the beach house, and she feared Ted was removing property. She asked for his help. No problem, Danny told her. He would take care of it. Danny told her that there were remote-controlled video surveillance sys-

tems that could be hidden in the beach house to catch Ted.
He had a friend who installed them and would give him a
call. They would be able to watch Ted when he was there and
he would have no clue.

One of the things Generosa liked about Danny was that
he was a can-do guy. She told one friend that Danny and his
workmen had begun following Ted around, trying to get pictures of him with women.

Generosa and Danny shared the magnificent $1,500-a-
night presidential suite. Danny had his own room, for appearance's sake, and the kids had their rooms. Then there
was the crew, who were put up in two other rooms. Occasionally, Generosa's butler Steven and Bruce the cook would
be given their own room and join the festivities. Adding up
the queenly accommodations, the food, the booze, and other
amenities such as laundry, tipping the bellman $100 twice a
day to walk Buddy, and another $100 to tip the guy who
brought the car up from the parking garage, Ted Ammon
was paying for the party to the tune of $60,000 a month.
When the children's private-school tuitions and other expenses were added in, Ted was forking over more than
$100,000 a month. Generosa had also demanded $153,000 a
month in tax-free spending money. In court papers, Ted
called the obscene requests "truly staggering amounts of
money, unrelated to any realistic need."

One night at the Stanhope bar, Danny later told people,
he was introduced to an affluent Manhattan society matron
named Jocelyn Wildenstein, who lived in a town house
nearby. Her scandalous public divorce the year before had
made her infamous in the press as "The Bride of Wildenstein," due to too many plastic surgeries, which had left her
face a disaster. She had caught her billionaire husband in
bed with a nineteen-year-old girl and he had pulled a gun on
her. He'd said that he was repelled by her unattractive, lion-
faced condition, an unfortunate situation that was not mentioned by polite society in her company. But Danny, seated

next to Generosa, was under sail when the introductions were made. He was not subtle about his curiosity.

"Oh, my God! What happened to you?"

Jocelyn was appalled at Danny's rudeness but she explained that it was the result of plastic surgery.

"You actually paid for that?" he asked, incredulous.

That settled it. Danny always felt that rich people were strange. Now he was convinced that they were all completely insane.

One of Generosa's few remaining friends, Ronnie, stopped by for a drink and to meet Danny. She was polite but immediately wondered what her friend was doing with the guy. Generosa was on the rebound and probably had to get the fling out of her system, she felt. Generosa detailed the latest in the campaign against Ted. Danny chimed in that Ted was an asshole and was trying to screw Generosa out of money.

Ronnie smiled at Danny, who reminded her of that Joey Buttafuoco guy, also from Long Island, who had slept with sixteen-year-old Amy Fisher, who had then shot Buttafuoco's wife. Ronnie was also introduced to several other men whom she decided were lowlifes. After observing Danny and Generosa for a while, she found it interesting that the new boyfriend seemed to have replaced Steven as the main figure in her life after Ted. Generosa also seemed to like playing godmother to a crew of husky guys. When they were alone, Generosa told Ronnie that she was happy, although she sounded like she was anything but.

"In bed, he's wonderful!" she gushed. "I've always wanted a tool belt kind of guy and now I have one."

Generosa's eyes were glassy and her speech was slurred. She was smoking and drinking heavily. She was not herself and Ronnie wondered what kind of drugs she was on. Valium? Cocaine?

When not at the Stanhope, Danny was also spreading copious quantities of cash among friends, family, and bar-

tenders, like a drunken sailor. Even when he was broke
Danny had been a good tipper, and he had not changed. Suddenly, he was giving barmaids hundreds of dollars for a
night of drinking and throwing car-repair guys thousand-
dollar tips for fixing his tires. Back in Manorville, where his
wife and kids lived, and in his hometown of Center
Moriches, word got around. Danny had hit the jackpot. He
was shacked up with the wife of a gazillionaire and every
day was a party for him and his entourage of pals and relatives, courtesy of a guy named Ted Ammon. Suddenly cash-
rich, Danny paid for renovations on his home in Manorville.
He bought a twenty-thousand-dollar outboard boat for his
son Danny Jr., a 17.5-foot Mako. By this time, it was obvious to Danny's wife, Tami, what was going on between
Danny and Generosa.

Generosa and Danny flew down to Barbados for a vacation. Their sex life was so revved up that they couldn't keep
their hands off each other. They coupled in the bathroom of
the jet on the way down and in a moving taxi on the island.
When they went skinny-dipping in the pool one night, a security guard politely suggested that they take it back to
their room.

Whether on a tropical island or back on Long Island,
Danny was Living Large. Some family members were saddened to see him drinking and acting like a different person.
Bob Pelosi told people that he did not like the idea that his
son was living off his rich girlfriend, like some kind of gigolo. But Danny wanted his father to meet Generosa; his
mother had already met her and liked her.

Bob Pelosi had moved with his new wife, Dorothy, across
the street from where Danny had been raised, into a waterfront home with a spectacular view of Center Moriches Bay.
On the horizon were lines of beige and green, the dunes of
the barrier beaches on the far side of the bay. The phone
rang late one morning. It was Danny, calling from his cell
phone. He and Generosa were in the neighborhood, looking

at property. Danny said that Generosa needed to use a bathroom and asked if they could stop by. They arrived a few minutes later and were greeted by Bob's wife, Dorothy. Bob came down the stairs and ran into Generosa, who was looking at family pictures.

"Who are you?"

"I'm Generosa."

"Is that a first name or a last name?"

"First name."

"So, you're Italian?"

"No," Generosa replied too quickly, her distaste evident in her tone.

"Did you come here to look at pictures or to talk?" Bob demanded.

Generosa knew that Bob Pelosi was a banker. She didn't like him. He reminded her of Ted. She turned to look at the view of the bay out the windows.

"Oh, that's nice," she said.

Her tone was always condescending, but Bob and his wife did not know that. It went downhill from there. Dorothy mentioned that they were retired, an attempt at conversation, but it didn't work.

"What do you do?" Generosa asked.

"We golf," Dorothy answered.

"Do you golf with your husband? I've never met a woman who could golf with her husband. Danny, take off your jacket," Generosa said.

"She says take off your jacket and you take off your jacket?" Bob asked his son sarcastically.

Generosa then began criticizing Danny's sister Barbara and several others in the family who were now on her payroll. Generosa thought she knew exactly what their supposed problems were, and suggested various solutions, including future plans for college, for his sister's kids.

"Italian women have no self-esteem," Generosa declared.

Bob and his wife later told others that they were offended

by Generosa's attitude and statements. What was she doing with Danny? She acted as if she had bought the Pelosi family and was now in charge.

"These people work for you," Bob snapped. "Where do you come off coming into my home and talking about my family?"

Danny asked to speak to his father in the garage and they stepped out. He asked his father to cut him and his girlfriend a break.

"Get that sophisticated slut out of my house," Bob said. "Take her for all she's worth."

Danny and Generosa went to the door. Generosa offered her hand, as if she expected Bob to kiss it.

"It's been short and sweet," Generosa told him. "So long."

"Well, it's been short," he replied, refusing to take her hand.

Soon after he began sleeping with Generosa, Danny told one person that his new girlfriend was rich and not too difficult to handle.

"She's a bitch. She's whacko, but she'll do anything for me," he said.

Later, he would claim that he had fallen in love with her. Danny informed his father one day that he had a check for him, and handed him one made out for forty thousand dollars—the amount that his father had estimated he had spent on Danny's bail and lawyers for all his past offenses.

"Oh really?" Bob Pelosi asked his son. "Did you work for it? Keep your money. Give it to me when you've earned it."

Generosa set up the Skypad Corporation, the company that would renovate the town house and turn it into her Jetsons pad in the sky. One of the first things the corporation did was to lease a $40,000 black 2001 Ford Explorer for Danny, befitting his new station as head contractor. Danny recruited friends and associates to work on the East Eighty-seventh Street project. One subcontractor, Charlie Daniels,* later claimed that Danny demanded a $20,000 kickback for an $85,000 demolition job. That way, the costs could be inflated, there would be enough to go around, and everyone would be happy. Except for Ted, who was footing the bills and was not invited to the party.

Generosa bought Danny a wardrobe and paid to have his crooked teeth capped. She told Danny that she had arranged for plastic surgery on her breasts. One was slightly larger than the other and she had always wanted to correct it, she claimed. Danny did not see much difference between them but didn't think it was odd because he already thought that rich folks were crazy. When she came back from the surgery, her breasts were indeed perfectly symmetrical. Generosa never told Danny about her former doctor and never mentioned the word *cancer*. It never occurred to him that the operation might have actually been to remove a tumor.

Generosa flew Kaye Mayne to New York, in an effort to talk her into coming to the States to work for her again. She wanted her to be the kids' nanny and help her run things. When she introduced Kaye to Danny, it was oil and water, from the start. After an evening of drinking, dining, and drinking, the soft-spoken Kaye decided that she was less than impressed with Generosa's new flame.

"You are a bigmouthed American," she told him calmly. "You are rude and obnoxious."

Danny reacted instinctively to any challenge.

"Listen to me, you ugly bitch," he snapped. "I don't know who you think you are, but this is my country and if you don't like it why don't you just go back home where you came from?"

Kaye was not intimidated by Danny. Generosa intervened and tried to get them to be friends but succeeded only in arranging a truce between the two strong-willed people who were competing for her friendship. Generosa felt that she needed them both to help her but each saw no need for the other. While the War of the Ammons raged, the battle between Danny and the nanny was postponed. For the time being, Kaye decided to stay in England. Generosa wanted to return to Coverwood after the divorce.

In Manhattan Family Court, Ted and Generosa were in front of Judge Diamond with their lawyers, trying to work out a civilized solution to their parting. But now Danny was there, seated in the audience. Ted and Adria Hillman noticed. Ted didn't know his name but he was happy to see him. Now that his estranged wife had a boyfriend, he hoped she would stop making his life miserable and they could settle the mess. He was very wrong. Generosa had spread the word that her boyfriend was a tough guy, mobbed up.

Generosa's lawyer, Ed Meyer, told the court that he had a receipt from a chic boutique for four thousand dollars' worth of ladies' lingerie, presumably spent on Ted's girlfriend. Generosa was not the recipient of the frilly undergarments, her lawyer said. It was okay to have a girlfriend but judges took a dim view of litigants spending excessive amounts of money—which should go to the spouse and the children—on lovers. As the lawyers discussed the pricey underwear bill, Generosa turned to Ted and got in a dig:

"What, are you—cross-dressing again?"

Ted glared at her but said nothing. She looked daggers back. After the court session, Adria decided they'd need more information on Generosa's new beau—starting with his name. She tried the direct approach. She walked over to Danny and introduced herself.

"Hello, I'm Ted's attorney, Adria Hillman."

"Howya doin'?"

"And you are?"

"Dan Pelosi," he said, extending his hand politely.

Adria smiled and shook his hand. She was pleased. Danny had just saved the private detectives she intended to hire days of work finding out what his name was.

20

LIES

Ted hoped that Generosa's loathing and spitefulness would pass with time and her campaign of vilification would end with a court settlement that would allow everyone to get on with their lives. He still thought he could do anything if he set his mind to it.

He had Alexa and Grego for spring break in 2001 and it was obvious that they were different kids: wary, distant—especially Alexa. He did his best to explain what had happened, but they were subject to powerful and terrible conditioning by their mother and they weren't listening to his side. They already knew they had to close their ears.

When Alexa and Grego got home from spring break, their crazed mother grilled them about their week with Ted.

"Did you have a good time?" she asked, sarcastically.

They denied it, but the fact that the eleven-year-olds could stomach a week with their father proved that they were disloyal. First, Generosa gave her children the silent treatment for three days. Steven the butler was a conduit for messages. Generosa was frantic because she feared that the kids would spend the Easter vacation with Ted at *her* house, the beach house in East Hampton. That would never be permitted. That was their mother's house. She owned it and he was not allowed there. When the twins tearfully begged her to stop being mad at them, she exploded into fury and threatened to kick them out.

"Go live with your father, if you like him so much!" she screamed.

During her cruel abuse and manipulation of her children, Generosa never once thought of Jo, the scared little girl she had been at the same age; the one who had been so hurt by being kicked out by her family over and over.

Terrified, sobbing, her children pleaded with her not to get rid of them. They swore that they would never go to the beach house with their father. Generosa told them all about Ted, all the evil, criminal things he was doing to her and to them. He and everyone around him was bad. They believed every word.

Meanwhile, Ted had just been unanimously elected the chairman of Jazz at Lincoln Center. Artistic director Wynton Marsalis announced that Ted "has an exciting vision of jazz, as a universal language." Ted was beginning what he hoped would be the best part of his life.

He got a strange fax from Generosa's butler, Steven. There was a picture of a table that had what appeared to be a sleep mask with a hypodermic needle atop it. The text was even stranger. Steven claimed that someone had broken into his and Bruce's apartment on East Eighty-sixth Street and not stolen a thing—just left the needle. He said he felt it was an attempt to intimidate or incriminate him. Steven had reported the alleged crime to the Twentieth Precinct but claimed in his fax that the mystery of the hypodermic needle was being investigated by an Officer Jim Pelosi, shield number 12174. Danny's brother was a hardworking up-and-coming narcotics officer across the river, in Queens, which was an entirely different jurisdiction. He did not investigate burglaries or any other crimes in Manhattan. Apparently, Steven, in cahoots with Generosa and Danny, was trying to run some kind of scam on him, Ted believed. Danny had actually gotten his cop brother to "run" a license plate number through the police computer, something that would later come back to haunt him. Ted took the odd communication as a bizarre and clumsy attempt to intimidate him. He shrugged it off and gave it to his lawyer.

Ted was looking forward to his Easter weekend with his kids, who had just turned eleven. His sister Sandi was flying up from Alabama to join them. His Porsche was too small for the weekend and he decided that even his BMW wasn't big enough for him, Sandi, the kids, and his dog Sophie and two new dogs he had just gotten. He went out and bought a big, black Chevy Suburban. When Ted and Sandi arrived at the Stanhope on Saturday morning, April 7, 2001, to pick up the kids for the Easter weekend, it was obvious from the start that Generosa's brainwashing of Alexa and Grego was complete. Steven brought the siblings down to the Stanhope lobby, where Sandi was waiting.

"Hello, Steven," Sandi said, with a smile.

He rudely ignored her. Instead, he whispered to the twins, "You tell them what the truth is."

The kids nodded mechanically. They seemed beside themselves with fear. They were being sent into the camp of the enemy with a mission. Uh-oh, Sandi thought. Instead of being allowed to enjoy their visit and get a break from the insanity, they've been set up to confront Ted.

Ted was waiting outside in the sunshine and they all walked to his apartment. In the living room, he told his children that he had already hidden eggs all around the estate in East Hampton and they were going to have a great time having an Easter egg hunt the next day, like they used to. No, the kids replied, they did not want to go to the beach house.

"That's Mom's house," Alexa protested, meaning that he was not welcome there.

Grego agreed. When Ted insisted, they panicked and cried and said that they would never go. They knew what awaited them back at the Stanhope if they did. Ted was appalled. His wife had made their kids afraid of an Easter egg hunt. He told them he would not force them to go to the beach house and they began to unload all the things they had been told to tell him, before they forgot it all:

"Mom only gave up the week of spring break because she thought it would look good to the court," said Grego. "The court's not on her side and the judge is mad at her because the court psychologist told the court bad things about her and you bribed the psychologist to say those things."

Ted was dumbfounded. He could not believe what he was hearing, but it was only the beginning.

"Mom says you have a secret girlfriend and she has a two-year-old son that's yours," Alexa said.

"What?"

"You asked the court to evict Danny from the Stanhope," said Grego.

"You haven't paid Steven and Bruce ninety-five thousand dollars," Alexa said, referring to money they had spent to move to England.

"Mom has no money! You cheat and you're dishonest in business," Ted's son told him. "That's the only reason you make a billion dollars a year. You should give all of your money to Mom, so the divorce can be over now!"

"Since you cheat in business, you can always make more money," said Alexa. "If you really loved us you'd do it. You must be dishonest because you're going to file for bankruptcy so you won't have to give Mom money."

Ted listened in horror as the kids spewed out the stories they had been spoon-fed by Generosa—her revenge, coming out of the mouths of babes. He let them speak, even though it was tearing him up. Apparently Generosa's message was not just one of blind hatred. She was using the kids to try to leverage a settlement on her absurd, one-sided terms. She wanted all the money. Everything. The kids told Ted that they knew he had bugged the telephones at the Stanhope to spy on them and also had used secret cameras, but he should know that their mother told them that she had installed a device outside that blocked his bugging. It would have been funny, were it not so sad.

"Why do you think your father would bug your phones?" Sandi asked.

"So he can catch us and Mom saying things that can be used in court against us," said Grego. "You hired someone to break into Steven and Bruce's apartment and plant drugs, so they would get in trouble with police and maybe go to jail."

"It's not fair you live in a nice apartment and we're stuck in a hotel," Alexa charged.

"I'm tired of the hotel food," Grego whined, bursting into tears.

"We don't want to see the new therapists," Alexa announced. "We can't trust them because the court psychiatrist told us to see them and you bribed her. So we shouldn't tell them what we really think."

What they really wanted was not ever to see him, as their mother wished. That way, they would not have to face their mother after being with their hated father. They wanted it all to stop.

"You have not been told the truth about any of these issues," he told them.

"We believe Mom!" they protested.

Sandi could not believe that Generosa had convinced them Ted was a burglar. No, Alexa said, they thought the culprit was his business partner, Mark Angelson, "Because he works for Dad and is a bad man." A car registered in Ted's name had been spotted in the neighborhood at the time of the burglary, she had been told by her mother. She said that the notional needle burglar had also left a note that read "I am watching you and I know everything you do." Alexa said it was obvious that her father was behind the caper.

"Who else would do that?" she asked.

Who indeed? Ted and Sandi sat in stunned silence for a few minutes. Ted was convinced that the needle thing was a scam to make him look bad in front of the children, or perhaps in court. He sighed, took a deep breath, and began to carefully and calmly respond to almost every issue his kids had raised. It had no effect. He would not discuss his dating life with the twins.

"I'm separated," he told them. "I have dated several people but there is nobody I'm ready to introduce you to."

"But we know all about Danny!" Alexa countered, meaning that they were acquainted with their mother's boyfriend.

By Saturday morning, their defiance was stronger.

"We believe Mom, not you!" they told him.

When Ted took a nap on Sunday afternoon, Sandi tried again to reason with the kids but they were well beyond that.

"You know your father loves you very much," Sandi told them. "No matter how you feel about him now, he's not going to give up his time with you."

"I know dad doesn't love me," said Grego. "If he did, he would give Mom all the money, so she could take care of us."

"You're wrong, Grego." Sandi gave up and hugged them both, saying, "I love you."

They did not hug back or say they loved her. She was one of the enemy. If they did, their mother might find out. On Sunday night, Ted realized that Alexa had Generosa's cell phone and Steven and Generosa had already called several times, upsetting the kids further. They tried to assure their mother and her butler that they were not having fun or being friendly with their father and were resolutely pushing the party line. Ted wanted to put a stop to the meddling during his time with the twins and asked Alexa to give him the phone. She refused.

"No. The only reason you want it is to get secrets off it."

"You guys might hate me right now, but I'm still your father and I expect you to do as I say."

Ted took the phone, telling his daughter that he wasn't interested in any phone numbers that might be programmed into it, but Alexa did not believe him. He paced back and forth in the kitchen, trying to defend himself and deflate his wife's lies, but the kids were not hearing it. He got angry and raised his voice but it did nothing to shake them. They were much more afraid of their mother.

"I don't cheat at business and I am furious that you would be told something like that. Your mother is not interested in what's best for you," he said. "She's only interested in telling lies about me."

But Ted declined to deny that his girlfriend Mary's child was his.

He gave up. He had deep concerns about his children's mental health and their ability to distinguish reality from fantasy. Ted had no choice: He would now seek sole and complete legal custody of his kids. Because of all the dangerous misinformation, the longer he waited, the worse off they would be. Later, Ted confided to Sandi that he had come to believe that Generosa's hatred of him went beyond what they had witnessed that weekend. Ted had heard that Generosa's new psychiatrist had prescribed a psychotropic drug to treat her mental problem—but she was refusing to take it.

"She's crazy," said Ted. "She wants me dead. I think she's going to kill me."

Sandi thought about it and agreed. In her heart, she felt that Generosa was capable of murder. She became alarmed and urged Ted to get a bodyguard, like he used to have for the kids, like Generosa had hired for herself. Later, Sandi's husband, Bob, a very cool-headed man, urged the same thing—constant armed protection. Immediately.

Ted was about to raise the stakes in the divorce and custody cases, something certain to enrage Generosa even further, if that was possible. Several other friends and associates, including Ted's partner at Chancery Lane Capital, Mark Angelson, also told him to get a bodyguard.

Ted did not take their advice.

21

PRIVATE EYES

GENEROSA glanced apprehensively over her shoulder at other people on the Manhattan sidewalk and whispered to a companion:

"We're being followed. Ted has someone following me," she said, taking another backward glance. "They're behind us."

The friend looked and saw a lot of people bundled against the winter cold, coming and going, none of them paying any attention to them. They must be really good, he thought.

"They're there," Generosa insisted. "He hired people to follow me and I'm not going to take it!"

There was no one following her. Not yet.

Danny hired a private detective to get information on Ted and to follow Generosa, to see who might be following her; a detective to follow a detective. Spy versus Spy.

Ted had also spotted people following him around that winter, but he was not mistaken. Some of the men looked rough and shady and stood out in Ted's surroundings.

In January, Danny made good on his promise to help Generosa in her battle with Ted. He contacted a friend named John Kundle, who was installing a security system on Generosa's East Eighty-seventh Street town house. Kundle

Prayers and Secrets: Generosa "Jo" Rand (*top left*) in her St. Catherine's uniform; (*bottom left*) high school graduation; and (*right*) as a flower girl at a family wedding.
Photo: Frances Thomas

The Reluctant Lawyer: Investment banker Ted Ammon.
Photo courtesy New York Post

Almost Paradise: Ted, Alexa, Grego, and Generosa Ammon when they were happy. *Photo courtesy* New York Post

Bedtime: Ted reads a fairy tale to his children. *Photo courtesy* New York Post

Growing Perfection: The beach house at 59 Middle Lane in East Hampton, with the yellow daffodils in bloom. *Photo: Jeffrey P. Gibbons*

Coverwood: The Ammons' manor house in Surrey, England. *Photo: Steve Stephens*

Tool Belt Guy: Danny Pelosi, displaying his tattoos, his rolled-up pack of Marlboros, and a diamond wristwatch. *Photo: Steven Hirsh,* New York Post

Million-Dollar Nanny: Kaye Mayne outside a Long Island courtroom, carrying a murder mystery. *Photo: Mary McLoughlin,* New York Post

The King and Queen of Center Moriches: Danny and Generosa at a wedding. *Photo courtesy* New York Post

Murder on Middle Lane: The pool of blood next to the bed where Ted was murdered. *Photo courtesy* New York Post

Officer Down: Danny's brother, NYPD officer James Pelosi. *Photo: Dennis Clark*

Newlyweds: Generosa and Danny out for the evening in England after their marriage with the press in pursuit. *Photo: INS*

Dying Wish: A gaunt and dying Generosa Ammon leaves a courtroom after designating Kaye Mayne as a guardian of her children. *Photo: Mary McLoughlin,* New York Post

For Ted: Ted's sister Sandi Williams and her husband, Dr. Robert Williams, after filing their lawsuit seeking custody of the Ammon twins. *Photo: Veronique Louis,* New York Post

Here's to You: Danny toasting the box containing Generosa's ashes at the Stanhope Hotel bar, where they met. (Note the cosmopolitan cocktail and cigarette in front of Generosa's remains.) *Photo: Robert Kalfus*

ran a security firm on Long Island that specialized in cutting edge video surveillance technology called the Rapid Eye digital video storage and transmission system. The concealed Rapid Eye video cameras, hidden inside burglar alarm system motion detectors at the corner junctures of ceilings and walls, took video images that could be viewed live or recorded from a laptop computer anywhere in the world where there was a telephone line. It transmitted and received instructions over Ted's fax line. Once it was hooked up, it was able to record and send pictures for up to a full year, using its hard-drive memory. Danny had John discreetly install a complete twelve-thousand-dollar system in the beach house, with eight hidden cameras inside and one camera outside. Ted, of course, had no idea that whenever he was in the East Hampton house, he was under constant surveillance. When Ted arrived and shut off the burglar alarm with his own subcode, John notified Danny that Ted was in the house. They also knew when he left, because, although Ted often failed to set the burglar alarm when he was there, he always armed it when he left. Cameras were hidden outside the master bedroom, in the guest bedroom, which Ted often used with girlfriends, in the den, the living room, the kitchen, the mudroom, and even in the children's wing. Another camera was placed outside, covering the side entrance to the mudroom. Once it was set up without Ted's knowledge or consent, every private moment could be viewed on any of three laptop computers. John had one, Danny had a second one, and Danny's friend Nick Short* had the third.

At the Stanhope, Danny showed Generosa live images of Ted moving around the beach house with his dogs. If Ted removed any property from the house, the cameras would capture it. Even though the court did not care about the sexual relationships of the litigants, Generosa cared very much about catching Ted with his pants down. The Rapid Eye unit, a flat, breadbox-sized metal box, was hidden behind a wall inside the secret safe room on the second floor of the mansion. The list of those who knew that the spy system existed, and where the main unit was hidden, was short: John Kundle and one of his workmen, Generosa, Danny and his pal Nick Short, Steven the butler, Bruce the cook, and Alexa and Grego. Of course, the list would grow if any of those on the list told others.

When Danny came out to use the beach house with Generosa, he would immediately go upstairs to Ted's study, reach behind the stereo and unplug the Rapid Eye—so that they would not be on display.

It wasn't long before Danny triumphantly flipped open his laptop and showed Generosa pictures of Ted during intimate moments with his girlfriend. Generosa exulted, although it was also painful to witness. Danny sometimes left his laptop at his sister Barbara's house in Center Moriches, while the computer monitored Ted's every move, including when Ted broke up with his girlfriend Mary and began bringing a sexy brunette to the house. Danny even set up his laptop on a table at the East Eighty-seventh Street construction site. His workers thought the video was usually boring but sometimes better than cable TV. One warm afternoon, while Danny was out, the construction workers noticed Ted getting amorous in the kitchen with the new brunette. All work stopped. The couple hugged and then her head moved down Ted's body as she knelt in front of him. The construction workers hooted, howled, and cheered as they realized they were watching a millionaire receive oral sex in the kitchen of his mansion. When Danny arrived, his workers told him what he had missed and he replayed it. Later, Danny showed it to a gratified Generosa.

On another night, Danny was spying on Ted and Mary with the laptop when he watched the beautiful, naked blonde emerge from the master bathroom and walk toward the bedroom.

"Nice rack," Danny said aloud, looking at her breasts.

Marie, at five-foot-four, looks like a soft-spoken librarian with mousy brown hair. Or a sarcastic sales clerk with cute chipmunk cheeks. Or a confused, nosy housewife with freckles whom you can't help but fill in on local gossip. Unless you see her sharp hawk eyes focus on her prey or hear her real voice, she could be any of those people.

Marie Schembri is a chameleon, the queen of blending in. She is a private detective, one of the best, whom celebrities, millionaires, and Teamsters call when they are in trouble. She is not listed in the phone book and does not advertise her services. She is so good, almost no one except a few top lawyers in New York knows she exists. She likes it that way. Like traditional detective agencies, she works with some off-duty or retired detectives, but most of her employees are gifted amateurs who look, speak, and act nothing like cops. That is her specialty: undercover operatives who don't look undercover. She is her own best operative and has a repertoire of disguises and tricks that would make a con man jealous. Sometimes she is the librarian, sometimes she goes formal, with another operative chauffeuring a rented limo, so that she can follow a subject to nightclubs. She has posed as a punk street person, an executive, and a Hasidic wife, complete with wig. It's not the disguise that does it, it's the whole persona she adopts that allows her to fade into the background.

Marie started out to be a lawyer but ended up as an accountant working for New York City. She backed into a part-time job at a detective agency, uncovering financial trails. It beat the hell out of her boring city job, so she quit and went to work for the detective agency full-time. After a few years, she went into business for herself. Her first customer was comic Eddie Murphy.

She had a childhood that was similar to, but in one way worse than Generosa's. Marie was taken away from a neglectful alcoholic mother when she was young and put into an orphanage and foster homes. She became good at blending in, at fading into the furniture, in order to survive. It later served her well in her chosen profession.

Like Generosa, Marie was driven and tenacious. The first thing Marie did when she was hired by Ted's lawyer was to

run a background check on Danny Pelosi. She hit pay dirt.
He had an extensive arrest record, mostly for drunk driving,
but also for assault and other things. A civil lawsuit he had
filed yielded a huge stack of documents at the county clerk's
office in Riverhead. Danny was bankrupt when he met Generosa and his house was in foreclosure. He needed money
desperately. A psychiatric report contained an interview
with him in which he admitted that he was an alcoholic involved in various illegal scams, and that he had used every
drug there was. The psychiatric report said he suffered from
an incurable personality disorder with antisocial traits. This
was the man Generosa had chosen, who was around her children. Ted's lawyer authorized Marie's operatives to stake out
the beach house.

Marie micromanaged the Ammon job by phone, constantly speaking to the four operatives she had in East
Hampton: Taylor and his wife Eileen,* two of Marie's gifted
amateurs, and Karl* and Stan,* off-duty detectives.

The surveillance began on Friday, June 22, 2001, at 6:30
P.M. Danny Pelosi arrived at the mansion at the wheel of a
blue Audi that was registered to Ted Ammon. The private
eyes drove by in cars and jogged back and forth down the
lane, in order to watch the house. That night, Taylor walked
up with a pair of mini-binoculars and hung out at the front
fence in the dark. He saw the kids, and saw Danny drinking
beer after beer. Generosa was drinking what looked like
screwdrivers. Danny did not leave that night. Later, when the
lights went out, he was still there. At 1:00 A.M., Taylor and
the other watchers left.

They were back at 7:00 on Saturday morning. An hour
later, Generosa came power-walking down the driveway
with Buddy the cocker spaniel on a leash. She did that silly
power-walk thing down the lane with the dog and then back.
After the healthful exercise, she lit up a cigarette. Later,
Danny came to the front door to check out the day. He was in
shorts and shirtless, his biceps and tattoos on display. It was
an uneventful day but the watchers' patience was rewarded

at 6:45 that evening. The blue Audi came out of the driveway
with Danny behind the wheel. Generosa was in the passenger seat and Alexa and Grego were sitting in the back. The
investigators took pictures but did not follow them. They
must have gone out for a long dinner, because they did not
return until 11:35. The big-screen TV went on and stayed on
until 2:30 Sunday morning, when the lights went out. The
detectives were back early Sunday morning and saw Danny
in his shorts again. On Monday morning, the servants
started arriving.

A silver-and-black Jaguar sped into the Ammon driveway
and stopped short by the side door. A woman dressed in a
coordinated and accessorized designer outfit got out in a flut-
ter and rang the doorbell. Steven the butler answered.

"Hello, I'm looking for my baby! He's missing! May I
come in?"

Steven invited the distraught woman into the kitchen,
where she pulled out a color snapshot of a dog.

"This is my baby! Have you seen him? I'll pay a reward,
of course."

Steven, an animal lover, looked at the photo and told her
that he had not seen her baby. The woman gave her real
name and phone number to him, begging him to call if he
saw her pooch. Steven promised that he would. She struck
up a conversation, explaining that she was a fashion stylist to
celebrities. She dropped a few names. While she chatted, she
looked around the house. She tried to engage Steven in gossip about his employer but he said he was busy and showed
her politely to the door.

Taylor's wife, Eileen, had pulled the lost-dog bit, a routine designed to get an operative inside the target home for a
look around. It was usually hit or miss but sometimes it paid
off big. Eileen really was a fashion stylist who worked with
a lot of celebrities. She was also one of Marie's snoops. The
photo of the dog was actually one of Marie's pooch, Doctor
Strangelove.

One night, Eileen saw sudden activity at two o'clock in

the morning at the beach house. Lights went on and Generosa was moving around in the master bedroom suite area on the second floor. Eileen trained her binoculars on the suspicious activity and watched a busy Generosa through a window. It took a while for Eileen to realize that the lady of the house, an insomniac, was up in the middle of the night doing laundry—washing, drying, and folding her underwear.

In a few days, the private eyes had what they needed and only one local resident had noticed that they were there. It wasn't Generosa. A woman neighbor saw the same cars and the same jogger going back and forth on Middle Lane and called the East Hampton Village Police. When an officer arrived, the investigators explained that they were licensed PIs running a surveillance. The officer wished them a nice day and left.

Near the end of the operation, Generosa and Danny came out of the beach house and split up, got into separate cars. One of the operatives followed Generosa, who went out on an errand and returned. Eileen saw Danny leave and then return in the Audi. He sped into the driveway and hit the brakes hard, skidding on the gravel. There was no one around to see his performance, so she wondered whether he was up to something urgent—or was just immature. When she later saw Danny and Generosa talking alone in the house, they seemed to be debating something very important. Eileen couldn't hear what they were saying but wished she could. She later told Marie she was just an amateur but she had a gut feeling that it might be a better idea to stick with Danny and see who he met and what he was up to, especially considering his record.

"We should be following where this guy is going. I think we're following the wrong person," she said. "I really don't think we should be watching her. I think we should be watching him."

But there was never close surveillance on Danny, just on the house.

A separate crew of private detectives working for Ted set up a different surveillance operation. They infiltrated a neighbor's backyard and found a spot in a tree along the fence line with a good view of the Ammon backyard, especially the pool area. One detective climbed up into the branches and got comfortable. Then he trained a video camera on the yard and started to roll. First, he panned over the landscape, the back of the home, the patio, the pond and bridge, the pool, cabana, lounge chairs, and Generosa's black-and-white cow, Elsie. Danny, wearing only cutoff denim shorts, and Generosa, in a two-piece bathing suit, emerged from the house at two in the afternoon and strolled out to the pool with their drinks, while the kids remained inside the house, watching TV. The camera caught Generosa reclining on a chaise longue in the sun. Soon, she got up and took off her top. She was saying something to Danny but the watchers could not hear them. Danny walked over to her and stood at the foot of the chaise. Generosa lifted a bare foot slid it up Danny's thigh, and began massaging his groin through his cutoffs. The camera wobbled because the watcher had it on maximum zoom and was nervous shooting such a scene. Soon, Danny dropped his shorts and stood naked before Generosa, while the videocam rolled. Generosa removed her suit bottom and Danny joined her on the chaise and they went at it. The watcher, who wondered if the kids could see the same thing from the house, filmed the action for several minutes, straining for position through the leaves. Suddenly, the detective lost his grip on a branch and fell out of the tree, hitting the soft ground with a loud thud and a grunt, but he never dropped the camera. Danny, although engrossed in amorous activity, heard the noise. It had come from the fence area, the bushes near the neighbor's property. He disentangled himself, pulled on his shorts, and ran over to the bushes.

"Who the fuck is over there?" he demanded, scanning the shrubbery.

No one answered. The detectives were already gone, hot-footing it out of there.

Later, the private eyes played back the X-rated surveillance video, which showed the sex and then a blur when the operative fell, and finally the dirt and leaves on the ground.

Meanwhile, in Manhattan, the judge in the divorce and custody case was presented with audiotapes made by Generosa of Ted talking to the kids on the phone. As a result, Judge Diamond issued an order banning all video or audio surveillance in the case—without knowing about the beach house sex tape or the secret spy system inside the mansion.

Ted's lawyer called Marie, who pulled her operatives off the case. Generosa ignored the court order and continued to spy on Ted whenever he was in her beach house.

For Marie, it was another successful job. They had confirmed that Generosa's boyfriend was spending the night with her in front of the children, despite the judge's order forbidding it. And Danny was drinking and then driving Ted's kids around, even though his license had been taken away. Generosa rarely took the kids anywhere. The weather was beautiful, but they stayed inside the house watching TV, while Generosa was busy spending time with Danny. Quality time.

In late June, Ted got the information about Danny's criminal record, his sleeping over, drinking, and driving the twins without a license. To friends, Ted said that "Sparky," as he called Danny, "has a rap sheet as long as my arm."

After the nightmare of Easter weekend, Ted was finally ready to fight back. His lawyer presented the evidence from the private detectives to Judge Diamond. The judge, who had already ordered that Danny could not live with Generosa and the kids, expressed great displeasure and strongly warned her to stop ignoring the court's orders. She did not tell the judge that she was secretly filming Ted at the beach house, a violation of the judge's last order. The combination of Danny's background and behavior coupled with Gen-

erosa's contempt of court did not bode well for her case, she
was told.

By this time, Ted had concluded that the town house renovation, which would soon be a year overdue, was a rolling
scam to cheat him out of money and put cash in Danny and
Generosa's pockets. He thought that the bills he was paying
were two or three times what the work was worth, if it was
ever actually performed by Danny's pals. First, Ted's lawyer
demanded a documented accounting of the whole project.
Ted also wanted to see the plans for the renovation. When
Generosa refused to provide either, Ted cut off the cash flow
and her credit cards and informed her through his lawyer
that he would not pay a nickel until he saw valid invoices. He
had no intention of continuing to fund the obscene expendi-
tures at the Stanhope for her and her construction crew. He
continued to pay all expenses for the children, of course.

The perpetual party at the Stanhope ended abruptly. Generosa and the kids decamped in the middle of the night and
moved into the Fifth Avenue residence. Suddenly, it seemed
as if Generosa might lose custody of the children and it did
not look like Judge Diamond was going to give her what she
wanted in a settlement. She downplayed her own arrogant
behavior and Danny's rap sheet and attributed all of her
problems to Ted, who, she told anyone who would listen,
was buying off the judge. Generosa, who had already borrowed large sums of money from friends before she needed
it, redoubled her efforts and hit up several more people. She
could not make the payments on the bank loans she had
taken out for the renovations. Work on the town house
slowed down. She told her new creditors and her kids that
Ted had cut her off without a cent for no reason. The Skypad
Corporation went bankrupt once Ted's supporting cash vanished. Danny was very upset when he had to sell the new
SUV Generosa had given him.

Ted had rocked their world but he wasn't done. The next
time he saw the twins he told them that their friend Danny
wasn't who he claimed to be, a struggling working-class

hero. He was a violent drunk, a drug addict, and a thief, and he had been to jail several times and had also cheated on his wife. The kids were shocked. They later asked Danny if it was true, and he had to admit that he had been arrested, although he denied almost everything else. Danny was furious at Ted for tarnishing his image.

After the hidden system had captured more images of Ted and his girlfriends in compromising positions, Generosa told her friend Ronnie that she had "a whole portfolio of pictures" of her husband with paramours that would guarantee that she got all the marbles: the fortune, all of the properties, and full custody of the kids.

"I'm going to hang him with it. Now I want everything."

It was bold talk, indeed, from someone who had just had her head handed to her by the judge. Ted, in fact, was better positioned to gain full custody, if he wanted it. But Generosa did not tell Ronnie about some other sensational documentary evidence that Ted would not want made public. Ronnie was confused and said so. Why would Ted give her the whole ball of wax? Nobody got everything in a divorce. Besides, Generosa was sleeping with Danny, just like Ted had his girlfriends. How was that going to get her anything, much less everything? Generosa refused to explain but seemed completely confident that she would get it all. It did not occur to Ronnie that Generosa was trying to catch Ted in bed with a man—and blackmail him.

"How can you get everything?" Ronnie asked again.

22

"I AIN'T DONE WITH YOU YET"

Danny had a real temper and he was mad at Ted for inform-ing the twins about his sordid past, among other things. He told Generosa that he could not take that lying down. "I've never talked to your husband but he's violated my boundaries and I've gotta confront him on that. What he did with the kids is wrong. He should never have told them about my arrest history and stuff like that, without saying something to me," Danny said.

In the summer of 2001 Ted had rented a house nearby, close to the beach in Amagansett. In a development reminis-cent of his first meeting with Generosa, Ted began dating a beautiful brunette real estate agent, Sherri Disalvo,* after he and Mary split up. On a warm July afternoon, Ted dropped the kids back at the East Hampton beach house after a visit. As the children went inside, careful to show no affection to their father that might be witnessed by their mother, Danny approached Ted's black SUV, waving and calling out to him.

"Ted!"

Ted ignored him.

"Yo! I ain't *done* with you yet!"

"I have nothing to say to you," Ted said coolly through the open window, fingering a switch that began raising the glass, cutting Danny off.

Ted was not about to chat. But before Ted could leave, the former boxer walked quickly over to the closed window and rapped sharply on it with his knuckles.

"Yo, pal! Not for nothing, roll down the window. We ain't done talking," Danny ordered, motioning for Ted to roll down the window.

Ted put the vehicle in park, hit the switch again, and the window slid down. Danny was angry that Ted had told the kids about his criminal record without warning him. He made it clear that Ted had violated his particular manly code.

"You should not've told them that without talking to me first," Danny scolded.

Apparently, in Danny's world, when you felt compelled to inform someone about the prior bad deeds of a stranger, you were required first to notify that person, so that they would be prepared for the event. Danny certainly wasn't challenging the accuracy of the information, the usual reason for a speak-to-me-first request.

"Listen," Danny continued, "you know my past. You've evidently done a huge background check on me. I'm no angel. I'm just in it for the moment, but what you're doing to the kids, that ain't right, man."

Ted agreed but felt that virtually all of the ugliness was Generosa's doing. Generosa had not consulted him before she told the kids terrible things about him—most of it lies or distortions. It was ridiculous that Danny was upbraiding him for telling the truth, an obvious attempt at intimidation.

But Danny presented himself as a peacemaker and told Ted that he would try to persuade Generosa to agree to a meeting to work things out concerning the kids. It was certainly possible that Danny was the more reasonable of the two, which would not have been difficult. Danny told Ted that he should speak to Generosa and that he had been trying to get Generosa to speak to him, to settle things and get it over with. He said it was dumb that they had not spoken for almost a year. Ted agreed but felt that Generosa was completely responsible for the impasse, not himself.

"I wish you would go talk to her," Danny said, tilting his head toward the house. "But, evidently, there ain't no talking with you two."

He stressed that Ted should never again speak ill of him to anyone, especially the twins, without consulting him first.

"If you're gonna down-mouth me, just do me a favor— down-mouth me to me before you do it to the kids. I'm the guy who defends you here."

"Thank you," said Ted, wondering if it was true.

"I got kids too, man. I wouldn't be appreciative if my wife got a new boyfriend and he was talking down on me. I wouldn't respect the man at all. I didn't do that to you."

Danny wants to respect me? Ted wondered. His analogy was inept but he seemed to be holding out an olive branch.

"Do we understand each other?" Danny pressed.

"Yes," said Ted.

Ted asked how Generosa was getting along and Danny said that she was doing better.

"I'm glad she's happy, but honestly, Dan? *Good luck,*" said Ted, as if he would need a great deal of it to survive Generosa.

Ted drove away and Danny went back into the house to tell Generosa about the encounter. Before August was over, Ted and Generosa actually had a civil phone conversation for a few minutes, long enough to arrange a meeting at the beach house to discuss the kids. Ted wanted to stop the madness and a poorer Generosa was now motivated to deal. The truce was arranged by Danny and assisted by a court ruling in which the judge ordered temporary shared custody of Alexa and Grego. Danny was acting as a go-between because he wanted to see an end to the kids' suffering, an end to the war—and a return of Ted's money.

Generosa told Ted that she wanted to move back to England with Danny, once things were settled. He said that he would consider it, but taking the kids out of the country at that point was out of the question. He agreed to fly in the kids' former headmaster from the Cranleigh School to par-

ticipate in a meeting at the beach house about possibly allowing the twins—after a settlement—to return to the Surrey boarding school where they had been happy.

Danny, who had suddenly become a good provider for his
estranged wife, Tami, and their three kids, often visited them
at their Manorville home. One night, after a few drinks, he
stumbled unannounced into the darkened house in the early
hours of the morning. Once inside, he saw a shadowy figure
pointing a shotgun at his chest.

"Tami! It's me! Danny! Don't fuckin' shoot!"

They were both shaken that she had mistaken him for an
intruder. Danny said that he was taking the shotgun away but
would buy her a stun gun for protection. Then Danny found
out that stun guns were also illegal. To get around the law, he
sent away for a mail-order Taser using the New Jersey address of a relative. When the package arrived unannounced,
the relative was perplexed. Danny told the relative that he
had mistakenly had his stun gun sent to her address. The relative did not like getting weapons in the mail for someone
else and did not want to get involved. She refused to give it
to Danny and told him that she had sent it back. Danny then
bought another one from the Spy Store.

A Taser is a plastic gun with a battery instead of bullets. It
explosively fires two darts using air pressure. The darts are
attached to thin wires that remain attached to the Taser and
dig into the clothing and skin of the target. The shooter then
pulls the trigger to deliver fifty thousand volts of muscle-
convulsing electricity that is incredibly painful and completely immobilizes the person getting zapped. Some
models also have two metal spikes, so the device can also
function as a contact stun gun. To guard against criminal
use, the manufacturers place thousands of tiny, colored plastic tags in some units that are ejected and spray outward
when the Taser is fired. Under a microscope, police can read
the tags to determine the manufacturer of the Taser and
other information that might lead them to the person who

used it. Because they are so small, it is virtually impossible to retrieve all of the tags. Once the weapon is fired, new dart cartridges must be loaded into the Taser in order for it to work remotely again.

When Danny got his new toy, he brought it to the town house job site while the workmen were still there. He was itching to test it but had no intention of inflicting pain on himself. The Taser also worked without firing the darts—if the barrel of the weapon was pressed against skin and the trigger was pulled. Danny asked for a guinea pig but no one stepped forward. He whipped out his roll of cash, peeled off a twenty-dollar bill, and waved it in the air. Still no takers. When he got up to one hundred, one crew member stepped up and snatched the bills.

Danny touched his arm with the device and pulled the trigger. The burly workman yelped and backed off. It hurt and made his whole arm numb. Danny was hot to test the darts. He offered the worker more money to take a full hit with the zapper but the man was not interested. One guy wanted two hundred but Danny thought that was too much. He later watched a video demonstration of someone getting the full Taser with the darts.

The victim twitched and crumpled into a heap on the floor. The guy was totally helpless and he only got one zap. With the darts, the victim continued to receive agonizing shocks for some time, while the user stood safely out of reach. He couldn't defend himself. He was helpless.

Ted later told his private detective, Marie, that Danny spoke to him again, this time outside a family-court courtroom in Manhattan that August. This time, Ted thought, Danny was trying a carrot-and-stick approach. Generosa had already told Ted that Danny knew mobsters but Ted dismissed it as Generosa's BS. But, in the courthouse hallway, Ted claimed that Danny issued what Ted took as a veiled threat:

"Don't think you're the only one with money or who knows people," Ted said that Danny told him. "I know people."

Ted said that Danny mentioned an Italian family name to him. It was unfamiliar to him. Danny didn't use the word *Mafia* and did not threaten Ted with death. Perhaps he meant that he knew rich people who might assist him. Coupled with Generosa's prior statements that Danny claimed pals in the Cosa Nostra, the statement apparently gave Ted pause.

"We don't give a shit who he's connected to," Marie said, when she heard of the conversation.

The professionals—Marie, the private eye, and Adria Hillman, the lawyer—saw no reason to hire a bodyguard because it was completely irrational for someone to harm Ted Ammon. Generosa and Danny would be the only suspects, and hurting Ted would accomplish the opposite of whatever they hoped to gain. They had never lost a client yet and Ted was smart enough to listen to the pros. But he was concerned enough also to mention the exchange to his sister Sandi. Again, she urged him to get protection and again he did not refuse but simply deflected the plea and changed the subject. His partner, Mark Angelson, again recommended a bodyguard, as well. Still, Ted did nothing. That night he had wine with dinner and slept like a baby.

On the Upper West Side of Manhattan, Ted's driver, Milton, was not resting easy. He tossed and turned in bed and was startled awake by a nightmare. The fear of the bad dream lingered in the air, like smoke. His heart was banging fast. In the vision, he had driven Ted to the office and gotten out to open the limo door. As Ted stepped out onto the curb, Generosa suddenly appeared on the sidewalk, her bulging eyes full of evil and hate. Frozen, Milton noticed that she had an ugly gun in her hand. She brought the pistol up and began firing wildly at Ted, but hit him, instead. Milton clutched at his gushing wound, but he was not bleeding blood. Clear water was gurgling out of his body onto the pavement. It was a strange dream.

Unnerved, Milton showered, dressed, and went to pick up Ted. As he drove Ted to the office, he told his boss his disturbing dream, which he felt strongly was a premonition of murder.

"You should get a bodyguard," he urged.

Ted just chuckled and stepped out of the car.

23

SPY KIDS

Alexa and Grego had been in the scorched no-man's-land between their parents for an eternity, but they quickly learned from their mother that they had to pick a side to survive the war. They really had no choice, since they lived with her and saw their father only on weekends and some holidays. To prove their loyalty to their suspicious and volatile mother, they became her eager spies against their father. Slowly, Generosa accepted the premise that they saw their father only so that they could help her defeat him. It was acceptable for double agents to consort with the enemy.

When Ted picked the kids up for a weekend visit, it seemed to him that they had suddenly changed for the better. They were friendlier and had mostly stopped accusing him of high crimes and misdemeanors with which Generosa had primed them. Working in tandem, they were still on a mission for their mother, but it had changed from open warfare to espionage. She had told them that Ted was hiding his criminal activities and secrets and that they could uncover them. Alexa excelled in the verbal arena, trying to worm secrets out of her father. Grego specialized in going through Ted's papers and secretly photographing documents.

Suddenly, after the deep freeze, the kids were very interested in their father. They wanted to know all about everything. What was he doing, where, with whom? Alexa zeroed in on Ted's love life. He responded, as he had previously, that he was dating but no one had yet become important enough to tell them about. If that happened, he would tell them, he assured them. Alexa told him that she was entitled to know all about his romantic life. She asked to meet Ted's girlfriend and do things with her but he deflected the request. Alexa overplayed her hand a bit when she revealed to her aunt Sandi that it was okay if Generosa got remarried to Danny but that Ted was not allowed to remarry.

"Why?" asked Sandi.

"I don't want a stepmother."

Alexa was still able to glean some nuggets of intelligence about Ted's dating habits by casually asking innocuous questions about the new girlfriend.

When Ted went out jogging or when he took a nap, the spy kids swung into action. Grego went through his address book, looking for girlfriends' names and numbers. He rifled Ted's business papers. He took out his small camera and photographed documents and Ted's personal notes. He took or copied Ted's appointment book and telephone logs—who called him and who he called. He also got the flight records for Ted's helicopter, which told Generosa that Ted was chopping up to Greenwich, Connecticut, presumably to see his ex-wife.

During the week, Grego had the film developed and both children gave full reports to their spymaster. When Danny saw the photographs he shook his head. He knew that if Ted found out, he would yell at the twins and would tell the court, which might throw another monkey wrench into the works.

"You're gonna get in trouble with your father," Danny said, trying to discourage them.

They looked to their mother, who accepted Grego's photographs and encouraged him and his sister to get whatever else they could. She seemed proud. The spy kids' missions would continue. In addition to being sad, they were unneces-

sary. Generosa had private detectives following Ted and the
equivalent of spy satellites snooping on him at the beach
house.

Ted never caught the spy kids. It never occurred to him that
his own children would spy on him. He still assumed that
there were moral limits. Because Generosa often switched
or canceled Ted's visits with the kids, the judge had granted
Ted's request that they both be given cell phones so that their
father could speak to them anytime he wanted. Ted bought
the phones and gave them to the kids during one of his
weekends with them. He felt better because he would be able
to stay in touch with them and, he hoped, undo some of the
brainwashing.

Generosa had other ideas.

On a Saturday when Ted did not have the twins, Generosa
and Danny took them to Danny's son Tony's Little League
baseball game. Before they left, Danny remembered that the
children were supposed to speak to their father that evening,
but they would not be back by then.

"Yo, guys, call your father, because your father's gonna
call here at seven," Danny said.

The kids headed for the phone but their mother stopped
them.

"Fuck it! They're not there. He'll talk to them tomorrow."

Danny had them do it anyway, because he knew that Generosa would get in trouble with the judge again. Ted was furious when he couldn't reach the kids on Friday night. Their
cell phones were already turned off. On Saturday, he got a
message saying that they were going out to Tony's ball
game. Ted called their cell phones over and over and got the
voice mail, getting angrier each time. Ted knew that Generosa had already gotten to them. Somehow, she had gotten
rid of the kids' cell phones and was violating the judge's orders again. When he reached Grego at home later that day,
Ted was on the edge. Generosa could hear Grego's side of
the conversation, but it didn't matter. She was taping all of

Ted's phone calls on her answering machine and the tape was rolling. Grego did not tell his dad about the secret cameras in the beach house. He did not tell him the call was being recorded.

"Where have you been?" Ted demanded.

"Oh . . . messing around."

"Yeah? Why wasn't your cell phone on last night?"

Grego did not answer the question.

"Dad, we called," he whined.

"I don't care, Gregory. That's not the point. You have a cell phone. You put it in your pocket and you take it with you."

"Dad, we were doing something at the time."

"I don't care, Gregory whether or not . . . Going to Tony's game is more important than talking to your father?"

"Dad . . . Dad . . . we—"

"Gregory, answer my question. I am your father. Tony is somebody you've known for two or three months and it was more important to you to talk to me. Gregory, I want your cell phone on, okay? I want your cell phone on so I know where you are. I carry my cell phone wherever I go."

"Yeah, but that's how lots of people get cancer!"

There it was. Generosa, using the unsubstantiated news report about a possible link between cell phones and brain cancer, had scared the kids into not using their phones. If they talked to their father, their brains would rot. Ted was fuming.

"Oh, Gregory, that's just your mother's—"

"No!"

"She's just playing . . . like she is about everything else in your life."

"Fuck you!"

"Well, Gregory . . . Your mother is just filling you with every kind of lie that—"

"We don't believe that. We believe Mom."

"Your mother is an evil human being."

"No!"

"Sorry . . . I hate her. . . ."

Gregory cursed his father again.

"Fuck you, Gregory!"

They both hung up.

Later, Danny called Ted and tried to mediate.

"Yo, Ted. I made the kids call you."

He brought up Ted saying "Fuck you" to his own son. After his son had cursed him out, he had lost it and told his son that he hated his mother. Ted was ashamed of himself.

"Yo, what are you, stupid? She's bringing the transcript into court. You know she tapes everything, just like you tape her," Danny chided.

"Dan, I was just angry and frustrated. I shouldn't have . . ."

"Whatever. You can't be caught doing that kinda shit, man."

Although Danny had assumed the role of mediator and was talking to Ted man-to-man, father-to-father, he did not mention to Ted that he and Generosa were putting his sex life on the Internet every other weekend.

24

BADA-FUCKIN'-BOOM

Danny and his cousin, Frank Parrone,* were drinking at the beach house while Generosa was out and about in the Hamptons. When they ran out of beer, Danny trooped down to Ted's basement wine cellar and grabbed the nearest bottle of vino and brought it back upstairs. It went down easily and they polished off the rest of the bottle quickly. When Generosa returned home, she walked into the kitchen, took one look at the empty bottle that her boozed-up boyfriend and his cousin had guzzled, and went ballistic.

"Do you know what this cost?" she demanded.

"Nope," Danny replied.

The vintage claret cost eighteen hundred dollars a bottle, she informed him.

"No wonder I'm so fuckin' smashed," Danny said, laughing.

Generosa was not amused. She made it clear that fine wines would not be wasted on them and they were not to raid the wine cellar again. The woman who had spent money like water was now preaching frugality. Danny and Frank were still thirsty, so they left. They drove into town, to the liquor store. As Danny grabbed a $9.99 bottle of Gallo red off the shelf, Frank expressed an opinion about Generosa:

"Yo, man. She's a miserable bitch," Frank declared.

Danny just laughed. He knew that Generosa was under a lot of pressure. Her sense of humor had gone south. One weekend, when Danny and his sister Barbara and the kids were having fun eating dessert in the beach house kitchen, Generosa walked in. She was appalled to see her pampered children eating Reddi-wip. They were supposed to eat only fresh, natural, homemade crème fraîche, prepared by Bruce the cook. They were not allowed to eat commercial products with added preservatives and colorings. She went off and yelled at Danny. He walked over to her with the Reddi-wip and told her it was good. He tried to prove it to her by squirting the whipped cream in her face. The kids laughed. Danny squirted his sister and the kids. They all laughed and giggled. Except for Generosa. She froze. It looked like the whipped cream would fry off her face, she was so mad.

Generosa was feeling the financial pinch. She had borrowed money from friends when she didn't need it and had poured it down the drain. She owed a considerable amount of money and had no income. She now redoubled her efforts and hit up all of her remaining friends and acquaintances, but with little success. Walking Buddy in Central Park with her friend and former neighbor Jurate, Generosa said that she had nothing and was desperate because Ted had cut her off without a cent. She asked Jurate if she and her husband, Roger, could help her with a loan. Jurate said that they would do whatever they could. She asked Generosa how much she needed to tide her over.

"Ten million dollars."

Jurate flinched. She had assumed that her friend needed money to pay bills and keep her household running, and bridge gaps on her loans. It turned out that Generosa wanted eight figures in cash so that she could complete her Jetsons pad town house, among other things, as well as continue to live in the style to which she had become accustomed. Jurate was at a loss for words. She said that she would talk to her husband and get back to her. Generosa did not like that answer. Apparently, she expected nothing less than an instant yes from a loyal friend. Jurate spoke to her husband, who said he wanted to speak to some people about possibilities for Generosa. Six days went by before Jurate called her back. Generosa had already decided that anybody who took six days to think about giving her $10 million was no friend of hers. She did not return Jurate's repeated calls. A few days later, she ran into Jurate in the park.

"Generosa!"

Mrs. Ammon turned on Jurate and lit into her.

"I don't believe it! You're all the same! You just want Ted's money! You don't care about anything except business and money! You're all the same! I asked you for help and you wouldn't give it."

"I called you back."

"Ha ha! You called me back? Why didn't Roger call me back? You don't know anything about business!" she screamed at the top of her lungs. "You went down to Necker Island. Oh, yes!" Generosa was literally spitting with anger. "When I did something, you took my money and went there and had yourself a good time!"

Jurate was shaking as Generosa stalked off. Generosa's anger was scary; it totally consumed her. Jurate went home and wrote her a note. She figured out what their share of the Necker Island vacation had cost and wrote a five-figure check.

"Generosa, this is what I owe you for Ted's birthday party. I have never been so insulted and so shocked. We care about both of you, but I have never been treated that way by anybody."

She dropped the letter in the mailbox.

A couple of days later, Generosa's butler, Steven, showed up at Jurate's door. He handed her back her letter, along with the check.

"I was going through the mail. Sorry, I wasn't paying attention and I opened it up. Generosa does not need this kind of insult at this time," he said.

"Steven, she needs the money. She asked for money."

He refused to take back the check and left. Jurate would never speak to Generosa Ammon again.

Danny dropped a Taser off at Tami's house. He told her that it was to protect her and the kids. Also, it could be used, he informed her, against dogs—in case the rottweilers down the block attacked their dog.

"Shoot 'em with the fuckin' Taser," Danny told her.

Tami later told people that she didn't like the gadget, didn't really want it in her house, and had no plans to use it against anyone or any animal.

Generosa was becoming increasingly possessive of Danny. When Generosa and Danny had a nice lunch for two at a sidewalk restaurant in East Hampton, an attractive young woman strolled up alone to read the posted menu. She smiled at them at their table and perused the bill of fare. Then several other women arrived to check out the place.

"Stop looking at them!" Generosa hissed. "Stop flirting with them!"

Danny, who, like most men, couldn't help looking, protested that he was not flirting.

One evening, one of Danny's older male friends escorted Generosa to a formal affair in Manhattan. Danny arrived in his tux about a half hour later. He found the forty-five-year-old Generosa and his fifty-year-old, silver-haired pal at a table and joined them. He kissed Generosa and realized that they were in a no-smoking area.

"Sorry I'm late. I need a cigarette."

Danny went to the bar and lit up.

"Well, hello," said a sexy barmaid.

"Hey, how are you?"

"Can I get you . . . anything?" she asked Danny.

She was flirting, making a move on him in front of Generosa. He ordered a drink and noticed Generosa glaring at him from her table. Her face blossomed red, the way it did when she lost her temper. Uh-oh. When the waitress returned with his drink, she nodded toward Generosa and Danny's buddy.

"So, you're here with your parents?"

"No, that's my date, and my friend," Danny corrected her.

He rushed back to the table. Generosa, still hot, began harassing the waitress. Over and over, she would take a napkin, crumple it into a ball, and wave imperiously for the young woman, who was in her mid-twenties.

"Here you go, *miss*. Take this garbage away."

Somehow, Generosa knew not only that the woman had hit on Danny but that she had mistaken Danny for Generosa's son. Later, Danny went back to the bar for another smoke. The waitress apologized for her faux pas.

"I'm so sorry," she said.

Danny looked at her face and her body. She was gorgeous, she wanted him, and he couldn't lay a finger on her.

"You're sorry?"

As he did every time he and Generosa arrived at the beach house, Danny immediately went upstairs to Ted's study, reached into the wall unit behind the stereo, and unplugged the cord from the Rapid Eye secret surveillance unit in the attic, shutting off all of the hidden cameras and the entire system. They had no intention of putting pictures of their private life on the Internet site or storing them on the attic unit, where someone, a hacker or perhaps even Ted, might spy on them. Of course, Ted still had no clue that the system existed.

Danny and Generosa were alone at the beach house when Ted made his first settlement bid in the divorce case. He offered Generosa $10 million, and the $8 million town house on East Eighty-seventh Street. Everything to do with the kids would also be taken care of by Ted. She could live happily ever after with Danny in the Jetsons pad. When Danny heard the offer, he thought it sounded great. He would never have to work again. It was like a lotto win. What more could

anyone need? Danny popped a Bud Light, strolled out to the
pool in the afternoon sun, and urged Generosa to accept and
settle it all for good.

"Gen, take the money and run. Let's do this."

Generosa looked at her boyfriend like he was insane. To
anyone else, Ted's offer was a fortune. To Generosa, it was
an insult. A resumption of hostilities. To her, it was losing—
big time. Ted was denying her Coverwood, the Soho loft,
and the beach house—the most important place in the world
to her. He was doing it to hurt her, she believed. He didn't
love the place like she did. And she still believed that he was
worth hundreds of millions of dollars and was trying to
cheat her. She began slugging back tumblers of Johnnie
Walker and cursing Ted. The drunker she got, the louder she
got and the more her rage erupted. Danny knew enough not
to argue with her and kept out of her way. It reached the
point where she was nearly jumping out of her skin with
fury and could not restrain herself. She ran into the mansion
and he heard her tearing around, ranting and banging.
Danny stayed where he was. He noticed that she had emptied a fifth of whiskey.

Next, the window to Ted's study opened. A minute later, it
was raining laundry. Danny stepped in for a closer look. She
was tossing Ted's clothes out the window. This was not Kmart
shit, either. It was very expensive designer suits and clothing.
Well, she had warned him not to leave his stuff at the beach
house when he left. The judge had ruled that Ted could leave
certain items there but Generosa didn't give a damn.

She's having a shit fit, Danny thought, popping another
brew.

Generosa emptied Ted's closet, creating a colorful pile on
the pavement. A few minutes later, a large, antique desk
from Ted's study appeared on the windowsill. The $41,000
mahogany and slate desk had been a gift to Ted from his
hated first wife. How had Generosa lifted the eighty-pound
desk by herself? Danny wondered. He gulped another Bud

and watched from a safe distance. The desk took flight out the window, flipped over in midair, and crashed onto the driveway stones like a bomb.

Bada-fuckin'-boom! he thought, shaking his head in disgust.

Forty-one grand was now a pile of splinters and shattered stone in the driveway. Terrific.

What a fuckin' waste, Danny thought.

Anyone who accused Generosa of caring only about money should see this, he thought. Generosa looked down at her handiwork, pleased, and then disappeared from the window. What would be next?

A $100,000 seven-foot antique grandfather clock, taller than Ted, was next. It was also a gift from another hated person to Ted. It went end-over-end and bonged onto the stone like Big Ben hitting the deck.

She was making one big pile and Danny knew what was coming. He winced. She was going to burn maybe ten grand worth of really nice clothes that fit him. When she ducked back into the house, Danny started grabbing shirts and jackets from the pile. He was trying to hide them around the side of the garage when Generosa came back out and caught him.

"Put that back!" she screamed, snatching Ted's garments out of his hands and tossing them back onto the sacrificial mound.

Then Generosa threw Grego's baseball glove onto the pile. Danny was confused, until he remembered that Ted had bought the mitt for his son and had played catch with him. Last, she emerged from the kitchen lugging Ted's shiny two-thousand-dollar cappuccino maker, trailing the cord, and heaved it atop the pile. Out came the lighter fluid and the lighter. It wooshed into flame and built, crackling and popping, as the flames hissed and spread. The bonfire was quite a barbecue. The flames shot fifty feet into the air, the acrid smoke swirling over the trees. Would the neighbors call the fire department? When the fire got to the cappuccino machine, something inside it started going off like gunshots.

Generosa was breathing heavily and sweating from her exertion and the heat. Her hair floated in the hot gusts from the fire. The flames flashed and danced in her eyes.

Danny went out of earshot and called Generosa's attorney to ask him what to do. He told the lawyer that she was going nuts, trashing stuff and having a bonfire.

"You better get over here," he suggested.

Danny later salvaged the works of the grandfather clock and sold them for a few hundred bucks, without Generosa's knowing.

Ted arrived at the beach house the following weekend and found his bedroom closet empty. There were other blank spaces in the house. He called Danny.

"Dan, will you tell me where my clothes are?"

"I can't do it, man."

Danny could not rat out Generosa.

"They're all gone."

"I know."

"Are they in storage?" he asked, hopeful.

"I can't tell you."

"My cappuccino maker is gone too."

Danny stifled a laugh, remembering the exploding machine.

When Grego got home, he also noticed that things had gone missing from the house. He went to Danny.

"Where's my baseball glove?" he asked.

Danny could not tell him that his mother had gotten bombed and burned it because he loved the glove his father had given him. He lied to spare the boy's feelings.

"Buddy ate it. I threw it out."

He told Grego that he would buy him a new glove.

25

BEACH HOUSE BINGO

Ted began seeing quite a lot of Sherri, the pretty real estate agent who showed him his summer beach-cottage rental in Bridgehampton. He took the house so that he would be close to his kids and not have to enrage Generosa, who got bent out of shape every time he spent a weekend in the East Hampton beach house. He never had to set foot there again. The house on Middle Lane had become the symbol of the conflict, the choicest bone of contention, only because Generosa valued it so highly.

Sherri heard Ted on the phone with his ex and listened to her push his hot buttons, but it took two to make an argument. Ted could not help but respond. He was the villain, because he had taken up with another woman, but it went way beyond that. But Ted still also said nice things about Generosa: about her good qualities as an artist, a decorator, an art collector, and as a person and a mother. The woman he used to know and love. He just wanted it over.

"There's plenty of money to go around," he told her.

Sherri liked Ted because he was so easygoing, a gentle giant. She didn't know him on the corporate level but she knew that there was no way he could be as successful as he was without being a tough guy. She had even heard him called a shark, but to her, he was a loving, sweet, generous man. He talked to her about how he intended to create a better life for Alexa and Grego, who were going through hell. Sherri had an eight-year-old daughter and understood Ted's concerns about getting his kids away from the situation that just kept dragging on and on.

At first, Generosa encouraged the twins to go to summer camp in July. But once plans were made and she realized that Ted would be able to see them there, she went berserk. When they left, she gave them a fax number and told them that, instead of writing letters, they could fax her butler, Steven. She refused to write to them unless they wrote her first. Then, she ordered them not to write. She claimed that she was too poor to rent a post office box in East Hampton because their father wouldn't give her any money.

Ted told Sherri that for the second time during the divorce, he felt that he was being followed. He had seen people, and he'd had that weird feeling when the hair on the back of your neck stands up and you know someone is looking at you. As he had told others, he said to Sherri that Generosa was mentally ill and had a vicious temper.

"She is crazy and wants me dead."

Sherri too, suggested that he get a bodyguard. As usual, Ted laughed it off. As negotiations dragged on, Ted became impatient and decided to pressure Generosa by once again demanding to stay at the beach house on alternate weekends, even though he had his own place a few miles away. He believed that it would get things moving. It was a bargaining chip and he played it. It was his house, built with his money, and the court had already said he had a right to be there. Ted was angry that every time he agreed to something, Generosa would up the ante, as if she wanted it never to end.

Sherri was shocked that Ted was going back to the beach house. He asked her to spend time there with him. She refused to set foot in the place. Coupled with Ted's statement that Generosa wanted to kill him, Sherri could not handle it. She knew the tremendous rage Generosa felt toward Ted and anyone around him, and she had no intention of getting in the middle of that battle. The situation did not feel right and Sherri made a hard choice. She decided to back up and create space. She told Ted that she had feelings for him but that he was consumed by his bitter divorce and now was not the time for them to work out a relationship. She felt that Ted was still in denial and was underestimating Generosa's rage. She also knew that Ted was still trying to work out a complicated relationship with a woman named Mary, whom he had begun seeing during his marriage and who had a boyfriend herself. Sherri told him that she would love to hear from him when it was all over. He assured her that would be soon.

Ted understood why Sherri had to back off but he was very upset. Generosa had frightened off a second woman.

That summer, Ted called Sandi and told her that Steven the butler and Bruce the cook had sent him a strange letter. Steven claimed that Bruce had been busy acting as a medium again, chatting with the dead. This time, it wasn't their dead cat. It was Ted's dead mother. Bruce, the letter claimed, was channeling the spirit of Bettylee Ammon.

"Bruce has been talking to Bettylee and your mother is very disappointed in you," Steven told Ted.

They were still trying to pressure Ted into paying them for their alleged moving expenses and were using the name of Ted's mother to do it. Ted found it creepy and outrageous. He thought that they were as crazy as Generosa.

Out in East Hampton, the social season was in full swing, with parties and charity events and the country club, yacht club, and nightclub scenes.

Sam Wagner strolled down Middle Lane on a sunny morning and walked across the Ammon lawn to the front door. He was carrying an engraved invitation for Ted to a Labor Day party at the nearby estate of Sam's employer, Barton Kaplan, who was infamous for his lavish and outrageous parties. His Labor Day party would cost two hundred thousand dollars and would be filmed by a gay cable-TV company. Kaplan always invited the neighbors, so that they

would not complain about the loud, live music, but Sam had
met Ted jogging around the neighborhood and he thought
that Ted was handsome and very nice. However, it was not
Ted's weekend to be at the beach house and Danny answered
Sam's knock at the door. Danny's hair had grown out so long
that it almost reached his shoulders, and his shirt was off.
Sam checked out Danny's manly chest and asked for Ted.

"Hi, could you give this to Ted, please?"

When Danny said that Ted wasn't there, Sam introduced
himself and handed the invite to Danny.

"Who is it?" Generosa yelled from the kitchen.

"A neighbor," Danny shouted back. "He wants to invite us
to a party."

"Get rid of him!" the ever-social Generosa ordered.

"Maybe you'll come?" Wagner asked Danny.

"Yeah, maybe."

Generosa and Danny did not attend Kaplan's party but
many did. The driveway of the Kaplan estate was lined with
six-foot-tall inflated penises for the occasion. The soirée,
which featured bowls of dildos and condoms as party favors,
and nude frolicking by some guests in the pool, was up—or
down—to Kaplan's usual standards.

Danny and Generosa spent time at the beach house, alone
and sometimes with some of Danny's friends and family,
since Generosa had few of either. At one barbecue, Danny
the clown became a cowboy and jumped on the back of Generosa's cement Elsie the cow by the pool and rode the bovine
sculpture like a rodeo rider on a bull.

"Yee-hah!" buckaroo Danny whooped, waving one hand
in the air.

"Get off my fucking cow!" Generosa screamed.

Danny had messed with her sacred cow.

Later, when Danny's pretty daughter Rachelle and several of her high school friends visited, they were all loung-
ing around the living room and chatting. Danny sat on the

couch, and his daughter, standing behind him, affectionately rubbed his shoulders.

"Get your hands off him!" Generosa shrieked at Rachelle, startling everyone. "He's mine!"

It weirded everyone out and put quite a damper on the party. The people there knew what they had heard—they just couldn't believe it. In private, Generosa later accused Danny of incest. He told her that she was nuts. Danny had been accused of many things but never incest. There wasn't a shred of truth to it. It was all in the mind of Generosa, who had not yet told Danny about the details of the massages she had received as a child and where they had led.

In September, Ted, Generosa, Danny, and the headmaster of the Cranleigh School in England had a meeting at the beach house about Alexa and Grego's future. Generosa's butler, Steven, also participated in the meeting, as if he were a party to the divorce and the custody case. Some positive things were accomplished, but Steven, still angry over Ted's refusal to pay his alleged past wages and expenses, clashed with his former employer, arguing over the kids. That led to a spat between Generosa and Ted. As a result, Ted ended the session.

"Fuck this meeting," Ted said on the way out.

He was holding all the cards.

On September 11, 2001, fanatical Islamist terrorists hijacked four airliners filled with unarmed civilians and crashed two of them into the two World Trade Center towers in lower Manhattan, shocking and outraging the civilized world. It seemed like everyone in Manhattan and the surrounding area, as well as millions of others elsewhere, knew or were related to some of the thousands who died. The acrid smoke of the massive funeral pyre could be smelled even on the exclusive Upper East Side, where it burned eyes already wet with tears.

Officer Jim Pelosi was playing golf that Tuesday, with his

father and stepmother, Dorothy, when his cell phone rang on the ninth hole. As soon as he learned of the terror attack, he rushed into the city to help. After weeks of dealing with the carnage and grief, Jimbo asked his war veteran father how to cope with the impact of what he had seen.

"How did you deal with it?" he asked.

Bob Pelosi explained to his son that time was a great healer but that he still sometimes had nightmares or flashbacks about combat that were triggered by loud noises or anything else that startled him.

The events of that day also had a profound effect on Ted, as it did on millions of others. He lost several business and social acquaintances but no close friends or family. Already in a reflective frame of mind, the tragedy spurred Ted to further reevaluate his life and priorities. He saw the beautiful, creative woman he had loved turn into what he believed was an evil creature, driven by hate and bent on his destruction. Now, he saw his city attacked by the daylight evil of terrorists bent on the destruction of America. It was frightening to all Americans and civilized people, especially to parents. What kind of world would their children grow up in? There had to be a force of good to counteract the force of evil in the world.

"I'm going to give something back," Ted told his sister Sandi. "I've been very fortunate and I'm going to give something back."

He began to talk about what new charitable project might be worthy. He thought perhaps he could work with former President Bill Clinton on something that would be part of a force for good in the world. This time, Generosa was not reinventing Ted. He was becoming who he could be, without her. He did not like what the money had done to Generosa. It seemed to act like poison on her. He was convinced that money was dangerous. Like many men who had wrested a fortune from business, Ted was seeking ways to even the scales; to turn the wealth into a positive force in his life, in Alexa and Grego's lives, and elsewhere. He feared that the money would be a burden, not a blessing, for his children. On one visit, Grego brought up the subject:

"Are we rich, Daddy?"

Ted thought before he answered.

"I'm rich. Maybe you will be too."

He turned it into a discussion of what Grego might want to do when he grew up. Ted decided that he would use trusts to keep the money away from the twins so that it wouldn't screw up their lives. He also was in the process of giving some of it away to charities, like Jazz at Lincoln Center. After the divorce was settled, he would draw up a new will. He would devote the next few years of his life to healing his kids, getting them whole, healthy, and happy again. He called it his five-year project to make them better.

When Ted wasn't at the beach house, Danny was the man of the house. He slept with Generosa in Ted's bed, and he drove Ted's cars. On the night of September 15, four days after 9/11, Danny and his pal Chris Parrino went for a spin in Ted's black BMW. They went to a bar, and played pool and drank beer until the early hours of the next morning. Danny was at the wheel when they left.

On the way back to the beach house, at 3:45 A.M., on Dunemere Lane, in East Hampton, a cop saw Danny speeding and weaving drunkenly across the road and began to follow him. He flipped on his lights and gave chase. Danny heard the siren and saw the flashing red lights in his rearview mirror. While they were still moving, Chris grabbed the wheel and they switched places, with Danny diving into the backseat before the Beemer came to a halt. When the officer approached the car on foot, Danny was stretched across the backseat, pretending to be asleep. The cop didn't fall for it. He roused Danny and told him that he had been speeding and driving in the oncoming lanes of traffic. He asked to see his license and registration.

"I don't have a license," Danny replied.

The officer asked if he had ever been arrested before.

"I had a DWI before."

Danny was being modest. He actually had three prior arrests for drunk driving, as well as other arrests for other charges.

"I wasn't driving," Danny protested.

The cop, who ignored the claim, smelled alcohol on Danny's breath and asked if he had been drinking.

"I had a few beers."

He gave Danny a field sobriety test in which he had to walk a straight line and then lean back, close his eyes, and touch his nose with his fingers. The cop told Danny that he had failed the test and he wanted to give him a Breathalyzer test to determine the amount of alcohol in his blood. Danny refused and the cop said that he was under arrest.

"For what? For sleeping?"

"No, for DWI," the officer told him.

"I'm not talking until I have an attorney present."

He was charged with DWI, speeding, driving out of lane, refusal to take a breath test, and driving without a license. Danny's hands were cuffed behind his back. The cop put him in the back of the police car for the trip to jail. He also asked for the name and address of Chris—who lied and told the officer that he was his brother, Frank Parrino.

Danny called his lawyer, Edward Burke, Jr., and arranged to be bailed out the next day. After he was released, Danny went to the Sag Harbor office of the prominent attorney and told him he wanted him to fight his new DWI arrest. He had used Eddie before for a drunk-driving rap, a legal specialty of his. When Eddie got around to his fee, which would run about eight thousand dollars, Danny told him it would be no problem.

"I hit Powerball lotto," Danny joked. "I got a new girlfriend with millions. I can pay in cash."

Eddie knew how broke Danny had been and that he'd had a hard time paying the last time. He assumed that Danny, as usual, was joking.

"So, how are you going to pay?"

"No, really, I'll go to the bank and get the cash. I'll be right back!"

Yeah, sure, Eddie thought, as Danny walked out the door.

A half hour later, Danny returned, walked into Eddie's office, and dumped ten thousand in cash onto Eddie's desk. The lawyer was stunned, wide-eyed. Now Danny was trying to tip his lawyer.

Oh, my God, Eddie thought, looking at the pile of bills. Did he rob a bank?

"Yo, it's real, bro," said Danny, chuckling at his lawyer's surprise.

Danny told Eddie that he was not driving the car. He claimed that his buddy Chris was the driver. The next month, Parrino went to the police precinct and claimed that he was the driver, not Danny. Danny had tried the same defense when he had been busted for DWI in 1983. It didn't work.

The next month, October, Danny took Grego and Alexa bass fishing. When they got off the boat, they brought their catch home in the beach car, the Buick wagon. Some of the fishy water slopped over onto the car floor, soaking into the carpet. In the summer heat, it quickly became an unpleasant stench.

Ted told friends over dinner that he had been assured that he could get full custody of the twins, if he wanted it. Because of Generosa's craziness and ignoring the court, he was about to win. He held his thumb and forefinger a quarter of an inch apart:

"I'm *this close* to getting full custody of the children."

But he decided not to press his advantage.

"The kids need a mother and she needs to play a role," Ted told his friends.

He made his final offer to Generosa—a cash-rich $24 million, the Jetsons town house, and split custody of the kids. They would spend one week with Generosa and one week with Ted.

Generosa thought that the split custody plan was like King Solomon splitting the child in half. But the one thing Generosa wanted most she would not get—her favorite place in the world, the beach house. The East Hampton estate and Coverwood, in England, would be sold. She did not want to swallow such a bitter pill but her lawyers told her to accept, that it would never get any better.

"Let me get this done," Generosa told her lawyer Mike Dowd. "Life's too short."

On Thursday, October 11, 2001, Ted and Generosa and their lawyers gathered in Manhattan to fix the final terms of the divorce and custody settlement. Generosa had reluctantly accepted Ted's $24 million offer, despite the fact that her creations on Long Island and in Surrey would be put on the block. Once the details were ironed out, the parties agreed to meet again in two weeks, after the papers were drawn up. Generosa had the beach house that weekend but she could no longer enjoy the beauty of her home because it was the last weekend she would spend there, while it was still hers. Ted had ruined it all. He had stolen her house.

On Saturday, October 20, Ted planned to spend the weekend in East Hampton. A few days later, they would sign the papers and it would all end. Despite the imminence of an agreement, Generosa made a videotape of the beach house before Ted's next scheduled visit. She filmed every room in detail, all the contents, so that she would have evidence if Ted took anything from her house.

The following Wednesday, October 17, Steven the butler and Bruce the cook filed a lawsuit against Ted, demanding $7,661,690 and 91 cents. In their suit, they claimed that they had laid out cash for everything from moving and storage to taking care of the horses and tennis lessons for the kids. They also said that Ted had promised them $2 million in cash and stock in one of his Internet ventures, and a house.

Ted laughed when he was served with the legal papers and handed them over to his lawyers. At first, Steven and Bruce had simply demanded money. Then, Generosa had tried on their behalf, followed by the kids, who also pestered him to pay. When that didn't work, they had enlisted Ted's dead mother. As a last-ditch effort, they were resorting to the Manhattan Supreme Court.

Now that a settlement was in the works, the mood seemed to relax a bit. Ted and Danny saw each other at Alexa and Grego's soccer games in town.

"Howya doin', Ted?"

Ted gave Danny good tickets to a Yankees game so that he and Alexa and Grego and Danny's kids could all go. Danny thanked Ted for the gesture.

That week, Ted attended an event with Wynton Marsalis and former President Bill Clinton. Amid discussion of jazz and charitable works, Generosa and Ted's problems seemed far away. Ted could not wait for the huge weight to be lifted from his shoulders. When Ted picked up Alexa and Grego for the next visit, Alexa took one look at her father and burst into tears.

"Alexa, what's the matter?" Ted asked, moving to embrace his sobbing daughter.

"I'm worried Mom hates you so much she's going to kill you."

Ted did not tell his child that he felt the same way. He did not press her to see whether she had overheard something that gave her such fear. Ted knew it was likely that Generosa, with her temper, would say such irresponsible things in front of the twins. Instead, he assured Alexa that everything was okay. Everything would work out.

Their mother would never kill him.

Ted invited his niece Wendy and her husband to come out to the beach house for the weekend. But Wendy told her favorite uncle that she had a wedding to attend. She decided to be honest with Ted. She told him that, even if they were free, she would not go out to the East Hampton place.

"I would never go out to that house," Wendy said.

"Why?"

"It's too scary."

It appeared to those around Ted that he was trying to get back together with Mary Belknap, who was still living with a man. Ted called Mary and asked her if she could spend the weekend with him in East Hampton. The young mother told him that she could stop by on Saturday but could not spend the whole weekend.

That week, Ted had lunch with the heads of another investment firm to discuss a merger. They reached a handshake deal to join forces. Ted was opening another door. He would fold Chancery Lane Capital into the new arrangement.

On Thursday night after work, Ted met his old friend Colin Hastings at a spot in Soho for a drink. When Colin arrived, Ted was sipping a glass of chardonnay at the bar and poring over some paperwork. It was a one-page printout of an estimate of Ted's net worth: almost $90 million. Generosa's lawyers had agreed to use the document as the basis for the financial end of the settlement. Finally, it seemed, Generosa was giving up on all her wild paranoia about how he was hiding millions.

"Generosa had American Express do this analysis," Ted said, showing the balance sheet to his friend, as he ordered a drink.

Ted talked about how he was going to be fund-raising with Bill Clinton and working with Jazz at Lincoln Center. He seemed full of energy and life, as he detailed a host of new plans and ideas. Colin had always joked that Ted didn't know what he wanted to do when he grew up, but now it looked as if he did. He also wanted to work with the World Bank, helping to grow struggling economies and people in third-world countries. When Ted began talking about music and mentioned his favorite piano player, a man sitting on the other side of Ted chimed in.

"I played drums with the guy."

Grinning, Ted turned to the drummer and spent the next twenty minutes talking jazz with him. Colin couldn't participate in the talk because he knew nothing about jazz. He looked at his friend Ted as he laughed and talked about something he loved. It was good to see him smile again. For the first time in a very long while, Ted Ammon was happy.

His nightmare would be over in less than a week.

26

CANDID CAMERA

Ted left Manhattan at midday on Saturday, October 20, 2001, and drove his Audi station wagon east, through the Midtown Tunnel into Queens. Morning clouds were beginning to break up and the temperature was rising. It was good to get out of the city, where the grief and terror were still heavy in the air, as was the smell of Ground Zero, which continued to burn. Fighter jets circled above New York, with orders to shoot down any jetliner that might be commandeered by terrorists bent on a second attack. The worst attack in American history had forced the postponement of the World Series. Game three—the Yankees and the Diamondbacks would eventually play each other—was scheduled to take place on October 20. If it had not been postponed, Ted would not have been driving to East Hampton. He would have been in his box seat at Yankee Stadium, watching the game with his kids.

He was still furious at Generosa for her latest stunt, which amounted to little more than thievery. Ted had asked his driver to drop off Alexa's soccer uniform at her mother's place, but Milton misunderstood and left Ted's entire sports bag, which also contained his clothes, shoes, business notes, and leather billfold. As soon as Generosa realized that she had Ted's stuff, she looted it of information and gleefully threw most of it in the garbage—just for spite. When Ted realized what had happened, he called his lawyer, who called Generosa's lawyer, who called Generosa. She lied, denying that she had ever received the bag.

Ted passed through Queens and Nassau Counties, where he picked up the Southern State Parkway into Suffolk. At the end of the parkway, Ted took Sunrise Highway into the Hamptons. On a summer Saturday, the trip would have taken at least three hours by car, but it was off-season in October. He was in East Hampton in less than two. First, Ted stopped at a local shop and bought an eighteen-hunded-dollar sweater. On the way to the beach house, Ted stopped at a market in the East Hampton Village for food and drink for Sunday breakfast, and a large coffee. Just after three o'clock, before he paid for his purchases, his cell phone rang.

"Hello?"

"Hi, it's Sandi."

"Hi, sis."

He told her where he was, what he was doing, and gave her the good news that the meeting with Generosa and her lawyers went well. It would all be over that coming week, when they would all sign the papers.

"I feel a tremendous sense of relief," Ted said. "I'm going to take a long walk on the beach and clear my mind."

Periodically, especially during moments of stress or change, Ted would go off by himself, ignore the rest of the world for a while and flush out his headgear. In silence, or walking with his dogs and listening to the ocean, Ted could hear his own heart. His penchant for occasional Hamlet-like solitude had sometimes caused concern and worry but everyone accepted it as a quirk of his personality.

Sandi and Ted talked briefly about what each other's kids were up to and chatted about the progress of the war against the terrorists in Afghanistan. When they were done, Sandi said goodbye.

"Love you."

"I love you, sis," Ted said.

Ted turned into his driveway on Middle Lane, crunching gravel as he parked by the side door. It was a magnificent, sunny Indian summer day, with barely a breeze, and the dogs were happy to be set free to run. It seemed more like April than October, except for the red and gold leaves on the trees. The clouds had rolled by, exposing a powder-blue sky, and it was a balmy seventy degrees. His new Porsche was already parked outside the garage. He grabbed his bag of groceries, his leather briefcase, and his overnight bag and let himself in through the side door. He punched in his code, 2760, to shut off the beeping burglar alarm.

At that same moment, eighty miles away, in Massapequa, John Kundle at the security firm noticed that someone using Ted's code had entered the beach house and shut off the burglar alarm. Kundle beeped Danny to inform him that Ted was in the house. Ted put away his groceries while the three dogs skittered around the kitchen floor.

He put his briefcase and a stack of newspapers he had brought along on the couch in the den. He sat down to read. There were copies of *Financial Times* and *The New York Times* that featured the latest on the Afghan war. There was also a copy of that day's *New York Post,* with a front page that had an arresting photo of a woman from the *Post*'s editorial department holding up her bandaged middle finger in a gesture of obscene defiance to terrorists. Her finger had been infected with anthrax sent to the newspaper inside an envelope. The bold headline filled much of the rest of the page:

ANTHRAX THIS!

That afternoon, Mary came over. She and Ted spent some intimate time together before she went back to her boyfriend, who did not know about the affair.

Unlike Ted, Generosa was not happy and not looking forward to the future. Surveying the ruins of the War of the Ammons, she despaired. As the date for signing the final divorce and custody papers approached, she became more and more angry and depressed. Ted had cheated her out of her beach house, and Coverwood, both of which would be sold to strangers. In days, it would be over and she would finally have to let Ted go. But it would never be over. She detested him but she still loved him, and she hated herself for that. At times, she wished they both were dead. Part of her would still rather see Ted dead than to have to watch politely as he married another woman, as he raised children she could not give him. With the joint custody agreement, she knew that Ted would eventually win the kids back with his charm. He would still have most of his money and he would make more. Danny was just spending her money. Ted was hanging out with ex-presidents and famous musicians. He was the darling of the Manhattan society that had rejected her. She was hanging out with electricians. She would have $24 million but the perfect life she had created in her head for Ted and the kids—her stone flower—had been shattered. Ted had won, she decided. Another woman, maybe that Mary, would probably create another perfect life for him and Generosa would have to watch it all, because the joint custody agreement would keep them chained together for life. She had Danny and his family. She loved Danny but her efforts to turn him into Ted had failed. He now had perfect teeth and wore expensive jewelry and clothing, but he was still drinking and driving. Instead of using her money to set himself up in business, all he did was party. Ted's idea of accomplishment was a billion-dollar takeover. Danny's idea of fun was a weekend drinking and gambling with his buddies in Atlantic City or Vegas. She suspected that Danny was a hound dog, just like Ted. Eventually, he too, would probably cheat on her.

Generosa was depressed. It would be a busy weekend in the Pelosi family. Danny's cousin was getting married on Sunday, the same day as the birthday party for Danny's eldest son, Tony. But Generosa refused to go to the wedding, where she would have met Danny's father again. She told Danny to go by himself. They argued about it on Saturday and then Danny left. He drove out to his sister Barbara's house in Center Moriches. For the first time in years, Danny was driving legally. The day before, he had taken his road test at the Department of Motor Vehicles and passed. When he arrived at his sister's house, her twenty-year-old son, Jeff Lukert, who worked for a swimming-pool company, was there, along with his sisters. They all watched television and Danny was going to spend the night.

Ted went out to dinner alone at a local restaurant and then went for a walk to a nearby beach. While walking in the sand, he used his cell phone to call Mary, but he got her voice mail. He left her a message saying he was at Two Mile Hollow Beach, which he believed was a gay beach. He added that he was afraid of some men there and was going home.

Ted closed the doors to the mansion before he climbed the stairs for the night, but he didn't lock them. He went to bed, naked, as usual, and turned out the light. He was alone in the house except for his three friendly dogs.

At two in the morning, someone logged onto the Rapid Eye program with a laptop computer and looked into the dark beach house. After twenty-one minutes without any sign of activity, the observer remotely shut off the entire spy-camera system and logged off.

27

KILLER'S MOON

Ted was asleep.

In the months that followed, police would struggle to reconstruct the events of that night.

There were no streetlights or other sources of light on Middle Lane. Once the house lights were out, it was country-dark, stygian, except for a sharpened crescent moon that began slicing through the stars and faint clouds above the trees. The temperature had fallen to a brisk fifty-three degrees. A slight breeze had come up below the moon. The leaves around the lightless house hissed.

One man quietly entered 59 Middle Lane without having to break in and silently passed through the kitchen. It was not yet cold enough for gloves but he was wearing them and waterproof workmen's coveralls. He held a black stun gun in his hand. On the counter in the center of the room were the keys to Ted's fifty-thousand-dollar Porsche and a wad of at least two thousand dollars in cash. The muscular man ignored the valuables and moved quietly into the living room. He soundlessly unrolled a plastic tarpaulin on the Persian rug at the base of the main staircase.

The concealed camera in the far corner of the living room was aimed directly at him as he completed his prearranged tasks, but it had already been shut off. He then tiptoed up to the

second-floor landing outside the master bedroom, where Ted
was asleep. His dark silhouette moved up the stairs with a long
metal object in one hand, and the stubby stun gun in the other.

The dogs began to stir at the noises outside their master's
bedroom. The man took a deep breath and strode into the
room toward the supine shape on the far side of the bed, raising the cudgel.

*He jabbed Ted's bare neck with the two metal points of
the stun gun probe and gave him a full charge. The Taser
sparked and rattled loudly. A smell of burning skin and
ozone filled the air.*

Ted jerked and twitched spasmodically in the bed, as the
electricity set his brain on fire.

The man brought the heavy metal down on Ted's head.

The first blow struck Ted in the head but did not knock
him out or kill him. The impact was slightly muted because
the force of the weapon was blunted and partially absorbed
by the cushioning of the bedding. Ted woke up, without
waking up, to a new nightmare. He did not know when or
where it was but, amazingly, he instinctively knew he was
fighting for his life, and his strong, fit body responded.

*Shocked that he was able to fight back, the man brought
the club down, over and over and over.*

Trying to defend himself, Ted put up his arms and hands
to ward off the blows cascading down on him, deflecting
several; the sharp pain shooting and fracturing the bones of
his hands and arms, not his head. Ted's startled dogs barked
and jumped up from sleep in the room.

*The man quickly poked the aroused dogs, one after the
other, zapping each. They yelped and rolled over onto the
floor, limp but unharmed.*

Ted groaned wordlessly with each clubbing and struggled
to gain his footing. The stun was wearing off.

*The man turned back to Ted, as he tried to fend off the
blows. He hit Ted in the back with another massive jolt.*

Ted went numb again. His arms and legs turned to rubber,
leaving him open to more blows from the poker.

The man clubbed Ted again and again and again.

Ted tried to shake it off and scrambled to the other side of the bed, near the door. He tried to stagger out of the room while simultaneously trying to stop the rain of pain to his upper body.

The man slipped in and got Ted in the back again with the stun gun, the painful explosion sapping his waning strength.

Ted was struck again on his hands and arms but he couldn't prevent the bludgeon from impacting his head.

Panicked that Ted had managed to get to his feet, the man grunted curses through clenched teeth, pivoted to the right, blocking Ted's escape, and struck harder and faster.

More and more explosions of pain flashed in Ted's skull, making it harder to think, harder to meet the engulfing waves of agony. They kept breaking mercilessly; striking him ceaselessly, the impacts alternating with flashing shocks. Ted could not withstand the two-pronged onslaught. His legs went out from under him and he went down. His arms moved slower, as if under water, blocking fewer hits, as his brain reeled from the concussions and could not communicate with his shielding arms, now numb and broken.

The man struck down and down and down.

In a few eternal seconds, Ted's flailing arms dropped and all his pain blew away like bow spray in a strong headwind. The fight was over. As he sank, the faces of his children appeared in his mind and he floated toward them as he lost consciousness.

The man kept pounding at Ted's head, bashing him out of existence; hot blood splattered all over him with each sickening thud.

It had taken more than thirty blows to Ted's head but only a few minutes to kill him. When it was done, the winded killer stepped over the still pool of Ted's blood on the bedroom rug and entered the bathroom, dripping red. He turned on the water in the shower and washed as much of it off his coveralls and weapon as possible.

The killer then went through Ted's study next door to the playroom and opened the closet. He slipped in through the

concealed door to the hidden safe room. He knew exactly
where to knock out the wall panel under the eaves to the
right of the door. He pulled out pink fiberglass insulation behind the wall and removed the Rapid Eye control unit that
had recorded the remote shutoff event. The killer brought
the metal box containing the computer hard drive back down
the stairs. The killer carried the washed coveralls and
weapons down the stairs and deposited them in a pile on the
plastic sheet at the bottom of the stairs in the living room.
The tarp was rolled up. He carried the metal Rapid Eye box
and toted the tarp across the living room toward the French
doors, dripping diluted blood onto the rug on the way out.
More trickled onto the slate patio stones as the killer left the
house to dispose of the evidence.

Then it was quiet inside and outside the mansion, except
for the faint sound of the rolling surf nearby. Above Generosa's perfect lawn, flower beds, and trees, above the briny
current of clouds, the crescent moon, white as a wind-filled
jib in the sun, sailed away toward the sea.

28

MISSING

Marlon was looking at the water lilies on the pond and daubing watercolors onto a large white paper pad with a sable brush: French green for the lily pads, Prussian blue for the water, Indian yellow and Venetian red for the turning leaves on the shore, which were reflected in the mirror of the pond. Sunday was another glorious autumn day, even warmer and sunnier than Saturday, but with gusty winds that played with the fallen leaves and Marlon's pad.

At eleven that morning, Marlon Windsor* heard a car in the lane turn onto a gravel driveway. He thought it was his friend returning from the store with food, so he put down his brush and walked to the driveway to help. But there was no one in their driveway. He turned and realized that the car was moving into the Ammon driveway, next door, crunching gravel thirty feet behind the bushes. He couldn't see what kind of car it was, moving on the far side of the foliage, or make out who was inside, but there was no reason to wonder about it further. He picked up his brush and turned back to his painting, feathering blue carefully, leaving little ripples of unpainted white paper to show the light dancing on the water. He did not hear any car doors slam at the Ammon place, no voices or barking dogs. Just birds singing. Soon, he was called in to lunch. When he resumed painting after one o'clock, Marlon heard nothing further from behind the foliage to distract him from his watercolor.

Mary played back Ted's voice mail message from the prior evening and became worried when she could not reach Ted at the beach house or on his cell phone. On Sunday afternoon, she and another man drove from her summer home two towns away to the Ammon beach house. They parked on the lane and the man walked down the driveway toward the house. Two of Ted's cars were there, but there was no sign of life. Mary dialed the house one more time, but there was no answer. They drove away.

Also that afternoon, a man driving down Middle Lane noticed two suspicious men, one of whom was wearing army fatigues, walking out of the driveway at number 59.

Danny went to Tami's house in Manorville on Sunday morning to celebrate his son Tony's birthday. Later, he attended the 2:00 P.M. family wedding of his cousin. After the wedding, Danny told everybody that he had lost a fourteen-hundred-dollar leather jacket he wore to the event, but at least one guest was certain that Danny had not worn the jacket. On Sunday night he went back into the city, to Generosa's place, where she claimed to have been all weekend.

That day, Ted's house phone and the beach house phone rang several times, as did Ted's cell phone. His sister Sandi called, as did Ted's partner Mark Angelson. They left messages and called back later in the day, when they had not heard from Ted. Then they called again. And again.

Ted was not present when the Monday morning meeting for Jazz at Lincoln Center was set to begin at an office at the arts complex on the West Side of Manhattan. As usual, renowned horn player Wynton Marsalis, Mary Fuss, and others were waiting for the new director, Ted Ammon. Wynton decided that Ted was a prince of a guy but he was always a few minutes late for everything. It was part of his charm. Mary Fuss dialed Ted's cell phone but he didn't answer. She left a message, pointing out, with a laugh, that the meeting had been Ted's idea. She called his office and left a message.

The group chatted about business for some time and eventually broke up.

When Ted did not arrive at the office in time for a meeting, his assistant, Kathy, called him at home in Manhattan, in East Hampton, and on his cell phone. He also had an Internet beeper on which he could send and receive e-mail from anywhere. But Ted remained unreachable.

Ted's niece Wendy was at work when Ted's chauffeur, Milton, called. Wendy and her husband had borrowed Ted's BMW to drive to the out-of-town wedding and had returned it to a garage near Milton's home on the Upper West Side on Sunday night. No, Milton, told her, nothing was wrong with the car. He was trying to sound casual in order not to alarm her, but she could hear the concern in his voice.

"So, have you heard from Mister Ammon today?" Milton asked.

"No, why?"

He told her that everyone was trying to reach him. He did not use the word *missing*. As Milton hung up, he felt a sense of dread. He remembered his nightmare, the one in which Mrs. Ammon was trying to kill his boss, the one Mr. Ammon had laughed at.

Obviously, Wendy thought, Ted had not been at his home when Milton went to pick him up for the drive to the office. Wendy called Ted's assistant, Kathy. She too, downplayed the situation but asked if Wendy had heard from her uncle.

Mark Angelson was worried as he tried once again to reach Ted. They were close friends and spoke virtually every day. Mark had begged him to get a bodyguard to protect him against Generosa's wrath, but his partner had continued to live his life as if he didn't have an enemy in the world. Mark called Ted's sister Sandi in Alabama, but she had not heard from him, either. In fact, she said, she too, had been trying for a day and a half to reach her brother.

"Why don't you call the police?" Sandi asked.

"This has happened before, where he has just disappeared for a day," Mark told her. "If he doesn't show up by noon tomorrow, I'm going to call."

That was too long for Sandi.

"If he's not there to pick up the kids this afternoon, don't wait until tomorrow," she said, her concern growing.

Mark agreed. Even in an emergency, Ted would never fail to pick up his children without calling. If he could, that is.

Everyone hoped it was 9/11 paranoia freaking them out and that Ted was fine. After the unthinkable terror assault, out of a clear, blue sky, anything—any terrible thing— seemed possible. Sandi began to think of reasons for Ted to be okay. She hoped that he was either purposely avoiding the world or had gone out bicycling, run into a ditch, and hit his head. Maybe he was unconscious in a hospital somewhere, without his wallet. The alternative was too terrible to think about. She called the Manhattan number of her daughter Wendy, who had declined Ted's invitation for the weekend. As she listened, Wendy felt sick to her stomach and a strange feeling washed over her. In her heart, she knew that her uncle was dead. She felt an eerie certainty that he had been killed and that Generosa had done it. She did not tell her mother.

Generosa's butler, Steven, called Ted's office to tell them that Ted had not called to make arrangements for his evening with the twins. Steven was told that they could not locate Ted, and he relayed this news to Generosa.

When Ted did not show up by the time the kids got out of their schools, Mark decided to act. He arranged for Ted's driver, Milton, to pick him up.

Ted and Mark were masters of the universe, take-charge executives who could handle anything. In the BMW, Mark asked Milton if he had a pair of gloves. Milton opened the glove compartment, took out a pair of heavy work gloves, and handed them to Mark. It would take too long to drive, so they pulled into a heliport on the East River and boarded a corporate chopper to East Hampton. The flight took about twenty minutes and they arrived just after five. At the same time, Wendy got home and told her husband what was going on. She tried to describe the weird gut feeling she had that Ted was dead, murdered.

"I think she did it," Wendy said.

They both knew who "she" was.

Milton got a cab at the airport and he and Mark were driven to 59 Middle Lane. As the cab pulled into the driveway, Mark's bad feeling worsened. Ted's Porsche was still parked there. Obviously, he had not driven away somewhere in his car. The estate was eerily quiet, except for crows cawing in the trees. They both knew the two possibilities: either Ted was off by himself somewhere or he was dead. If he was alive, Mark did not want to invite scandal or embarrassment by calling the police. If he was dead, he knew he should not leave fingerprints in what might be a crime scene. Mark put on one of the gloves and Milton donned the other.

Mark opened the unlocked garage door and went in with Milton following. The whining dogs, the chocolate Lab and the two golden retrievers, were barking. They were now in the rear yard.

"Ted?" Mark shouted into the house.

No answer.

He looked around and saw no one. He moved to the stairway and went up, his heart beating faster. At the top of the stairs, he saw Ted's body sprawled on the floor near the bed. Blood was everywhere. He gasped and backed away, down the stairs. It was 5:19 P.M. Outside, his palms sweaty, Mark pulled off the glove, took out his cell phone, and dialed 911.

29

MURDER ON MIDDLE LANE

M ark Angelson told the 911 operator that he had to report a murder. He gave the information and the address and he and Milton waited.

When he heard the news, East Hampton mayor Paul Rickenbach, a former cop, realized that it was the first slaying in East Hampton in almost twenty years. The previous murder in 1982 had been no mystery. A man got drunk in a bar and picked a fight with the wrong guy. The victim brought only his fists to a knife fight and was stabbed to death. They quickly locked up the bad guy. Case closed. The only other murder in the village that Rickenbach could remember was a decade before that, and it was a bit odd. A reclusive, homosexual theatrical-set designer died in a suspicious blaze. It was written off as a possible arson-suicide, which would have required that the victim set the fire himself and then waited to be burned alive. The murder of Ted Ammon would become the biggest mystery and the most infamous killing in the 353-year history of the village and of the entire Hamptons. But the village cops handled only natural and accidental deaths. When it was murder, they dialed the Suffolk County Homicide Squad, who worked out of police headquarters in Yaphank. The local force roped off the block, closed the house, posted officers at every door, and

waited for the homicide squad and its commander, Detective
Lieutenant John Gierasch.

The doors of the mansion were found unlocked and the
burglar alarm had been shut off before the murder. The
victim had been found near his bed in the master bedroom
upstairs. Pending an autopsy, the cause of death appeared
to be repeated blunt-force trauma to the head. There were
defensive wounds to the hands and arms and the victim
also seemed to have severe cuts as well. Was it a knife or
just the edge of a not-so-blunt weapon? Blood had soaked
into the rug and splattered on the wall beside the bed.
There was also what appeared to be blood outside the bedroom, at the base of the stairs, on the living room rug, and
even out on the rear patio. The killer should have been
covered in blood. Had the killer or killers taken a shower
after the murder? The plumber's traps in the drains would
have to be opened to search for evidence that might have
washed there. The body was room temperature, so the
death had likely occurred quite some time before it was
discovered by the victim's business partner. There was no
murder weapon found at the scene. The area would have to
be searched, the troops called out to beat the bushes. The
pond in the backyard had to be dredged. There were no
witnesses and the body had remained undiscovered for a
day or more. Hopefully, an autopsy would narrow the time
of death further than the forty-eight hours between Saturday night and Monday night.

To the right of the living room fireplace stood a black
wrought-iron stand that had held fireplace implements. It
was conspicuously empty. Where were the heavy metal
poker and the shovel? Were one or both of them the murder
weapons? Was there one or more killers? A preliminary can-
vass of the neighbors indicated that no one had seen or heard
anything significant. One woman neighbor wondered how
Ted could have been killed apparently without any noise.

"Why didn't I hear the dogs barking?" she asked.

The only strange events in the area recently had been a

series of crimes by a man the local folks called the Wyborg Wanker, a naked man who had been exposing himself to women in the neighborhood. He had been seen in the vicinity of nearby Wyborg Beach, on foot and in a red car, flashing females, masturbating, and then running or driving away. The naked, well-tanned sex criminal had been spotted around the corner at eleven o'clock Friday morning. Had the pervert suddenly become a killer? It was unlikely, but first they would have to catch him.

The crime scene technicians began taking samples, cutting up rugs to preserve bloodstains and dusting black or white fingerprint powder everywhere in the house. The experts collected, bagged, and tagged evidence, including Ted's wallet and its contents. They worked well into the night but they were only getting started. They would be there for a solid week, going over the estate with a fine-tooth comb, with every light in the place on day and night. Later, tests would reveal a blood sample that did not belong to Ted and several sets of unidentified fingerprints. It was routine to eliminate prints left by dozens of people at a murder scene. The blood also could have been routine. Or perhaps it was the blood of the killer, who had been injured in the frenzied assault? Unlike their portrayals on television, real detectives are not psychic. They have to search painstakingly for evidence and witnesses who will stand up in court. It takes shoe leather.

The press release issued by police in the early hours of Tuesday gave little information but asked for the public's help and urged the press to use the phone number of the Suffolk County Homicide Squad, or Crime Stoppers, so that anyone with information on the murder could report it to authorities.

At eleven o'clock that morning, Danny got a call in the city from Hamptons contractor Wilbur Gant,* who told him that Ted had been found dead in the beach house. Danny asked how Ted had died, but Gant said he didn't know. Later, Gant called back with a neighborhood rumor that said Ted had OD'd.

At 2:00 P.M. that day, two Suffolk County detectives arrived at the Manhattan apartment where Danny and Generosa lived. Danny told the investigators that they could not talk to Generosa because she did not know Ted was dead. Also, Danny explained, Generosa's divorce lawyer had advised them to get criminal lawyers.

"Why would you need a criminal attorney?" one of the detectives asked. "Were you involved in the murder of Ted Ammon?"

"No, I wasn't," Danny replied.

Later that day, Generosa and Steven went to Ted's apartment to get the kids, who had been dropped off there after school. They were with Ted's housekeeper. The twins listened, in tears, as Generosa told them that their father had died out at the beach house over the weekend.

"Your father took too much medication and drank too much," she said.

Later, when it became public that Ted had been slain, she told her kids that—and suggested a strange motive: "Maybe one of your father's boyfriends killed him."

When the press heard that a well-known millionaire had been murdered in his mansion, it was obviously a hell of a story—the story of the day for newspapers, television, and radio. Millions of people heard for the first time about Ted Ammon. It looked like it was going to be an unusual case. It wasn't every day that homicide detectives were called to an English-style mansion to solve the mysterious murder of a millionaire. The estate looked like the kind of place where the tweedy fictional detective Miss Marple might stroll by at any moment to help with the murder most foul, to say that everyone was a suspect.

That day, Lieutenant Gierasch spoke to the crowd of press outside the murder scene.

"We're looking at every possibility. We haven't ruled out anything or anybody," he said.

Gierasch would not comment when asked if the divorce played any role in the murder.

"Everything is a possible motive—his money, his status—but nothing is focused on one thing. The house is clean and neat. It's not ransacked. The house is in general good order, but that's not to say that we've ruled out robbery as a motive."

Investigators could not yet rule out the possibility that Ammon had been killed by a burglar who had fled without completing the crime.

That day, they learned of the Rapid Eye system. Instead of Miss Marple, they contacted John Kundle, the burglar alarm guy, and asked him to come to the scene and help them. It was a chilling moment for the investigators. There was a secret video surveillance system, with each camera taking one frame per second, on a ninety-day loop. Someone, maybe even the killer, could be watching them at that very moment, as they investigated the crime scene. As a precaution, a police technical team shut off all phone lines to the house.

John arrived and told them that the Rapid Eye system was hidden behind a wall in the secret safe room, under the eaves. He told them that it worked off Ted's fax phone line. He offered to show them but they would not let him go anywhere near it. Detectives located the concealed door and entered the safe room.

Inside, Alexa's white china tea things were still set for the Mad Hatter's tea party at the long table in the middle of the room. A fortune in Monopoly money was scattered around. The detectives found piles of what looked like cotton candy on the floor. It was fiberglass insulation that had been pulled out of the nearby wall. Inside the triangular hole where the Rapid Eye had been, a bundle of black wires that had obviously connected to a power source and the cameras led off into the dark innards of the house. The video system had been ripped out and taken away. It was a good bet that the killer had inside knowledge that the system existed and knew exactly where it was.

The detectives went back downstairs to question John but did not tell him that the central unit was no longer there.

"Who put the cameras in?" one detective asked.

John said that he and a workman had installed the system.

"Who knew about it?"

John told them that, in addition to himself and his employee, Danny Pelosi knew about it, as well as Generosa Ammon and their lawyers. Also Danny's friend Nick Short, who had recommended John for the job. Steven the butler and Bruce the cook, who had been there during the installation, also had knowledge of the system.

"Did Danny know how to unplug the system?"

"Yes."

Detectives had to keep certain things secret—information that only they and the killers would know—in order to exclude the innocent and implicate the guilty. The investigators would remain mum on the subject of the video surveillance system.

The main hard drive of the spy system, John said, could not be changed once the photos had been taken—at least, not without leaving a trace in the computer that erasures had occurred. Cameras could be shut off remotely, using the laptops—one or all of them—but, again, the main hard drive and the separate laptop hard drive would have a record of that. John said that he had never shown anyone how to shut off the cameras. If the hard drive was changed, it would have a different serial number from the original. That meant that John was also a suspect until he was later cleared—because his position and expertise could be used in any possible murder plot.

John told them that the system could also be foiled by someone with a working knowledge of electricity—by popping the electrical meter outside the house before going in. The power cutoff would shut down the system but there would be a record of power interruption and then rebooting on the hard drive. There would be a time difference on the system clock. The difference between that and actual time would reveal the length of any possible outage. Also, a burglar-alarm keypad in Ted's bedroom would have started beeping as soon as the power went out. It might have awakened him. The power had not gone out.

The existence of the hidden system presented a tantalizing possibility to the detectives. This might be a slam dunk—if the surveillance cameras captured pictures from the time of the murder. It would be a homicide detective's dream—pictures of the killer, perhaps even committing the crime. It didn't get any better than that. But how many killers would be willing to have their deeds filmed? Had they been wearing masks? If the system had been shut off before the murder and then the main unit had been removed—taking along the hard-drive record of who had shut off the cameras—Ted Ammon's murder had not been broadcast live. The only way to find out was to locate the control unit and download the drive—if it hadn't already been destroyed—or to seize any laptops that had been used to access the system remotely, and hope that their hard drives contained the vital evidence of shutting down the system just before the murder. The problem was that any computer anywhere in the world could have been used. All that was needed was a copy of the Rapid Eye software and the password.

But, even if they never located any of the computers, they had leads: a short list of people who knew about the system and knew where it had been hidden.

The Ammon story was the lead that night on television and in the next day's papers. The *New York Post* headline read:

L.I. MURDER MYSTERY
BANKER IS FOUND SLAIN IN THE HAMPTONS

There was a photo of the mansion, a shot of detectives comparing notes, and a nice picture of Ted with Wynton Marsalis. As news of Ted's brutal murder spread, hundreds of people who knew him were shocked and saddened, one at a time. Many immediately suspected Generosa.

Ted's former girlfriend, Sherri Disalvo, was turning pages in *The New York Times* when Ted's last name caught her eye. To her horror, she read that Ted had been murdered in that house. She cried but, somehow, she wasn't surprised. She had warned Ted to stay away from Generosa's beach house.

The morning after the murder, the friends whom Generosa had spit on, after they had talked to Ted, saw Generosa walking toward them in Central Park. After the spitting incident, Generosa had always avoided their eyes when they passed on the street. Now, she glared right at them, without speaking. They discussed it and wondered why she was suddenly, defiantly acknowledging their presence. When they got home, they found out that Ted had been murdered.

Ronnie too, saw Generosa on the street. Her friend seemed to be in shock, numb, walking in a cloud. She looked right through Ronnie. Was it just grief? She wondered what Generosa knew about Ted's death. She couldn't imagine her friend doing that to Ted, but had her hatred led to the murder?

Architect Jeff Gibbons answered the phone at his Southampton office.

"What do you think of this murder?" a friend asked him.

"What murder?"

"Ted Ammon."

With a chill, Jeff thought about what he had said to Ted when they last spoke, when he had yelled at Ted for his and Generosa's shark behavior and warned him that what goes around comes around. And now Ted was dead and Generosa would surely be a suspect.

First, private detective Marie Schembri felt shock when she heard about Ted's murder. Next, she felt sadness. Then, she felt guilt. She had not seen it coming. She felt that she should have known. She had never had a client killed before. She felt that she had let Ted down. Last, she felt anger.

Mary Fuss, at Lincoln Center, got a call from a reporter.

"Do you have anything to say about the death of Ted Ammon?"

The news hit her like a punch.

"What? Oh, my God!"

On Wednesday, Jurate spotted Generosa walking the dog in Central Park with her butler Steven. Jurate had not seen Generosa since her former friend had castigated her in the same spot months earlier—because she would not lend her $10 million. As she neared them, Jurate realized that Generosa was sobbing, wailing, as she walked. Jurate wanted to offer her condolences but the hateful glare she received from both of them changed her mind. They passed without speaking.

In Colorado, Generosa's cousin Al Legaye, Jr., was saddened to hear about Ted. He wondered how long it would take police to arrest Generosa.

In California, Howard Ashe, who had once dated Generosa and been stunned by her obsession with money, got a call from a friend who had heard the news.

"She's been implicated in the murder," the friend said.

"What?" Ashe asked, disbelieving.

"Boy, you dodged a bullet."

At first, Generosa's divorce lawyer, Ed Meyer, also represented Danny, who refused to talk to the cops. Generosa and Danny needed lawyers who specialized in representing people charged with murder. Generosa did not want any big-name Manhattan people because she distrusted them.

"I don't want anyone who has anything to do with the major law firms because they're all hooked in with each other," said Generosa. "They're all in Ted's pocket."

They hired Manhattan lawyer Mike Shaw, who had represented a woman who shot and killed her husband in 1996 while he slept in bed. Shaw issued a statement from Generosa in which she denied any involvement in the murder. But Generosa quickly dropped Shaw after he made the unforgivable faux pas of saying in her presence that she lived in Westhampton—not East Hampton. Westhampton, Generosa felt, was not really part of the Hamptons—it was for middle-class people and beach bums. It was another place in which she wouldn't be caught dead.

Shaw's associate Michael Dowd took over representation of Generosa, and she paid attorney Paul Bergman to be Danny's criminal lawyer.

Dowd was a politically connected criminal lawyer from Queens. He was stripped of his law license in 1990, years after he blew the whistle on a city scandal. He admitted that Queens Borough President Donald Manes had ordered him to pay bribes to get a city Parking Violations Bureau contract. Dowd became the star witness in the scandal and was granted immunity from prosecution in exchange. But a court later ruled that he had violated professional ethics by waiting years to report the illegal payments. The scandal tarnished the Koch administration and Manes committed suicide rather than face the consequences. Dowd later won his license back and championed the cause of battered women who struck back at abusive husbands. Because of his reputation for defending women who had killed their husbands, Generosa's choice of Dowd set tongues wagging.

Danny and Generosa were sitting in Dowd's Manhattan office, discussing the case, when Danny suggested that perhaps money would move things along and end the suspicion.

"Why don't we offer five hundred thousand dollars for the arrest and conviction of anyone who did the murder?"

"That's a good idea," Generosa said.

"No way," Dowd replied.

Later, after a group of Ted's old friends put out a twenty-five-thousand-dollar reward for his killer, a reporter called Dowd and asked him if the Ammon widow was interested in adding to the relatively small reward fund.

"No comment," he said.

Meanwhile, the homicide squad had its hands full with the rapidly expanding Ammon murder investigation. They were working on likely and unlikely suspects at the same time, trying to eliminate people and narrow their focus on suspects and motives. In addition to the short list of those who knew about the secret surveillance system, detectives had to investigate everyone around Ammon, including his estranged wife and her new boyfriend. It was a much longer list, especially for the small squad. The list kept growing every week:

- One executive at Ted's firm had been fired after a dispute with him. The split was so acrimonious that they had changed the office locks. A second executive had also had a falling out with Ammon and would have to be checked out.
- A group of investors got burned when a stock that Ted recommended tanked about a year and a half before the murder. They lost millions and were very angry at Ammon. A few in the group could not afford to lose what they had lost.
- The dead man had also had business disputes with several other people. He had arranged to sell his home at 1125 Fifth Avenue for $9.5 million to a second bidder. When the first bidder had tried to back out after the 9/11 terror attacks, Ammon wouldn't let him and, according to their contract, Ammon kept the bidder's $1 million nonrefundable deposit. The guy sued Ammon. Was he angry enough to kill for his $1 million? People were killed over little $20 bottles of crack all the time.
- Ammon was also battling the board of his Fifth Avenue co-op building, which was headed by actor Kevin Kline. Ammon had sued them because they would not approve his sale to the second bidder. Had the famous actor-singer or the condo board bumped him off?
- Ammon's first wife, Randee Day, whom Generosa suspected of having an affair with Ted, had borrowed a million dollars from him. Day's second

husband was a Greek shipping magnate who had his head blown off with a shotgun in July 1998—while he was in the middle of a nasty divorce with her. That possible murder or suicide occurred while the husband was in Greece with his girlfriend, with whom he had a child. Day was in Connecticut at the time of the violent death. Under the provisions of the shipping magnate's will, everything went to Day's son. But her alimony and expenses were cut off. Was it possible that Day, an educated banker, had taken out a murder contract on her estranged husband? Had she done the same thing to Ammon to avoid paying him back his million?

Most of it was very unlikely, even laughable, but it all had to be investigated thoroughly and eliminated or included. It took time. These were not street punks and junkies who could be put in a chair and interrogated. These were rich people with expensive lawyers. Ultimately they would all be cleared because they all had alibis and were no longer suspects.

The investigation kept returning to the likely suspects, the victim's angry wife and her bad-boy boyfriend, even though they claimed to have good alibis. There was a lot of money floating around. Had they hired someone to get rid of her inconvenient husband? Had she gotten his fortune? If so, that would make one hundred million reasons for murder.

The local animal shelter got a call from the police to pick up Ted's dogs. A week later, Danny called and told them that Generosa did not want Ted's dogs back and they should be put up for adoption. A cop adopted one and two delighted civilians took the other two and gave them good homes.

The first weeks of the Ammon investigation were not going as well as the police had hoped. There were apparently no photos of the murder or the killer. The two prime suspects claimed to have ironclad alibis. A week of hunting for clues inside the beach house did not yield any strong forensic evidence. The combing of the neighborhood and the dredging of Generosa's pond had failed to turn up any bloody murder weapons or clothing or any other evidence.

The only witnesses to Ted Ammon's murder were his three dogs.

30

TED'S CARS

Oscar Emerson* opened his Center Moriches auto body shop on Monday morning, October 22, and was surprised to see a blue 1999 Audi parked outside. The keys had been dropped through the mail slot. He had no idea whose car it was or what he was supposed to do with it. It didn't need any body work and no one had made any arrangements for a drop-off. He quizzed his staff, but they didn't know either. A license-plate check revealed that it was owned by a Robert Theodore Ammon in Manhattan. Emerson shrugged and got on with business.

The car had been left there Monday morning by Danny's nephew. It sat there for two days until Oscar was informed that Danny wanted new brakes installed, and he wanted it detailed, inside and out. Detailing involved washing and waxing the outside of the car, cleaning, vacuuming, and shampooing the rugs, and chemical treatment for all vinyl surfaces. Oscar checked the car. It didn't need new brakes but he did as he was asked and installed a new set. Then he sent the car out for detailing.

Danny remembered the Taser stun gun he had given to Tami. He called his younger brother Jim, the city cop, and asked him if it was a violation of his probation to have a Taser.

"You retard," Jim scolded. "They're gonna violate you."

"Can you get rid of it?" Danny asked.

"Yeah, I'll put it in the drop box at work."

Danny called Tami, who called Jim and asked him to come and get the Taser because she did not want it around. He picked it up and drove away with it.

A drop box is a large, curved metal tube at police precincts that looks like a fat periscope coming up from the floor. Anyone who has an illegal weapon they want to dispose of can drop the gun inside, no questions asked, and the police will dispose of the weapon. After checking serial numbers and possibly ballistics—to see if the weapons have been used in any crimes—the firearms are melted down.

When detectives began knocking on Pelosi family doors, Danny offered to get his father and other family members lawyers. Several accepted the offer but his father and several siblings declined.

The Saturday after the murder, Danny figured that Alexa and Grego needed to get away from their problems and have some fun, so he put them in the station wagon with his sons and drove west into the city. Danny drove to the apartment of one of Generosa's lawyers and gave him the laptop computer on which he had watched Ted and his girlfriends at the beach house. After dropping off the computer, they drove into New Jersey. They went to Six Flags Great Adventure amusement park. The kids spent the day screaming on terrifying noisy rides, eating hot dogs and cotton candy, and having a blast on attractions such as the Great American Scream Machine roller coaster, the flipping, spinning, rotating Chaos, and Houdini's Great Escape. After the sun went down and the lights came up, flashing on the hills of the roller coasters, it was time to go. The escape was over and Alexa and Grego had to return to the more frightening real world.

After a week, the police were finished going through the beach house, and Generosa hired a cleaning company and replaced expensive rugs in the bedroom and living room that had sections cut up and removed. Generosa was furious at the thirty thousand dollars in damage done to her house. But, before the cleanup, Generosa and Danny's lawyers hired top private detectives and forensic investigators to come in and do their own investigation and take after–crime scene photos.

On November 6, Danny had his first encounter with the press. Driving Ted's station wagon from the beach house, he went to Manorville to check on a few things with his estranged wife, Tami. When he pulled into the driveway and got out of the car, a reporter called to him.

"Hey, Danny!"

He turned, and the reporter knew he had the right guy. He introduced himself to Danny and got right to the point.

"Did you kill Ted Ammon?"

Danny smirked. He was not yet used to the question.

"Call my lawyer," he replied.

Danny appealed to the reporter, who had been joined by a photographer, not to take pictures of his estranged wife or kids and made a deal to meet them at a convenience store down the road, where they could take his picture. The journalists agreed and waited at the store. Danny approached the meeting point in the wagon, then he suddenly turned and sped in the opposite direction and was out of sight in seconds. The reporter had gotten the license plate of the vehicle, which was still registered in Ted's name. The next day, when he saw the newspaper headline, Danny had his first taste of how the press would treat him:

LATEST SLAY TWIST

"OTHER MAN" DRIVES DEAD MOGUL'S CAR

The unsolved murder case—full of money, sex, and betrayal—was made to order for New York City's two fiercely competitive tabloid dailies—the *Daily News* and the *New York Post*. *The New York Times* and Long Island's *Newsday* covered the story, as did magazines such as *Vanity Fair, People,* and *Time*.

Two days later, homicide detectives went to court in East

Hampton, where Danny had a brief court appearance on his
September DWI case. The investigators asked his lawyer if
they could question Danny about the burglar alarm and the
video surveillance system at the beach house.

"We need to speak to your client. Tell him not to be
afraid," one detective said. "We need some information that
we can only get from him."

Lawyers for Danny and Generosa passed information to
the police but they refused to sit down with detectives. The
detectives probably approached Danny when he was with
his lawyer for legal reasons, so that, just in case he said
something incriminating, it couldn't be thrown out of court.

On Monday, November 13, another vehicle showed up on
Oscar Emerson's auto body shop lot without warning. It was
Ted's 1995 Buick station wagon used at the beach house.
The keys had been left on top of the car. Oscar's wife, who
worked in the shop, got a call from Danny. He asked her to
change the brakes and tires and detail the car, inside and out,
including the cloth upholstery, just as had been done to Ted's
Audi. Danny said that Generosa would be driving the wagon
and he wanted it perfect for her. Money was no object.

"Pretend as if the Queen of England is gonna ride in the
car," Danny said, chuckling.

Again, Oscar knew that the car didn't need tires or a
brake job or even detailing, but he did as his customer asked,
and even added a shiny almost-new grille on the front. Later,
police would charge that Chris Parrino took the Buick to a
car wash just after Ted's murder.

Homicide Chief John Gierasch retired and was succeeded by
Detective Lieutenant Jack Fitzpatrick, a tall man with silver
hair and a mustache that reminded some members of the
press of a lawman from the Old West. He had a dry sense of
humor and a reputation for straight shooting. Fitzpatrick
pushed his detectives on the Ammon investigation to press
as hard as they could on the case.

From some of their scores of interviews, detectives

learned that Danny had Ted's cars cleaned after the murder. They were immediately suspicious, because of the possibility that the washing and cleaning was meant to erase any blood traces or other evidence. Their suspicions were deepened when they heard about a supposed red stain on the passenger-side rug and a bad smell. Could it have been blood? They approached Oscar at his shop and quizzed him about the cars. They had several conversations and were later joined by Suffolk County Assistant District Attorney Janet Albertson, who told Oscar about the alleged red stain.

Wow, Oscar thought when he heard the claim. It was Danny. I can't believe this. He realized that, if the cops were right, his shop had been used as part of a cover-up.

They asked who had done the detailing and he gave them the name of the place. He told them that he had not noticed any stain in the wagon, although he might have missed it.

"He told me when this guy was killed, he was at a wedding," said Oscar.

Then he told the detectives something that surprised them.

"Danny told me he heard that the man was hit in one room and he was found in another room," Oscar remembered. "He said there was a lamp missing and they thought the lamp was the thing that was used."

When asked for the exact words he heard, Oscar said that Danny had said, "Allegedly, he was bashed in the head, murdered, and dragged into another room."

Oscar noted that Danny had prefaced his remarks by saying that the private detectives he and Generosa had hired had told him. To a reporter, Oscar said that Danny had asked him if he could fly him out of the country—but he told detectives that it was just a joke.

They asked Oscar if he would be willing to testify before a grand jury, if one was impaneled. Yes, he told them. He would tell the truth.

Oscar told Danny that the cops had been around, asking questions about him and the cars. Danny had had many such calls from friends, neighbors, and shopkeepers in the close-knit village of Center Moriches.

"Tell the truth and give them whatever they want," Danny told Oscar. "I got nothing to hide."

Investigators spoke to the man who said he saw two men leaving the Ammon property on the Sunday afternoon after the murder. Was it Danny and a pal coming back to the scene of the crime because they had left something incriminating behind—perhaps the leather jacket that Danny claimed was lost or stolen that weekend? The detectives showed the witness a photo array, which included a picture of Danny, but the man did not pick Danny as one of the men he saw that day.

A lady Danny knew well approached him with a proposition about Ted's murder, he later told people. She wanted money from him not to tell a story.

"Give me ten thousand dollars or I'll go to the *New York Post* and say you did it," Danny claimed she said.

"Suck my dick!" Danny replied to the blackmail threat. "Get the fuck outta here!"

Danny told her that he hadn't killed anybody and the cops would never believe her. He told her that they would see it for what it was—an extortion. The woman thought about it and then lowered her demand to one thousand dollars. Danny laughed and made it clear he wouldn't pay her a dime. The woman sighed.

"Well, could you lend me three hundred and eighty dollars for my car payment?"

31

DIDN'T HE RAMBLE?

Generosa, Alexa, Grego, and Ted were together one last time, exactly a week after his death was discovered. They gathered at the church on Park Avenue where the couple had exchanged wedding vows fifteen years earlier. Generosa held her husband's ashes in a container on her lap during the simple religious service. There was no press in attendance at the secret memorial because Generosa wanted it private. There certainly weren't any crowds. Virtually none of Ted's legion of friends would have attended a service that involved being in the same room with his widow, because most of them suspected her of being involved in the murder.

After the service, the twins' godparents, who were still friendly with Generosa, took the kids and Ted's ashes across town to Lincoln Center, where more than five hundred of Ted's friends and family were arriving for a public memorial service.

Generosa and Sandi had worked out the arrangements in advance. Sandi told Generosa of Ted's wish to be cremated and Generosa agreed. It was painful to Sandi that, because the final divorce papers had not been signed, Generosa was still Ted's wife and was calling the shots. Sandi told Generosa that she felt it would be better if she did not come to the memorial service at Alice Tully Hall at Lincoln Center.

Sandi did not mention that several of Ted's friends had made it clear that if Generosa set foot in the hall, they would make a scene. One had threatened to scream, "Arrest her!" at the first sight of Generosa. Of course, Ted's widow was not interested in attending any event that lauded him and featured so many people she hated and to whom she would not speak. She agreed to have Ted cremated and to turn the ashes over to Sandi, but she declined to go to the large memorial. The children's godparents brought them to the service, through a back door, to avoid the horde of press and TV crews outside.

As he was entering the building, Ted's friend Roger Altman, who was scheduled to speak at the service, clutched his chest. He was having a heart attack. He was rushed away in an ambulance. Later, he would have a heart transplant and recover.

Inside, the group of more than five hundred mourners, who happened to represent billions of dollars in net worth, hugged, comforted one another, mingled, and took their seats. Alexa, who had recently told her father that she was afraid her mother was going to kill him, looked terrified. Grego was not. He chatted with the family and friends. The full import of the events had apparently not hit him yet.

Wynton Marsalis and his musicians took to the stage that was the home of the New York Philharmonic and began playing New Orleans funeral music from the Dixieland era, one of the many jazz styles Ted loved. The music was played by some of the best jazz masters in the world. Marsalis's trumpet sounded like a bell in the middle of the mournful cadence, sorrowful bass and moaning trombone. After the first number, the band launched into a Dixie jazz song that after a few measures revealed itself as an evocative New Orleans version of "Danny Boy."

Bob Burton was the first to mount the stage, step up to the simple wooden lectern with a microphone, and speak.

"For the past twelve years, I've had the pleasure of being a business associate and personal friend of Ted Ammon," he told the mourners.

He was a big, husky guy, a former football player, but he told the crowd that his religious faith was the only reason that he was able to get through the moment. He evoked laughter with several anecdotes about Ted, which somewhat lessened the tension. Sandi spoke next and recalled their childhood days, how competitive Ted was. She told about how Ted, even as a youth, had offered her sage advice on the boys she dated in high school.

"Sis, lose the guy in the white socks."

His defining characteristic, she said, was his love for his family, especially Alexa and Grego, who were his true wealth. A courageous Jurate stepped to the podium to read the eulogy that her husband, Roger, had intended to read before his heart attack: Roger reminisced about being neighbors with Ted, talking and always laughing. He said that he thought Ted should have a wall of filing cabinets in his office labeled "Ted's Ideas," and a small cabinet in one corner labeled "Ted's Good Ideas." Roger felt that Ted was "the financial equivalent of the baseball player Roy Hobbs," of Bernard Malamud's book *The Natural,* a golden boy who was the best there was and did it all for the love of the game. Jurate said she would always remember the handsome, fit Ted, jogging toward her in the park, smiling and jogging on. One of Ted's London friends spoke, as did his partner, Mark Angelson, who was under the protection of a bodyguard he had hired right after Ted's murder. Mark read a letter from another of Ted's friends, with a message for Alexa and Grego:

"Your father was a wonderful human being. He loved you deeply. You were the most important thing in his life."

But Wynton Marsalis gave the most humorous, moving, heartbreaking, and lasting tribute to Ted, first with poetic words and then with soaring music. First, Marsalis said that he and the band would play a Gershwin song Ted loved, "Embraceable You." Later, Marsalis told the mourners, he would speak at the spot where the minister in a New Orleans jazz funeral would give a eulogy for Ted.

"We have to send him off right and that's what we're going to do."

The old Gershwin standard sounded new and sophisticated as an offbeat jazz instrumental, yet still sentimental. The musicians doubled, parted, and counterpointed in a one-of-a-kind performance. There had been no applause or response from the mostly white audience when Marsalis stepped to the podium and delivered his elegy to Ted:

"In the loneliness of loss, we seek the comfort of friends. In the shock and confusion, we scurry for conclusions.

"In anger and pain, we cry out for revenge. In the abrupt finality of death, we experience, with horrid elation, ultimately, the sweetness of living. We are afraid. We want to know the particulars of death. It repulses us. It calls us. It fascinates us. And, even when the cold, hard facts are known, we who are alive remain still ignorant. Only the dead know the facts of death, and they never tell," he said.

"But there is a place, oh yes, where the soul of a full-grown man, with the perfect optimism and freshness of youth, has gone; a grown man with the smile of a Little League pitcher throwing his first strike, has gone.

"There is a place where the soul of a man with a sharp and original mind, a desire to uplift the human spirit, an unflinching integrity, and the will to live a life of lyricism, has gone. And, in this place, he dunks his sushi in too much soy sauce," he said, to ripples of laughter.

He joked about Ted's mismatched clothing colors and the fact that he was always three and a half to six minutes late for everything.

"He would want us to move on, past the inert melancholy of this long, long moment," said Marsalis. "Move on past this moment of oppressive, thunderous silence, to the place where men and women and boys and girls mourn with such intensity, that all tears and sinking of spirits becomes broken down into a symphony of joy and euphoric celebration. Then, a life well lived is not lost; but incorporated into our own, to nourish our future," he said.

"For now, he is in a place where time does not pass, so the music goes on and on. So, it doesn't make a difference whether he's late or not."

The grieving listeners chuckled again. Before Marsalis and his amazing musicians played the final number, he explained that it had been a traditional New Orleans funeral piece, the kind—like his elegy—that starts out profound and climbs to joy.

"We hope he hears this one. It's entitled 'Didn't He Ramble?'"

Marsalis intoned the lyrics first, so that his audience would know the sentiment that went with the instrumental:

> *Didn't he ramble?*
> *Didn't he ramble?*
> *He rambled all around, in and out of town.*
> *He rambled all around,*
> *'Til the butcher cut him down.*
> *Didn't he ramble?*

The words chilled the mourners, as if they had been written about Ted. The driven, up-tempo piece swung fast, each part distinct as it flew past. It was sad and sweet, with the clarinet fluttering high above the piano, trumpet, and saxophone, while the trombone slid in between. The strains spoke far beyond words, as if the instruments were the expressive mouths of the silent assembly. The music seized the beating heart, squeezed it until it ached with love, and then dragged it up into the sunlight, where it could breathe again. All the melodies and bouncing harmonics then slid and crashed to a sudden finale, as the mysterious musical spell vanished into the air, like a soul.

Didn't He Ramble?

There wasn't a sound for the Grammy-level performance because the mourners were not used to applauding at funerals. The silence was, indeed, thunderous, until Marsalis told the people:

"You don't have to be so quiet."

The applause was thunderous. They applauded for the music, for Ted, until their palms smarted, and then they wiped their tears and moved to the lobby for a reception with the family.

Ted got an artistic, royal sendoff: unique and more moving than the last rites of many presidents and kings. It was the kind of event that made some observers reflect on their own lives and accomplishments. The quality of the memorial did not provoke jealousy but it certainly caused some introspection and inspired a few to try to become a bit more like someone who deserved to be sent off right.

32

FROZEN

Generosa and Danny were sitting at a long table in the glass-walled conference room at lawyer Mike Dowd's Manhattan office. Out the window, the silver spire of the art deco Chrysler Building glistened in the morning sun.

Also in the room was lawyer Gerry Sweeney. Dowd had recommended Sweeney, an old friend of his from the Queens Democratic Party, because he specialized in estates. The politically connected Sweeney had been appointed the lawyer to the public administrator and collected fees from every estate in Queens in which the deceased had died without a will or next of kin. He collected about a million dollars a year from the position.

Sweeney was hired by Generosa because the assumption was that Ted had changed his six-year-old will during the year-long divorce process. The question was: What were the provisions of Ted's new will? They were preparing for the case. She would have to elect against the will and challenge it in court for her one-third, as the surviving spouse. If she was successful, Generosa might win anywhere from $10 million to $30 million from Ted's estate. Their discussions were interrupted by a call from a lawyer with the big law firm that handled Ted's will. Dowd put the lawyer on the speakerphone.

"I have Ted's will," the lawyer said.

"Why are they calling us?" Dowd wondered.

The lawyer said that he was providing copies of Ted's will to Dowd's office, for Mrs. Ammon, and a second copy to J.P. Morgan Chase bank, the coexecutors of Ted's old will. After some legal talk, Dowd hung up. He was shocked but Generosa and Danny did not react at all. They didn't get it. Dowd explained that the only reason they got a call and a copy of the will was that Generosa and the bank were still coexecutors. That meant that, for whatever reason, Ted had not changed his old will.

"Okay," Generosa said calmly. "Well, what's in it? What does it mean?"

Dowd told her that she was the major beneficiary. Without a lengthy court fight, she would get it all. When it was finally probated, Ted's estate would total $97,424,628.03, before paying any outstanding debts.

Generosa said that she couldn't believe it but took the news quite calmly that she suddenly would be getting the house that meant so much to her, as well as Coverwood, and everything else. All of it.

But Danny almost fell off his chair.

"You gotta be fuckin' kidding me! This guy didn't change his will? What's in the will? What does it say?"

"Well, she gets it all," said Dowd.

"Get the fuck outta here!"

Danny was amazed. Ted hated Generosa; she hated him. He had figured that the first thing Ted had done was to change his will. He had the best lawyers in the world, he was a multi-bazillionaire, he knew his wife was going for his throat—and he had done nothing. He hadn't changed his will.

It was good news for Generosa but not for Sweeney. He would no longer be needed for a court battle.

Danny was happy but couldn't believe it. It had to be a mistake. As events began to sink in, that Generosa was the sole beneficiary, other than the kids' trusts, it became clear that the good news had a downside. The press was already pointing a finger. Now, everyone, including the police, would wonder if Generosa had killed Ted to get all the things she would not have received in the drafted but unsigned divorce agreement. It was a reason for murder. It was ninety-seven million reasons for murder.

"I bet if you go to the guy's office and you go through his files, you'll find one of those new wills," Danny predicted.

"Don't even say that," Dowd said.

"Well, what happens when the police go through the files? This guy ain't no fuckin' dummy. You really think he left that fuckin' thing that way?"

"Just keep your mouth shut," an angry Dowd told him. "Don't talk about that to anybody. Don't give anybody any ideas."

But they already had those ideas. Whenever police questioned those around Ted, they asked their routine question: Did they know anyone who hated Ted, who might want him dead? Over and over, detectives heard people say that the only enemy Ted had was Generosa and she wanted him dead. Very quickly, they also learned that Generosa would get everything. They knew about Danny and his criminal record and were also questioning people in Danny's neck of the woods.

All of this made Danny and Generosa very nervous and they talked about it. If they arrested him for the murder, the police would assume that she had put him up to it. Who would believe that she had not? She was petrified at the prospect of going to jail. She became even more isolated from others than she had been.

Generosa told her friend Ronnie that Ted had not changed his will and she would get everything that was not held in trust for the kids. She was the coexecutor with a bank. She got her favorite beach house and the place in England, the whole enchilada.

That's strange, thought Ronnie. Just before Ted was killed, Generosa had predicted that she would get it all. Now she had it all, just like she'd said she would, and Ted was dead. Her thoughts led only in one unpleasant direction.

But on November 16, J.P. Morgan Chase bank, acting as coexecutor, froze everything. The bank's lawyer said that they wanted to wait until the murder investigation was completed before settling the estate or distributing any assets. A bank was taking sides. It was very unusual. The lawyer attached a copy of the report written by the court-appointed psychologist who had interviewed Generosa and the children during the divorce and custody cases. That was also very unusual. The report, written two and a half weeks after Ted died, was very damaging to Generosa. It said that she was suffering from many features of a borderline personality disorder, narcissistic personality disorder, and paranoid personality disorder. It said that she was paranoid, delusional, and had a violent temper. It concluded that she was a bad mother who had involved her children in the vicious divorce and had emotionally abused them. It described in great detail her unremitting hatred for Ted.

To Generosa, the message was clear: They suspected her of being involved. They wanted to wait until she was arrested. She desperately tried to borrow money but she was almost tapped out. The court gave her a fifty-thousand-dollar monthly allowance until the matter was settled. She had inherited it all but it was all tied up again, frozen, just like it had been when Ted cut the purse strings.

Generosa Ammon had new people to hate.

Sometime after the memorial, Sandi called Generosa about seeing the twins.

"Are you calling to apologize?" Generosa asked her.

She wanted Sandi to say that she was sorry for suggesting she not attend Ted's funeral, perhaps even express regrets that she had sided with her own brother during the divorce, but Sandi did not apologize. Generosa complained about having no money and how the bank wanted to deny her access to it until after the homicide investigation was over, which was good news to Sandi. It was still all about money. Generosa refused to let Sandi see the kids. Sandi was still the enemy.

"You can't just have lunch with the children, like nothing's happened," Generosa said.

"Believe me, Generosa, I know something's happened," Sandi replied.

Again, Generosa was hurting for cash. She borrowed more money but couldn't sell anything because all of the properties were held jointly and could not be sold without the permission of the bank. The only property of significance she held in her own name was the old East Hampton car dealership property that she was planning to redo. She had told the East Hampton mayor, who wanted to make it part of the village green, to buzz off. Now, her lawyers called the mayor. Generosa wanted to deal. She soon sold the East Hampton property for $3.7 million. She had doubled her money but was still furious at being forced to sell. East Hampton had won and she had lost. Mayor Paul Rickenbach noticed that the entire transaction was accomplished by lawyers. The unpleasant Mrs. Ammon never showed her face. Rickenbach was only sorry that it took the death of Ted Ammon to help the village.

On the evening of New Year's Day, 2002, Danny was drinking in the Mustang Grill bar on the Upper East Side with his nephew Jeff and a few other pals. An attractive blonde was one of several others hoisting a few at the nightspot. She chatted and drank with Danny's group and ended up sitting on Danny's lap. A real estate agent named Ricardo Escobar* was also drinking down the bar. He overheard Danny telling people that his name and photo were featured in that month's *Esquire* piece on the Ted Ammon murder. Danny was buying drinks for everybody with a wad of hundreds, like he had won the lottery, like his ship had come in. He tipped the barmaid three hundred dollars. Ricardo thought that the guy was a loudmouthed showoff who was trying to pick up the blonde, but it was none of his business. But, as the drinks flowed and things got louder, the blonde suddenly slid down the bar next to Ricardo and began flirting with him.

"I think I'll go home with you tonight," she told Ricardo, who had requested no such thing.

Danny came down and tried to get the woman to rejoin his group. Ricardo wondered if Danny was angry that he had bought the woman so many drinks and here she was threatening to go home with some other guy. The two men had words over the situation. The possibility of stepping outside was mentioned.

"You know who I am, don't you?" Danny asked.

"No."

"Write it down!" Danny said, grabbing his arm.

Danny thought that the man was a detective who was going to write down what Danny did and said. Ricardo didn't know what Danny was talking about. He didn't like Danny's mouth and told him so. He gave Danny a couple of quick shots in the face with his right fist and then another shot to the ribs. Danny went down, as bar stools banged over. Danny got up from the barroom floor with a bloody nose.

"I think this guy is a cop," Danny confided in his nephew Jeff.

"I know who you are," Danny told the man who had decked him. "I know what you're doing and I don't want no trouble, you motherfuckers. I'm outta here."

As they left, Jeff could not believe that his tough-guy uncle had walked away from a fight. It was a first. Danny, getting a bit paranoid, mistakenly believed that the guy was a cop trying to provoke him so that he could be arrested, a violation of his probation.

"Uncle Dan, you're going to let that guy do that to you?" Jeff asked.

"Just get in the fuckin' car."

A full account of the bar fight appeared in the press, including Ricardo's claim that Danny was picking up the blonde. Generosa saw the story and confronted Danny. He told her that the woman came on to him and the guy was a police plant. Generosa believed Danny.

Many months earlier, Generosa and Danny had exchanged rings and talked about getting married when the divorce was over. They wanted to get married but they were now public figures and preferred to do it in secret. They decided on a quickie marriage but first Danny had to get a quickie divorce from Tami. Once that was arranged, Danny and Generosa planned a honeymoon at Coverwood, where they would remain with the kids—who were now free to go back to the English boarding school they loved.

Gerry Sweeney helped by arranging to help get them a marriage license quickly in Queens. They kept everything secret and drove out to Borough Hall in Kew Gardens in mid-January.

Generosa surveyed the scene and smirked. It was a busy spot, on a main thoroughfare, next to the courts. Outside was a subway stop, jammed with working people on their way to jobs. Across the boulevard were ugly apartment buildings, cheap markets, and steamy eateries jammed with people of every color and from every country, wearing tacky department store clothing and munching greasy fast food. It was a scene she looked down her nose at. She was forced to spend some time there but would flee as soon as the civil marriage ceremony was over. Queens was just the kind of place that Generosa Ammon did not want to be caught dead in.

33

BODY HEAT

Generosa and Danny flew to England with the twins but left their dog, Buddy, behind, which upset the kids. The English countryside reminded Danny of Upstate New York. He tried to fit in. He stopped at the local pub and bought drinks for everybody. Danny and the rehired English housekeeper, Kaye Mayne, still did not like each other but they got along because Generosa wanted it that way.

Danny noticed a weird pattern developing between his bride and the housekeeper. Suddenly, Generosa, who did not watch television, was watching it a lot with Kaye. The housekeeper began renting Hollywood movies and she and Kaye would watch them. Kaye loved reading and watching murder mysteries. The ghoulish part was that most of the movies were about women who had murdered their husbands. One evening, Danny saw the women watching one of the films, the sexy 1981 *Body Heat,* with John Hurt and Kathleen Turner, a tale of arson and murder.

"You're not too smart, are you? I like that in a man," Turner told Hurt at their first meeting. The story was about a lonely, smoldering blonde who lived in a mansion and was married to a rich, older man. "Jesus," said Hurt when he saw the huge mansion for the first time. Hurt had violent sex with Turner, who complained that she hated her husband but couldn't leave him because she had no money of her own. The only way she could get his fortune was if he died. In one scene, the husband, played by Richard Crenna, confronted Hurt, saying that if he caught his wife with another man, "I think I'd kill him with my bare hands." Crenna lorded his wealth and power over the younger man, telling Hurt that he was "like a lot of guys you run into, they want to get rich, they want to do it quick, they want to be there with one score—but they're not willing to do what's necessary."

"Yeah, I know that kind of guy," Hurt replied. "I hate that. It makes me sick."

"Me too," said Crenna.

"I'm a lot like that," Hurt confessed, and both men laughed.

After the meeting, Hurt told Turner to be careful about talking on the phone "because we're going to kill him—we both know that. It's what you want, isn't it? It's the only way we can have everything we want, isn't it?" After the murder, they both became paranoid and squabbled. It turned out that Turner had planned to frame Hurt for the killing all along and get all her husband's money using a trick with his will. Hurt became the patsy and went to jail for killing her husband—and a body the police incorrectly believed was Turner. The movie ended with the beautiful icy blond wife sipping an umbrella drink on a tropical beach and living happily ever after.

Danny did not like the ending.

"Hey, you're setting me up!" he complained.

"Oh, don't be silly, sweetie," Generosa assured him.

By the time Generosa, Danny, the kids, and Kaye had settled into a routine in Surrey, the press in New York found out that Generosa and Danny were married. It was big news in the States and the London press descended on Coverwood. They staked out the estate and got pictures of Generosa driving Danny in her SUV. Danny, wearing a new leather jacket to replace the one that he said he had lost the weekend of the murder, looked surprised and annoyed in the

photos. Generosa had an odd, faraway look in her eyes. The
shots and the story were front-page news in London and
New York. The *New York Post* called the couple the "Hamptons murder mystery newlyweds." The *Daily News* called
Generosa the "Merry Widow" for marrying three months after Ted's murder.

When an English reporter knocked on the door of the
manor house and asked Danny about the marriage, Danny
clenched his fists.

"Get the fuck off my property now," Danny said. "Just go
away now."

The headline on the story read: HE'S LORD OF THE MANOR.

Later, Danny calmed down and told reporters that they
had left New York because of the bad press.

"We want to calm down for the kids. The bottom line is
the bad press. It was coming back to the kids and had a large
emotional impact. There were horrible things written about
their father and they were being bullied at school because of
that. That's why we relocated."

Generosa, he said, "wants to move on with her life but is
still mourning for her ex-husband. She has been under a lot
of stress."

He denied being a suspect in the murder.

"I would not be here now, if any of that were true."

But there was an uproar on Long Island with Danny's
DWI case. When he did not show up for his court date, the
judge asked Danny's lawyer Eddie Burke where his client
was. He said that he did not know. The judge issued a bench
warrant for Danny's arrest. Suffolk County D.A. Thomas
Spota made a statement that the investigation of the Ammon
homicide would continue and it did not matter what country
the widow or her new husband were in. It looked like Danny
was a fugitive—until the next day, when the probation department said Danny's probation officer had given him permission for the trip. The arrest warrant was voided. Danny's
lawyers told him that he had to return for the next court date

the following month, on St. Valentine's Day. It meant the newlyweds would spend their first Valentine's Day apart.

Danny flew back to the United States in February. He later told several people there that he thought Kaye was strange. He claimed to have seen the soft-spoken house-keeper walking backward around a tree under a full moon, at midnight, muttering mumbo-jumbo. He said that he wondered what the hell she was doing. Was she some kind of witch? he wondered.

On the way into court in Riverhead, Danny made no comment, as usual, on the advice of his lawyers, a situation that frustrated the press, who peppered him with questions. There had been speculation that the judge might throw Danny in jail.

"Hey Danny," quipped one reporter, trying to get a rise out of the defendant. "Did you bring your toothbrush?"

"Nah," Danny replied. "I left it back with your wife."

The press laughed and the reporter was suddenly at a loss for words. Score one for Danny. In court, the judge, citing Danny's less than perfect record of showing up for probation appointments, took away his passport. One of those missed appointments had been a few hours after Danny's bar fight. Because Danny was now grounded, Generosa decided to return to America to be with him. She would bring the kids and Kaye too.

While still in London, Generosa went to the dentist for a routine examination. The dentist told her that he didn't like the look of a lesion on her jaw and suggested a biopsy. She delayed, telling Danny by phone that she would have it done back in the United States.

"When I get home, I'll get checked out. These doctors over here are assholes."

While Generosa was taking her afternoon nap at Cover-wood, she awoke to the smell of smoke. Ted's study in the manor house was on fire. The Peaslake Fire Brigade was summoned and they extinguished the smoky blaze before it

could spread throughout the house. The fire had trashed
Ted's desk and his files and burned a hole in the floor. There
was some smoke damage, of course, but it could have been
much worse. Fortunately, no one was hurt and Generosa was
home to smell the smoke. The only things burned beyond
recognition were Ted's personal papers and a laptop computer that had been brought from the States: one that had
been used to spy on Ted.

34

OFFICER DOWN

Jim Pelosi was husky, almost six feet tall. He was built like a football linebacker, with a handsome face, strong jaw, and black hair with a flattop haircut. He smoked. He was an NYPD officer in the Queens Narcotics Division. He had received commendations and decorations on the job and was highly regarded by his fellow officers and others who worked with him, including prosecutors at the Queens D.A.'s office. He did the job and got a lot of armed dopers off the streets and into jail. He was on his way up in the department.

In late February, he received a call at the 113th Precinct in Queens, from a newspaper reporter, who asked him if he knew that his name and badge number had been used by Generosa's butler, Steven, in his fax to Ted, which claimed that "Officer Jim Pelosi" was investigating the alleged Manhattan burglary.

"Really?" he asked, with a laugh. "That's news to me. I don't like my name being thrown around like that."

He asked for the spelling of Steven's last name, and when the alleged incident had occurred, and he made it clear that he would have nothing to do with investigating crimes in Manhattan.

"Unless they sold the hypodermic needles in Queens," he said with a chuckle. "It doesn't make any sense at all."

Jim said that he thought that Danny and Generosa were probably suspects in the Ammon homicide.

"He's within the scope of people, I'm sure."

After the story about the alleged needle break-in ran in the paper and was picked up by other media, Jim was questioned by NYPD Internal Affairs detectives. By "running a plate" for Danny, Jim had violated department policy. The check had yielded the name and address of the owner of the car that Steven the butler claimed was connected to his strange, alleged hypodermic incident.

In addition to his concern about Danny's problems, Jim now had his own. He might be reprimanded for unauthorized access to the DMV system. Having a brother who was a homicide suspect who had involved you in the case might not adversely affect a cop's career. But it certainly wouldn't help, especially when it was in the press. Being investigated by Internal Affairs was no career booster, either, and Jim would be on edge until the investigation was over.

Generosa flew back to the United States and moved in with Danny, who was staying in the basement apartment at his sister Barbara's ranch house in Center Moriches. To Danny, it proved that Generosa loved him. She could live in a palace anywhere in the world but she chose to live in a small, viewless apartment with him. But they soon decided that they were imposing on Barbara and needed a new place. They began house hunting. They decided to look nearby, in Center Moriches, Danny's hometown, so that he could be near his kids.

Meanwhile, their lawyers had decided to cooperate more with the murder investigation and had advised them to provide fingerprints and DNA samples to the police. The cheek swabs, which took microscopic amounts of epithelial cells from inside the cheek, were given to authorities. Lab tests isolated Generosa's and Danny's DNA configurations and they were then compared to samples found in the murder house. But since Danny and Generosa had lived in the house, their traces were all over the place. Unless they had left one of their fingerprints in Ted's blood, none of their fingerprints or DNA traces at the beach house had any dates attached. Investigators had isolated several fingerprints and one blood sample in the mansion that matched neither Generosa's nor Danny's, nor any of their other samples of people who had known access to the house. Was it the blood of the killer, who had been injured during the murder, or was there some more innocent explanation for the mysterious blood spot?

Since the beginning, Danny had wanted to speak out and defend himself. That was his instinct and he said that he had nothing to hide, but his lawyers told him to keep his mouth shut. At his next court appearance on his DWI case, Danny came out swinging, claiming that DNA evidence had cleared himself and his wife—and perhaps pointed to the real killer.

"Here's a headline for you," Danny told one reporter. "The DNA does not equal DAN. Police have some other DNA in the mix, and it isn't me. The big picture is far away from me. I would look at me, if I were the police, and anyone reading the papers would look at me—but enough, already."

As he called for suspicion of him to end, Danny was sartorially resplendent in an expensive suit and tie. He tugged at the collar of his white dress shirt.

"I'm blue collar. This isn't me."

He even had kind words about Ted.

"Ted didn't deserve to go that way. Nobody deserves to go that way. He was a good guy. He really loved those kids," Danny said.

The murder and the resulting suspicion and publicity were very hard on Alexa and Grego, he said.

Two days later, Danny prepared a written statement with his lawyer Paul Bergman, who released it to the press. In it, Danny claimed that they had found at the beach house a note in Ted's handwriting with figures that indicated that Ted was actually worth $300 million more than his estate claimed. The alleged missing fortune was the key to the killing and proved that the solution to the murder lay in secret financial dealings Ammon had had before his death, Danny claimed. He said that they had turned the note over to police. He stressed that he had no motive to kill Ted. In the statement, Danny said that he hoped the Suffolk County homicide detectives had the interest and commitment to unravel Ted Ammon's complex financial affairs. If they did that, Danny believed, they would be closer to solving the crime.

When called and asked for comment, homicide squad commander Detective Lieutenant Jack Fitzpatrick declined to identify anyone as a suspect in the murder, or eliminate anyone either.

"The investigation is certainly active," Fitzpatrick said.

That week, Suffolk County Homicide Squad detectives and NYPD Internal Affairs Bureau detectives arrived at Jim Pelosi's precinct in Queens to question him.

"My brother might be a fuck-up, but he's not a murderer," Jim told the detectives.

But Jim's certainty was shaken when the investigators told him that Danny had bought a Taser, ordered a second, and had tested one of them on a construction worker. Tasers had serial numbers, just like guns, and could be traced. They told Jim that Ted Ammon's body bore stun gun burns on the skin—evenly spaced round red burns, like the marks of a vampire.

Then the detectives gave Jim other information that made his stomach turn: The probes on the Taser model Danny had were the exact same distance apart as the double marks on Ted's skin in the autopsy photos.

Danny, by asking him to get rid of that Taser, had dragged his brother into a murder investigation. Jim did not mention the stun gun. Already, he was withholding something from his fellow officers.

The investigators then ticked off their version of the case against Danny. Ted was beaten to death and had stun gun marks consistent with the Taser Danny bought, the one that was missing. Danny was with the dead man's widow, who had vowed to have him killed. She got all she wanted and grossed $100 million because of the murder. Danny had a secret video surveillance system installed to spy on Ted and watch his every move. Danny's alibi on the night of the murder apparently rested on his family and friends alone. They suspected Danny's alibi was either faked or the murder was committed by Danny's pals. It was a circumstantial call, but it looked bad for Danny.

After he was questioned, Jim called Danny.

"We gotta talk," Jim told him urgently.

He did not believe that Danny was a killer. But what if he was wrong? Rumors had been circulating among family and friends that Danny had two or even three stun guns. Why would he need more than one? Danny had denied the rumors and said that he had only one. Even if Danny was innocent, Jim might be charged with destruction of evidence and his career could be over. He could go to jail. If the stun gun had been destroyed, it would look like Danny—and he—had destroyed it because it was used in the murder. Jim was between a rock and a hard place. He did not want to hurt his brother but he did not want to do anything illegal or get jammed up on the job.

Jim drove back to Long Island. He called Danny again on his cell phone when he arrived outside the murder house in East Hampton, where Danny was supervising a crew of workmen who were cleaning up the mansion. He told Danny to come out, that he wanted to talk alone. Danny tried to tell him that he was busy but Jim was insistent.

"Danny, this is serious. It could cost me my job."

"What's up?" Danny asked once he was outside.

"Get in the fuckin' car," Jim ordered.

Jim drove to a nearby beach and parked in the deserted lot. The two of them got out and walked toward the rough March surf.

"Danny, you've got nothing to worry about with the fuckin' Taser, have you?"

"Jimbo, I got nothing to worry about," said Danny, who believed that his brother had already disposed of the stun gun.

"I'm going to ask you something and I want you to think and tell me the truth," Jim said. "Danny, did you do this? Did you stun Ted?"

"What the fuck are you talking about?" Danny asked.

"The detectives were in my office, with my sergeant," Jim said, anger and panic in his voice.

He said that the detectives had told him that there were marks on Ted's body from a stun gun—like the one Danny had.

"I don't care! It wasn't from my gun!" Danny protested. "I swear on my kids. . . ."

"Yo, bro, if you did this, come clean, get it off your chest, and at least I'll bring you in," Jim said.

"What are you—fuckin' nuts?" Danny asked.

"You'd rather have me bring you in than Suffolk bring you in."

"Jim, I didn't do this—enough already!"

He told Danny that the detectives had also told him that the Taser came with three dart cartridges—and there were only two with the one Jim had taken from Danny's house. Danny vehemently denied that he had fired one of the cartridges into Ted.

"But there's three darts, Danny! Where's the third dart?"

"It wasn't there! Maybe the guy I got it from might have used it."

"You're a fuckin' liar, Danny! They're gonna fuckin' have it!"

"The dart cartridge wasn't there when I got the gun," Danny maintained.

"You better hope to God . . . If you did it, let me arrest you," Jim tried, one last time.

Jim did not beg but he was desperate. The only way he could redeem himself now was to break the case—to bring in his own brother. If he didn't, he might be arrested or fired. Even if he was not fired, his career would grind to a halt.

Danny made the point that it didn't matter, because the Taser no longer existed.

"But you dropped it in the drop box at the precinct, didn't you?" Danny asked.

"Never mind where it is," Jim said.

Danny wondered whether Jim still had the Taser and, if he did, what he intended to do with it.

That Thursday, Jim played golf with his father before going to work. The young officer looked exhausted and depressed. He told his father that he had been about to be made detective when Danny's stun gun mess came up. Now, he feared that he would never get his gold shield. He was afraid that the best that could happen would be that he would remain a ground-pounder, a foot cop, for his entire career.

"Dad, I'm afraid I'm gonna lose my job over this," Jimbo said.

Bob Pelosi told his son not to worry, that he would set him up in business the next day. Jim wasn't interested. He had always wanted to be a police officer and he loved the job.

"I want to stay a cop," he said. "If I find out Danny did this, I'm taking him in."

Bob Pelosi was very troubled. First, Danny had left his wife and kids for that Ammon woman, and then there was the murder, and now, one of his sons was ready to arrest the other.

Early Saturday morning, after working a double shift of sixteen hours on the streets of Queens on Friday, Officer Jim Pelosi made the long drive to Center Moriches. He arrived home on the morning of Saturday, March 30, and went into the bathroom. He suddenly felt dizzy and smelled an odd odor. His strong muscles contracted in a huge spasm and his arms and legs became rigid. Jim had no idea that these were symptoms of ideopathic seizure disorder. He fell to the bathroom floor and his body went stiff for several seconds. He then went into a full seizure, his body shaking violently and uncontrollably on the tile floor. As his own muscles squeezed the air out of his lungs, he made a slight moaning sound. He quickly passed out and never woke up.

Sometime later, his wife walked into the bathroom, look-ing for him, and was horrified to find him dead on the floor. She did what she could and called 911 but it was too late. Jim Pelosi was dead at age thirty-six.

His death rang alarm bells, in the form of phone calls and beepers, in two police departments. The sudden death of an officer under investigation caused NYPD's Internal Affairs Bureau to investigate the circumstances of his demise. The death of the brother of a suspect in the Ammon homicide got the attention of the Suffolk County Homicide Squad. Was it a suicide? A murder? Or was it the result of natural causes? There was no sign of foul play but it was always possible that a subtle poison could have been used. Much later, an au-topsy revealed that Jim had died of natural causes, from ideopathic seizure disorder, a massive, sudden-death epilep-tic attack. *Ideopathic* was a fancy Latin word for "unknown cause." Jim had appeared tired but healthy before his seizure, which made his death surprising to police and to his grieving family. The toxicological testing—to make sure that he had not been poisoned—took months and no traces of poisons or drugs ever turned up. There was no reason for further investigation and Jim's house was never searched by police.

The startling death caused an angry rift in the Pelosi fam-ily. Danny felt that some blamed him for Jim's death. Some were mad at him for dragging Jim into his problems, which caused him the added stress that they felt might have con-tributed to his death. Others blamed Generosa for Jim and Danny's problems. Some blamed the press.

A wake was held at the local funeral home, which was at-tended by his divorced parents, Robert and Janet, as well as his siblings, Janet, Joan, Barbara, and two brothers, Robert and Danny. An honor guard from NYPD was dispatched. The local fire department where Jim had been a volunteer also honored him. If he had died in the line of duty, Jim would have received the honor of an inspector's funeral and thousands of brother and sister officers would have attended.

Hundreds of cops and friends and coworkers in law enforcement did arrive to pay their respects, along with the family. When the press showed up across the street, some family members, in their anguish, threatened the reporters and photographers with violence if they did not leave.

"My mom is already on pills for depression, and if she dies, I'm going to kill each and every one of you!" a female relative screamed.

"You want to know where she is?" asked another relative, referring to Generosa. The relative mentioned the address where Generosa was living with Danny. "She's there right now! Go talk to her!"

"James was the nicest man in the world, but Danny has his own problems," a female relative told a reporter. "Don't mix the two together."

Later, Danny went to Jim's house to see if the Taser was there. He went right to the kitchen and lifted up the linoleum, exposing the floorboards. Under the boards was a hidden cement box, a secret hideaway put there by Jim. Danny lifted the lid. No stun gun. It was empty, except for a few live bullets. Danny turned to his brother's widow, Lee.

"Nah. That would have been the only place he could have put it," Danny said.

35

THE KING AND QUEEN OF CENTER MORICHES

Generosa, like a new CEO after a hostile takeover, began selling off the real estate assets left to her by Ted, because she needed cash to pay her mounting bills.

Generosa's lawyers succeeded in getting a judge to rule that the bank could not freeze Ted's estate. Also, she sued to obtain a $15 million settlement from Ted's business insurance.

Ted's estate dropped his lawsuit against actor Kevin Kline and the board at 1125 Fifth Avenue, and Generosa sold the place for $10 million. She evicted Ted's niece Wendy and her husband from a $3 million condo on West Sixty-seventh Street, where they had been living courtesy of Ted. The twenty-six-year-old graduate student paid $1,200 a month for taxes and maintenance but could not afford to buy the home. Eventually, Generosa would sell Coverwood for $8 million and liquidate at least $30 million in assets.

With the homicide investigation apparently stalled and the money flowing again, the good times for Generosa and Danny began to roll again, better than ever. Generosa took care of Steven the butler and Bruce the cook. She settled their lawsuit against Ted for a secret sum rumored to be in the high six figures. They sold their place in England, left New York, and bought a chateau in the south of France, which was not a bad retirement plan for domestic servants.

Generosa spoke often to Kaye Mayne by phone and arranged to bring her to the United States, ostensibly to be the twins' nanny but actually to be Generosa's personal assistant, Steven's replacement.

"I hate my life here," Kaye told a shopkeeper near her home. "And this will be an opportunity I can't miss. The children are great and my life will be completely different there."

Behind a white picket fence on a wooded lane in Center Moriches, Generosa and Danny found a white ranch house on a grassy knoll overlooking the brimming Senix Creek. There was a dock for the family boats and a thirty-foot flagpole flying Old Glory. They quietly bought the $700,000 home and, of course, began renovations, including remodeling the basement into a two-bedroom apartment for the kids. It was a house, not a huge estate, and Generosa did not go crazy with the remodeling. Alexa and Grego had attended the finest private schools in the world and had flown in their father's private jet to Switzerland for ski trips. Now, they walked down the block to the public-school bus stop and swam in the canal behind the house. They loved it and they loved Danny, who sometimes offered them cash rewards for competitive activities, such as fifty bucks to the first one to swim to the dock.

Of course, it was difficult to forget about Ted's murder when stories appeared regularly in the newspapers and on TV, and detectives followed Danny around.

Police located Ted's Buick station wagon in a remote area of East Hampton. The investigators suspected that they had been unable to locate the vehicle because it was being hidden from them. The police towed the vehicle to the police lab for testing. The preceding month, detectives had impounded Ted's Audi and also brought that in for tests, to see if any blood, DNA, or other evidence could be recovered. But still, no one was charged with the murder.

Danny was now living in an expensive waterfront home in his old hometown. The high school dropout with the arrest record, the screw-up, had returned as a rich man. Danny had once bragged that half the town was afraid of him, and now he was back as a generous man of leisure, a sportsman, who went on gambling junkets with his pals to Atlantic City and Las Vegas. He stayed at luxury hotels there with his buddies, where they ate and drank well and hit the gaming tables. Danny spent hundreds of thousands of dollars and told Generosa that he had lost most of it at the tables. As Generosa and Danny settled into their new arrangements, they were affectionate and seemed quite in love. However improbable it seemed, it appeared that the formerly snobbish Mrs. Ammon was happy in a place in which she previously would not have been caught dead. They were content but felt harassed by the press, the police, and public innuendo. To many who knew Generosa, not to mention much of the public, it looked like she had gotten away with the perfect murder and she and Danny were living happily ever after.

Danny was heard to brag that he had more money than his father, who lived in the same town, just a few miles away. One day, Danny arrived at his father's dock with friends in his brand-new boat, *Generous*, which Generosa had bought for him.

"How do you like my new boat?" Danny called out to his father.

Bob Pelosi asked his son if he had earned the money that bought the boat. It was a rhetorical question. When Danny didn't answer, Bob shouted out another question:

"What do you call it? Ammon Joy?"

Danny sped away across the roiling bay.

A visitor to Bob and Dorothy Pelosi's house one day was saddened to find Bob in the garage, staring at a poster-size photo on the wall of Danny and Jimbo when they were kids. Tears were rolling down Bob's face.

"What happened to my two boys?" he asked the visitor.

While golfing one morning, another duffer, who did not know their last name, told Bob and Dorothy Pelosi about the latest newspaper story on the Ammon murder case.

"You just know it was that electrician," the golfer concluded.

More and more stories were appearing in the press about Danny and Generosa. Enough was enough, Bob Pelosi told people.

The next time Danny dropped by, Bob told him that he had nothing to say to him and handed him a letter that he had just written. Danny read the letter. In it, Bob said that he did not know who Danny was anymore and had nothing to say to him again. He said that he had lost two of his sons. It was not Jimbo's fault that he had lost Jimbo but it was Danny's fault that he had lost Danny. It was a hard letter to write and a hard one to read.

"Well, you are my father," Danny said.

Danny began telling people that his father and others in the family blamed him for Jimbo's death—even though the letter did not say that.

In June 2002, Generosa came down with an illness that gave her chest congestion and a fever. As the flu worsened, her lungs began to fill with fluid and she had difficulty breathing. She became dizzy and collapsed. Concerned, Danny brought her to a local doctor, who recommended X-rays and tests. Danny thought she might have pneumonia. After obtaining the films from the testing facility, Danny took them first to a friend who was a nurse. The nurse took one look at the X-rays and saw shadows in the breast area, lungs, and kidneys.

"Oh my God, Danny! Your wife has cancer!" she said.

"What!"

It had spread throughout her chest and abdomen, the nurse said. It was very serious and advanced. Danny was stunned. A doctor came to the same conclusion, but Danny did not want to tell Generosa until they could find out what, if anything, they could do for her. That way, it would be bad news/good news, not just bad news all at once. Danny wondered why the cancer hadn't been picked up the year before, when she had breast surgery. Had they missed it? How could she not know? Danny had not considered the possibility that Generosa already knew she had cancer—because she had already had surgery to remove the tumor.

Generosa went first to a hospital on Long Island, where they asked about her medical history and were shocked that she claimed never to have had cancer. Then Generosa went to Beth Israel Hospital in Manhattan for a series of tests, which determined that the cancer had spread too far to make surgery an option. The disease had invaded her lymphatic system and was already attacking her brain, just like it had in her mother, Babe. Chemotherapy could extend her life by a few years. Nothing would save her. Danny could not give her the news and called Generosa's former doctor, Mark Borelli, the one she had cut off because he had spoken to Ted, the one who had written her the letter she had never opened. Borelli was not surprised at the news Danny gave him.

"Oh, so you knew she had cancer?"

"She's going to die," Borelli said.

Danny was shocked. The doctor had known almost two years earlier.

"Why didn't you tell her?"

"Well, I tried to, but she wouldn't take my calls."

"You drove past the Stanhope every day."

"Didn't Ted tell her? Didn't she know about this?" Borelli asked, incredulous that Generosa had ignored his medical advice.

Danny didn't know what Ted had told her but Generosa claimed that she knew nothing.

"What can we do?" Danny asked.

"There's not much we can do," Dr. Borelli replied.

"This doctor here is talking six months."

"Well, maybe we can get her four or five years."

Finally, some good news.

"I can't tell her," Danny admitted.

He asked the physician to come to the hospital and tell Generosa the truth. At first, she refused to see him, but Danny insisted, and Dr. Borelli walked into the room to perform the sad duty of telling his patient that she had only a short future.

"I want you to know that I'm still not happy with you," Generosa told her former doctor, as she lay in bed.

"Well, let's put all that aside," Danny urged. "Why don't you two talk and I'll step outside?"

Danny waited just outside the door.

"I have to tell you something that's very shocking," Borelli told Generosa.

"What is it?"

"You have cancer and it has metastasized."

"What does that mean?"

"We caught it too late."

It took a few seconds for the meaning of those words to sink in. Then Danny heard Generosa crying. He walked back into the room and they discussed radiation and chemotherapy options, in an effort to give her hope.

"Hey, kid, don't worry about it," Danny told his wife. "Everything's gonna be okay."

But Generosa was still resistant to the idea of radiation and chemotherapy. She didn't want to do it. Very quickly, Generosa blamed Ted. He knew and he had kept it a secret from her, she claimed. He had told her to go for tests and treatment but it had all been a trick. It was all his fault. The idea that Ted had conspired to kill *her* seemed to give her comfort.

None of it made any sense. She had hung up on Ted when he called after speaking to the doctor and had refused to talk to him for a year. It was Ted's fault that he could not tell her she had cancer over the phone before she slammed down the receiver. She broke off with her doctor, ignored all of his calls, and threw away his letter, unopened; but it was Ted's fault. The man had been dead for eight months and still her hatred for him burned hot. Not for an instant did she consider that her own fear and denial might be to blame, that she had killed herself; or that it was no one's fault.

She told Alexa and Grego that she was sick but not the terrible, inescapable fact of terminal cancer. Of course, she told them that their father had tried to harm her by keeping her illness a secret from her. It was all his fault.

Although she had registered under the name Genna Pelosi, the press got hold of the story and reported about her "cancer scare" and about their new house. Danny told one reporter that Generosa had had some tests but did not need surgery. That was a white lie for the kids—because her cancer was inoperable.

Generosa's lawyer Mike Dowd visited her in the hospital and urged her to hire back Gerry Sweeney, the estate lawyer, and she did. Soon after she got out of the hospital, she relented and scheduled chemotherapy and was fitted for a wig, for when her hair fell out. She made up a new will, using Gerry Sweeney, that left everything to Danny, except what was already in trust from Ted's estate for the kids. The twins would get almost nothing further.

But when Danny realized that the children had been cut out from most of Generosa's estate, he told her that she had to change it. He told her that it wasn't right not to take care of her kids. Also, Danny felt that the police would point to that as a motive. If he, as Generosa's husband, got all the millions, that might convince a jury that he had killed Ted. Generosa went back to Gerry Sweeney and changed her will accordingly. In her second will, she left one-third of her estate to her kids. One-third went to Danny and the last third would be held in trust for him.

Danny devoted himself to Generosa and she demanded all of his attention. He had no time for his friends and not much more for his own family. Pain invaded her lungs and other organs, taking over, slowly, steadily. She lost weight and became pale; her arms and legs slowly began to dwindle.

One morning, she looked in the bathroom mirror and

gasped. The hopeless, sunken eyes, the hollow cheeks—it was like looking at the face of her dying mother, Babe. Generosa now looked just like her. It was eerie and terrifying.

Generosa began to talk of suicide. This was not unusual in terminal cancer patients but Generosa had seen her mother waste away from the exact same thing: untreated breast cancer that spread through the body and into the brain. She wished she would die before she suffered like her mother had. When the pain medication did not dull the pain and the anguish, Generosa began taking more and more and then drinking on top of it to achieve oblivion. When no one was around, she gobbled a leftover bottle of muscle relaxers and passed out. Danny's sister Barbara noticed that Generosa was drinking scotch and beer and whatever else she could get her hands on, as her breathing became more difficult. She had to sleep propped up in bed or on the living room couch because she could no longer lie flat.

When Kaye arrived in the United States at the start of the summer, she saw to Generosa's needs and took charge of her medicine. Because Kaye was so busy with Generosa, the twins had to be taken care of by someone else.

Luke Johnson,* who had known Danny in high school and then lost touch over the years, was hired to take care of Alexa and Grego at his home nearby, where he lived with his wife and their two children. Generosa needed peace and quiet and wanted all of Danny's attention. When Generosa was introduced to Luke's daughter, she flinched at the teenager's name.

"Hi, I'm Babe."

Babe. Generosa's mother's name. Babe, again. Generosa was the only one who got the joke. She even had blond hair and resembled Generosa's mother a bit, as a child. But Generosa took to Babe, who was the only one she allowed to hug and kiss her. What started as weekends over at Luke's house quickly became whole weeks, as the twins were spared the sight of their mother's suffering. She did not want them to see her ill and weak, dying. She did not want anybody to see her. Alexa became friends with Babe, who was two years older than she, and Grego got tight with Luke's son, Charlie, who was three years his senior. As Generosa languished in her new house, her kids were becoming part of someone else's family. It quickly became more than a job to Luke, and his wife, Ann, and their children. Suddenly, they had four kids, not two, but everyone liked it.

In the morning at eight, when housekeeper Joanne Matheson arrived to clean the Pelosis' house, she would usually find Danny and Generosa asleep in the living room, Generosa propped up on the couch and Danny sprawled in a chair. Danny would sleep on a chair or on a makeshift bed on the floor next to the couch while Generosa napped. He would rub her feet and wait on her when she was alert. They would play Scrabble for hours every day. It bugged her that she, with her college education, was often beaten by Danny at the word game.

"You're a fucking ignorant high school dropout," she moaned, sounding a bit like Danny.

"I went to Whatsa-mattuh U," Danny said, laughing.

Every moment had become precious. Kaye dispensed Generosa's medicine and took care of other household tasks, but her toilet-scrubbing days were over. That was now Joanne's job. For a time, Generosa improved a bit, but, as is common in such cases, she would worsen again later. Her biggest fear was that a course of chemotherapy or radiation would cause her to lose her blond hair. She didn't want to look unattractive for her new husband.

Generosa and Danny were not living happily ever after as the king and queen of Center Moriches. They were together in their lovely, new waterfront home, but their kingdom had shrunk to their living room, a couch, a chair, cigarettes, a game board, pills, pain, and a clock.

36

GENEROSA'S NANNY

Kaye took over more and more responsibility for Generosa and the house, as Danny was forced to spend increasing amounts of time in court on the DWI charge, and with his lawyers and the private detectives preparing to defend him against a potential murder charge. Kaye did the laundry and Generosa allowed her the singular honor of touching her underwear, because she loved the way Kaye folded it.

Danny arranged to get lawyers for some members of his family, his friends, and even for the doorman at the Stanhope hotel after detectives tried to talk to him. The more people who were lawyered up and not talking, the harder it was for investigators to put together a case. Danny's friend Chris Parrino had told police that he was the one driving— not Danny—the month before the murder, when Danny was charged with DWI. But, after an investigation in which police interviewed several other people, Danny's defense collapsed and Chris was charged with making a false statement. After consulting with his lawyers, Danny reluctantly agreed to plead guilty to his DWI charge, take a deal offered by the prosecution, and serve four months in jail.

Generosa was often out of it, zonked on pain medication and booze when the pain was bad. On other days, she could get around. Fear of poverty began to haunt her.

"We're not going to have money for food this winter," she told her children.

She continued to smoke cigarettes because she no longer cared about many things.

When Danny brought home his lawyer, Eddie Burke, Jr., and introduced him to Generosa, he politely said, "How do you do?"

"How the fuck do you think I do?" she snapped, puffing away in bed.

"I hate lawyers. I hate bankers," she said.

But later, she warmed to Burke and appreciated his manners and his help. However, when she was loaded on pills and booze, she appreciated nothing. Her terror and rage erupted and she sometimes hallucinated. One night, she saw a ghost and grabbed a butcher knife from the kitchen counter to defend herself, snicking it around in the air.

"Ted, you fuck!" Generosa wailed, coming at Danny with the flashing blade.

"Yo, honey, it's me," Danny protested.

"Get away from me!"

"Okay," Danny said, backing off.

"You ruined my fucking life!" she sobbed, slashing at Danny, the steel slicing into the left side of his abdomen, which began to gush blood.

In a few minutes, she came out of it and was sorry for what she had done. The ghost had evaporated. Danny bandaged his wound but did not go to a hospital because he feared the press would find out.

Early one evening, Danny's sister Barbara found an empty prescription bottle and realized that Generosa had taken the whole bottle of Xanax with alcohol because she was despondent. Generosa told Barbara that she had seen her mother's suffering and she didn't want Alexa and Grego to go through what she had experienced as a child. And she was vain about her hair. She said that she had decided not to go through with her chemotherapy because it would make her bald.

"I don't want to look ugly for Danny," she said.

Barbara noticed that Generosa was becoming very dependent on Kaye, as if the Englishwoman, who was only ten years older than her employer, were her mother. But the kids did not like Kaye very much. She was capable of being sweet but more often was tough on the twins, which seemed to be what Generosa wanted. Kaye became an instrument of Generosa's will and then, slowly, the servant ceased to be a servant. When the children did not get good grades or misbehaved in any way, Kaye would order them down into their basement apartment, forbidden to use their computer or to watch television. They would have to do their own laundry and clean their own bathroom. Kaye, the former housecleaner, would sniff the toilet bowl to rate their job. Generosa thought it was character building. To the kids, after what they had lost and were losing, it seemed like a gothic fairy tale in which the brother and sister were being kept in a dungeon, away from their sick mother, by the evil stepmother. Kaye knew that the twins did not care for her but that didn't matter as much as the difficult job she had with Generosa. Alexa would give a little bit more than Grego, who clashed with Kaye regularly and was punished almost daily. Both children wanted to talk to their mother without Kaye listening, but she was always there.

The kids were happy to stay at Luke's house more and more, because it meant being away from Kaye, but they missed their mother. It was obvious to Luke that Alexa and Grego were smart but seemed not to have any play left in them. Their father had been killed, their mother was sick, and the joy in their life was gone. Kids at school taunted them:

"Who killed your father?"

"Are you really rich?"

"Just say it isn't you," Luke advised them.

Every time a story about their father's murder hit the papers, the big, husky guy would drive around town in his SUV and buy up all the copies from the newsstands and convenience stores so that the kids—and their schoolmates—would not see them. He threw them in the garbage.

Alexa and Grego were bright, with a lot of love to give, and they started to explore their own interests. Alexa wanted to be a writer and had a talent for writing poetry. She won an award for one of her poems and someday hoped to write her life story. Grego made and raced miniature cars. He was in the local newspaper when he made the racing finals. Luke framed it and Grego proudly presented it to his mother. Grego was a natural baseball player. One day, when he dropped the kids back at Generosa's house, Luke chatted with Generosa, who was on her couch. First, she made it clear that she didn't want Luke to go out drinking with Danny and join that crowd. He promised that he wouldn't.

"How's Grego doing?" Generosa asked.

Luke told her that he was so good at baseball that he should go out for it—maybe even get a college scholarship or even go pro.

"Absolutely not!" Generosa exploded. "He's not going to be that and he's not going to be what his father was—he's going to be an architect."

Ted had played baseball and other sports.

When they were at Luke's house, Alexa and especially Grego vented their hatred of Kaye, who, by then, was running the house. Kaye herself made that clear to Luke when she told him, out of her mistress's hearing, that "Generosa wants to feel like she's in charge."

To Luke, Kaye also sounded like she was Generosa's mother.

The twins' grades at school improved. They used one of Danny's video cameras to make a video in which they pretended to commit a murder—of Kaye. Grego also began creating hip-hop lyrics about how he hated Kaye and wished she were dead.

When Danny and Kaye got into arguments, Generosa made him apologize to the nanny—or Kaye might go back to England.

"I'll just leave," Kaye threatened Generosa, more than once.

Suddenly, it was clear to everyone who was in charge.

One night, Danny came home and discovered that Generosa had taken huge amounts of Klonopin and lots of alcohol. The kids were in the house and Kaye was in charge of Generosa's medications—which meant that she was supposed to guard against overdose. Danny accused Kaye of giving his wife an overdose or allowing her to do it herself. Danny found Generosa insensate, sprawled on the couch, fading away. Danny was furious. He forced Generosa to vomit on the couch and he called poison control, as the kids watched. Generosa had swallowed enough dope and booze to kill two people but her tolerance had been built up by too many pills and too much alcohol for months. She began to come around.

"C'mon, how long ago did you give her this shit?" Danny asked Kaye.

"It's time for her to go," Danny later said Kaye replied.

"You ain't doing this in my house!" Danny screamed, turning on Generosa. "You wanna die? You go out to fuckin' East Hampton. I am not gonna be part of this. It goes against everything in the goddamn world!"

He turned back to Kaye.

"I got fuckin' police lookin' at me for a murder I didn't do, and she's gonna fuckin' die? They're gonna tell me I murdered her! I don't want nothin' to do with it!"

37

DANNY AND THE NANNY

Kaye didn't have a good word to say about Danny but she became quite friendly with Danny's mother, Janet, whom Generosa also liked. They would go to dinner and the movies and have a nice time but that did not prevent Kaye from talking Danny down to Generosa and others.

"Danny came from a bad gene pool," Kaye said one day, with a smirk.

Kaye criticized Danny for his crudeness, his spendthrift ways, his gambling, and his rumored womanizing, which Danny vehemently denied. Generosa knew Danny's past and was sensitive to the possibility that he might cheat on her, especially now that she was sick and felt unattractive. Joanne, the housekeeper, liked Danny and lived next door to his sister Barbara. Joanne thought it was obvious that Kaye, who had replaced Steven—and then some—was trying to get rid of Danny. Joanne noticed that Kaye seemed to be doing things beyond her job description, such as having long phone conversations with Generosa's lawyer Mike Dowd. What was that about? she wondered. Joanne had already heard Dowd refer to Danny as "Shady."

One sunny afternoon, while Joanne and Kaye were relaxing in the backyard and looking at the canal, Kaye casually mentioned something that stunned her.

"Danny told me that he killed Ted," Kaye said.

Kaye claimed that Danny confessed that he had sneaked into the beach house, put down a plastic sheet in the living room, beaten Ted to death, and then cut off his penis. Joanne's jaw dropped. She didn't believe it.

"Why would Danny tell you that he killed Ted?" Joanne asked. "He would never be that stupid to make a statement like that to anybody. Do you actually believe he killed Ted?"

"No."

"Well, why would he say it if he didn't do it? Nobody in their right mind would make a statement like that," Joanne said. "I don't think so, no. I don't think he would ever tell you that. You can sit here and say that you think he killed Ted?"

"No, I don't believe that. I know he didn't kill Ted," said Kaye. "I know he didn't do it."

"Okay, thank you," said Joanne.

Joanne wondered if Kaye was making up the story. Was this how she was going to get rid of him? If he had done it, Kaye was probably the last person in the world Danny would admit it to. Or, was it just Danny and his sarcastic sense of humor? Joanne had read that the rumor that Ted had been sexually mutilated was not true. When she asked Danny about his alleged confession, he angrily denied it.

Joanne felt that Kaye was now the control freak, acting in Generosa's stead, and didn't want Danny around. Joanne was also the housekeeper at the beach house and felt that Kaye hadn't liked Ted, either. Now, she heard that Kaye was saying bad things to Generosa about her and Barbara and Danny's family. Kaye whispered that Barbara was a bad mother, which Joanne considered untrue, and she told Generosa that Danny's nieces "dressed like sluts. You don't want Alexa hanging around with them."

Kaye wants to get rid of us all, Joanne decided.

Danny had angered Generosa with the speed at which he spent her money and by asking for a million dollars to pay what he claimed were his past gambling debts. One morning when Generosa felt well enough to be driven to the local bank's cash machine to withdraw money, she was startled and embarrassed to get a DECLINE message on the computer screen when she inserted her bank card. Danny had cleaned out their checking account. After talking to Kaye and her lawyers, Generosa made up a new will, in which his two-thirds of her estate would be reduced by $2.6 million, the amount that she said he had thrown away on gambling and other pursuits. Danny would get one-third in trust and one-third right away. The other third went to the kids, as Danny had suggested.

When Danny went to Las Vegas for a second time with a dozen pals, he was concerned that Generosa would kill herself while he was out of state but his wife said that she did not think she could.

"Danny, I'm afraid I can't do it. Sweetie, I promise you I'll kiss you before I leave you."

But, before he left, Danny warned Kaye not to assist Generosa if she became suicidal.

"Lady, anything happens, I'm gonna put you in jail."

Danny flew to Sin City with his amigos. He loved Vegas. With half a million in cash, they lived like Frank Sinatra and the Rat Pack for ten days, throwing Ted Ammon's money around at Caesars Palace. Nothing but the best. Danny was somebody. He and his pals had a great time, eating, drinking, gambling, swimming, catching shows. There were also women, along with the wine and song, but Danny later told his wife that he had courted only Lady Luck, who had not smiled on him. He said that he had lost big time at the tables. But when he called home, he became more and more concerned that Generosa was, indeed, going to try an assisted suicide while he was out of town.

He called Mike Dowd. "What do I do? Do I come home?" Dowd told him to stay a bit longer, until they figured out what was happening.

"Danny, I don't think it would be smart for you to come home. She's really ticked off," said Dowd, referring to

Generosa's anger that Danny was losing so much money gambling.

When he got home, Danny was relieved to see Generosa alive. But she was doped up and drunk and she had burns all over her arms. He didn't know if they were from cigarettes or from the stove or something else. He screamed and cursed at Kaye and blamed her for Generosa's condition.

It was obviously open warfare between Kaye and Danny, with a weak Generosa in the middle. Kaye told Generosa that she had heard from someone in town that Danny was sleeping with some barmaid. Generosa confronted Danny and he swore he wasn't messing around with anybody.

After a year without speaking to her, Generosa called her girlfriend Ronnie for advice. Generosa told her that Danny had not come home the night before and she believed that he was shacked up with a local woman.

"I don't know what to do. He didn't come home," Generosa said. "I'm hearing from people that he's with this girl."

Ronnie was not surprised to hear that Generosa suspected her husband of cheating.

"Generosa, I can't advise you," Ronnie said. "You've got to follow your heart."

Ronnie felt terrible for Generosa's suffering and all her troubles, but, in her heart, she knew that Generosa had killed Ted.

Generosa told several people that her lawyer Gerry Sweeney had told her that money was tight and claimed he would have a problem getting the bank to free up money from Ted's estate—because she was married to Danny, who was the prime suspect in Ted's murder. Already frightened by her terminal illness, she now became frightened that she would die poor. Generosa was sitting in a living room chair dotted with black ovals, burned because she had passed out while smoking, when she told Alexa and Grego that they had very little money and had to cut back.

"There's no money for horseback riding," she told them.

"The bank is not giving me any money, because they think that Danny did it."

But the bank had never told Sweeney that they would withhold payment because Generosa had married Danny. The bank would claim that Sweeney never asked for the money. Sweeney later responded that he did not ask because he believed the request would not be granted.

After consulting with Kaye and the lawyers, Generosa decided to leave the kids, among other things, to Kaye. She told Sweeney that he would have a tough time handling Danny "because he is a handful and Mike Dowd is going to need you to take care of the kids." Generosa wanted Kaye to take care of the twins but she wanted the lawyers to control the money through a trust. Kaye wanted Generosa to move back to East Hampton, where she belonged, and get out of Center Moriches, where she did not. Generosa agreed, even when her children freaked out at the news. Alexa and Grego felt that it was a double horror—they would spend all their time with Kaye, and would be forced to live in the haunted house where their father had been murdered. They immediately began having nightmares about the house, in which the killer was coming after them next. They wanted to stay with Danny and their new friends but their mother paid no attention to their pleas. She had spoken. If Grego didn't like it, they would send him away to boarding school. Generosa always wanted to return to her beloved beach house, her special place, but she did not because everyone was against it as ghoulish, something sure to set the press off again. Now that she was dying, she wanted to end her life inside her best creation. Ted had ended his life there and she would do the same. In the same bedroom. She had finally won her beach house and now she was going to enjoy it. Her kids would just have to get over it. She came first.

Generosa and Danny had a meeting with Generosa's lawyers Mike Dowd and Gerry Sweeney in the city. Danny also had his lawyer Edward Burke, Jr., with him, and Kaye

Mayne was there, at Generosa's insistence. Danny tried to get her out of the room, because of the confidential matters to be discussed, but Generosa would not budge. Wherever she went, Kaye went. It would be Kaye, not Danny or his sister Barbara, who would get custody of Alexa and Grego. Kaye had won. A steaming Danny glared at Kaye and stated his position that an assisted suicide by Generosa would incriminate him.

"I got this sneakin', fuckin' worm, who threatens to call the police on me, okay? You want to call the cops on me, lady? I see your setup. I see what you're doing."

Kaye did not respond.

"Danny . . . ," Generosa interrupted, but Danny turned to her.

"You snap, you black out—you don't even know what you're doin'. I live with it. It's very hard."

"Then move out," Generosa told him.

"No, I won't move out, because I love you, that's the problem."

The lawyers interrupted briefly.

"If you want to move out, you'll move out," Generosa repeated.

"And if that's what you want, that's where I'll go," Danny said.

"At least I'll get a good night's sleep," Generosa said.

"Gen," Danny said. "It's gonna be better. Who's going to put out the fire on the chair, huh?"

"Kaye will stay with me."

There it was. Kaye would replace Danny.

"I see Kaye has done a fantastic job for you, already," Danny said sarcastically. "You say that she's here for you and the kids. She does nothing for your kids. What does she do? She comes over here, she cleans up, she sits down and fills up your head with shit. Me and you have never had a money problem. All of a sudden, you forget what's going on in the real world—everything's a blur and I'm just out, reck-lessly spending your money. Look . . . you bought the boat,

not me. You don't see me traveling around with all these exquisite things. All I've done is what we had to do. Now, I had
the proof . . . I'll call the kettle black. I'll go the extra mile.
Yeah, I spend a million dollars on old gambling debts, all
right? Because you told me to deduct the money."

He argued with Mike Dowd, and Danny returned to his
biggest fear—that Kaye was planning to incriminate him in
the murder.

"Here's the thing, okay?" Danny said to Dowd. "If you
represent Kaye and Kaye comes to you after Generosa
passes and says, 'Look, Mike, Danny told me this,' okay?
This is a problem for me. This is a big problem."

"Boy, you are so wrong. You don't know how wrong you
are . . . ," Dowd began.

"I gotta woman here, who—she wants me out of the box,
all she has to do is make a statement."

Danny addressed Generosa and accused Kaye of fortune
hunting: "I don't trust her. She has turned on you, on Bruce
and Steven. She sits here and talks behind everybody's back.
Evidently, the whole thing has erupted over money. There's
been a lot of money spent, a lot of money, okay? All I
wanted was to make sure these kids are taken care of, from
day one."

Danny pointed out that he had insisted that Generosa
change her original will that left him everything and cut out
the kids.

"So, if anybody thinks I'm here for the money, please
stand up and tell me."

"Nobody's saying that," said Gerry Sweeney.

"Nobody's saying that," echoed Dowd.

Danny noted that he had revived Generosa twice, rather
than let her die from drug overdoses.

"Kaye had come here and she was going to assist her in
suicide," Danny charged.

No one in the room spoke up to disagree with him, so he
continued.

"I threatened Kaye that if I find out that she helped Generosa kill herself, I'll turn her in. I'll be so fuckin' mad I might even kill her. . . . I will not allow her to take her out of this world—and, since that has been said to her, there have been major problems."

"Look, that's a decision your wife makes," Dowd said.

"That's a decision that my wife makes? That I brought back two fuckin' times?"

"Okay," said Dowd. "I guess, what I'm saying is that none of us—except one of us—in this office is facing . . . none of us deals with the pain. I'm not a philosopher, but want to know where I stand? If I decide at a certain point that my quality of life isn't worth it, I'm going. And I'll take whatever means and remedy I have."

Dowd asked Danny to get specific about what was troubling him. Danny repeated his fear that after Generosa died, "Kaye turns around and says that 'Danny Pelosi told me that he murdered Ted Ammon.'"

Dowd pointed out that the police already had a woman who was saying that, the woman who Danny claimed had asked him for money and tried to get money from him because she couldn't pay her car loan.

"So now we have two statements," Danny said.

"Kaye's not going to do that," Generosa said.

"Generosa, Kaye is a liar. I have proof, okay? I'm worried about your kids. Yes, I want research done on Kaye."

Research was a lawyerly phrase Danny had picked up, meaning an investigation by a private eye. He told Generosa that Kaye was two-faced.

"She calls me up and tells me you're dead drunk, you're dead fuckin' drunk, you're a miserable bitch—everything. When you're awake, she turns around and says, 'Generosa's taken a turn for the worse. You should be home.' I'm like, 'You lyin' bitch.' I mean, Gen, she played you like a puppy. That's one thing I don't like, to take advantage of . . . I love you. I will do anything in the world for you. Anything."

"Then why don't you try getting along with Kaye?" Generosa asked.

"Because I don't trust her," Danny said. "She sits here, talking behind everybody's back. I have your children making videos of killing her, of killing this woman. I mean, you gotta see the real picture."

"You're afraid that after Generosa . . ." Dowd began.

"I'm set up, I'm knocked out of the box. Then Kaye has total control, just what she's trying to do, right in front of my face."

"Whatever control she's going to have, she's going to have—whether you're here or not," Dowd said.

The meeting ended where it had begun. Generosa was going to make Kaye the guardian of her children, and Danny could either leave or stay and lump it. He was no longer in the driver's seat.

After he left the meeting, he reached into his jacket pocket and retrieved the tiny, silent digital recorder and checked it. It had recorded every word of the meeting. Danny had started to make recordings of many of his phone calls and conversations, and they were piling up. He wanted to protect himself because he felt that he was being set up to take a fall for the murder.

Danny regretted his earlier decision to plead guilty to his DWI charge. He would receive an eight-month sentence in the county jail but would have to do only four. The good news was that after he got out, Danny would be free of the criminal justice system. He would have paid his debt to society and would not be facing any other charges and would not be on probation or parole. He and Generosa would be free to live anywhere in the world. But the decision had been made before his domestic situation fell apart. The last thing he now wanted to do was to leave his sick wife with Kaye Mayne while he was locked up. It was too late to change. As his sentencing date approached, Danny not only felt that he had made the wrong decision, he claimed that he had been maneuvered into it by Mike Dowd, who had convinced him that it was the best thing to do. Danny suspected that Dowd had been working against him all along. People were choosing up sides: Generosa, her lawyers, and Kaye on one side, Danny and the kids on the other.

In February 2003, Generosa went to Riverhead with her lawyers and Kaye to ask the surrogate court judge John Czygier, Jr., to appoint Kaye as the standby guardian for Alexa and Grego. Danny was totally against it and did not attend. Somehow, a *New York Post* reporter had learned about the proceeding and was sitting in the courtroom as the cordial, smiling Kaye and the silent, emaciated Generosa entered with the lawyers, who immediately asked the judge to close the courtroom. The judge held a brief hearing in which the *Post* reporter and the *Post* lawyers argued by phone that public proceedings should not be closed to the public or the press. The judge decided to close the hearing. Once the reporter was excluded, the courtroom doors were closed and Gerry Sweeney called Generosa to the stand. In a weak, raspy voice, she discussed her terminal illness and denied that the cancer had reached her brain. She seemed lucid and rational, if fragile. Kaye, she said, would "carry out my wishes—morally, spiritually, educationally, and practically." She said that they had become very close and understood each other and what the other would do in a crisis.

"What should I call you?" Judge Czygier asked. "Ms. Ammon or Ms. Pelosi?"

"You can call me Generosa," she said with a charming smile.

When the judge asked, Generosa also denied that she had any close relatives. She claimed that her kids did not have a close relationship with Ted's sister Sandi, other than to visit "once a year, and it wasn't even that. Once every eighteen months." She did not mention Sandi's daughters, who lived in Manhattan and saw them much more frequently.

"But since my husband decided upon the divorce three years ago, my sister-in-law did have interaction." She said that this was "not in the same universe" as the closeness

Kaye had with the twins; she was one of the family. She did not mention the kids' strong dislike of Kaye.

"Sandi and I have opposite views on how to raise kids but Kaye shares my philosophy," Generosa told Czygier.

Generosa said that it was shocking how well the children were doing, considering how much they had been through.

"Kaye understands our particular type of normalcy," Generosa explained.

Kaye then took the stand and explained that she took care of Generosa and paid the bills and took care of the kids. She did not mention Luke Johnson or his family. The judge asked whether she could be responsible for the person and the property of the children.

"As I understand it, the lawyers will be responsible for the property of the kids," Kaye replied.

Judge Czygier determined that Generosa was competent to make arrangements for her children and appointed Kaye Mayne as their standby guardian. He sealed the court record and transcript, saying that it would be detrimental to the kids if information about them, or about their mother's medical condition, was released to the public. A photographer shot Generosa leaving court with Kaye and the lawyers. They had no comment. The next day, the headline of the story was shocking:

DYING REQUEST
AMMON WIDOW THINKS OF KIDS
AS HUBBY FACES JAIL

One evening, while Danny was napping on the couch in the living room, Generosa, high as a kite, glared at his sleeping form and began acting strange. She slinked into the kitchen and picked up Buddy's large, heavy ceramic water dish. It weighed perhaps five pounds and was hard as a rock. She tiptoed back into the living room and raised it high over her head, some of the water slopping over the side as she brought it over Danny's head. When she reached the couch, another hand blocked the downward arc of the bowl and pushed it aside. The heavy bowl flipped in midair, spraying Danny with water on the way down. The bowl bumped off the couch and banged onto the floor. Danny sat up with a start, wet, wondering what the thump had been. He saw Generosa standing over him with a mad look in her eyes.

"Ted, you fucking scumbag!" Generosa wailed, talking to Ted's ghost again.

Kaye told Danny how Generosa had tried to hit him on the head with the dog's bowl while he was asleep, how she had seen it and was able to knock the unusual weapon aside at the last second. It would have fractured his skull. Kaye had stopped Generosa from killing him. She had saved his life.

Generosa, while high in a fog of pills, booze, and free-floating murderous rage, had tried to bash her sleeping husband over the head with a blunt object.

38

POWERLESS

Danny slipped on his leather jacket. Generosa reached up from her chair to him before he stepped out into the cold February sunshine to go to jail.

"Give me a kiss goodbye, because you're never seeing me again," she told him.

He, along with his lawyer Eddie Burke, was going to court in Riverhead, where Danny would be sentenced and sent directly to jail for four months.

"You know what? I'm not gonna kiss you," Danny told Generosa. "You promised me you would give me a kiss goodbye before you did something stupid."

It was Danny's way of trying to keep Generosa alive until he got out of jail.

Danny went to court with his dead brother Jim's badge clipped to the inside pocket of his jacket. On the outside, he had pinned the gold numbers from his brother's uniform that denoted his precinct: 113. With Danny were his elder brother Robert, his sister Barbara, and two friends. Burke asked the judge to delay the sentencing because of Generosa's illness. The judge refused but said he would allow "a short grace period" if Generosa went downhill suddenly.

Once the four-month sentence was handed down, Danny put his hands behind his back and a court officer clicked a

pair of handcuffs onto his wrists. He was led away to a
holding cell and later was walked through a tunnel from the
court building to the adjacent county jail. He turned in his
personal effects and clothes and was issued a pair of lace-
less sneakers and a dark green prison shirt and pants. When
they took his mug shots, front and side, Danny looked quite
angry. He was certainly unhappy about the situation he had
left behind in Center Moriches—Kaye having total control
of Generosa for four months. Prison is not a nice place. No
one wants to go to jail, especially anyone who smokes and
drinks. The Suffolk County Jail was a smoke-free facility
and Danny would not be able to light up or have a drink for
four months. He was already undergoing instant cold
turkey.

Danny was also concerned that police might plant an undercover cop inside, to try to worm a confession out of him,
or that an inmate looking to get out from under would invent
a confession to get out of jail. He also wondered what the
homicide squad was doing out in the world while he was
locked up. Danny, who had been behind bars before, got
along well with most other inmates because he walked the
walk and talked the talk. He had that "I'm okay, you're okay,
but don't fuck with me" attitude that cons respected. He was
a funny guy and a celebrity, so his problems were few.

When a friendly guy was thrown in jail with Danny,
claiming to have been arrested for DWI—just like Danny—
Danny became suspicious. He thought that the guy was a
plant, an undercover cop trying to trap him. He became convinced that a tape recorder was hidden in an air vent behind
the cells, and he was sure that the correction officers would
service the recorder at night and change the tape when the
inmates were locked in.

Danny was able to negotiate for a lot of phone time on the
collect-only, one-way phone in the "pod" of cells. He spoke
to his lawyers but spent most of his phone time talking to
Generosa. He was on the line with her for several hours each
day. After his calls, Danny went back to his small, elongated

cell, which had tan cinder-block walls, a bed platform with a
mattress, a stainless steel sink/toilet combo, and a thin, vertical, sealed window with a partial view of the pine woods
surrounding the lockup. Slowly, as the days passed, the winter sun crept north above the trees.

With Danny locked up, homicide detectives kicked their investigation into high gear. They targeted those around
Danny whom they suspected of involvement or who might
be witnesses. The first step was to find a reason to take them
all into custody. The next step was to round them up, turn up
the heat—and see who cracked.

On Friday, April 4, Danny's ex-wife, Tami, left her
Manorville home at eight-thirty in the morning, as usual, on
her way to work as the director of a preschool center. When
she merged onto the Long Island Expressway, a marked Suffolk County police car pulled up behind her with the lights
flashing and the officer signaled her to pull over. When she
parked on the shoulder, the officer approached and asked her
to stand behind her car. The cop told her that he had stopped
her because she had failed to signal when changing lanes.
She denied it and handed over her license, registration, and
insurance card. The officer went into his vehicle and then
emerged. As Tami later claimed in a lawsuit against the police, he informed Tami that there was a warrant for her arrest. She was stunned and asked what the charge was. The
officer said that he did not know and that she was under arrest. He pulled out a pair of handcuffs and ordered her to put
her hands behind her back. Tami began crying and protest-
ing her innocence. She told the cop that she would not be
handcuffed. He told her that if she did not allow it, she
would also be charged with resisting arrest. He slapped the
cuffs on, and put her in the back of his patrol car. He drove
her to the Seventh Precinct in Yaphank. In an interrogation
room, he undid the cuffs and then recuffed her with her
hands in front. He left her there. Later, he returned and told

her that she was being arrested for felony theft of services.

"What does that mean?" she asked.

"I don't know."

After a few minutes, two homicide squad detectives walked in, showed Tami some paperwork, and told her that the charge was for theft of electrical power from the Long Island Power Authority, LIPA. It was about Danny bypassing the electrical meter at the Manorville house, which he had done years earlier. Tami recognized one of the detectives because he had interviewed her twice after the Ammon murder. They began questioning her about the case again, asking her who had killed Ted Ammon.

"I have no idea," she said.

The detective she knew slammed the table with his hand.

"You know what happened!" the detective yelled, saying that she had better tell what she knew.

Tami claimed to know nothing about the killing—not even when Ammon had been killed.

"Your son Anthony's birthday, October twenty-first!" the detective yelled back.

The other detective, in a classic good-cop, bad-cop play, asked the yelling detective to leave the room.

"I am not going to smack you," the good detective told her. "We are the good guys. We're just trying to do our job. If you want a get-out-of-jail card, tell us what you know."

Tami, still crying, repeated that she had nothing to tell. They let her call her job but cautioned her not to mention anything about the murder interrogation. When Tami's mother arrived at the precinct to help her daughter, she too, was questioned about the homicide. Tami asked for her lawyer. The detectives took her to another precinct for processing on the power-stealing charge. There she collapsed and had a panic attack, sobbing and gasping for breath. She was hysterical. She was fingerprinted and photographed. After paying the fifty-dollar stationhouse bail, she was given a desk-appearance ticket to return to court at a later date and then released.

• • •

The next morning, Danny's friend Chris Parrino claimed he was surrounded by police as he drove away from his home. Some of the cops had their guns drawn. Chris would be the first of four men taken into custody by detectives that morning.

"Get on the ground!" they shouted, as he opened his door.

The thirty-five-year-old carpenter was swiftly cuffed and driven away. Inside the car, when he asked what he was under arrest for, an officer told him:

"Murder."

"Who did I murder?"

Parrino was driven to police headquarters in Yaphank and grilled about the Ammon homicide.

"We have you all," one detective told him.

Danny, he was told, had "blabbed" about the killing in jail. It was not true, but the Supreme Court has ruled that detectives are allowed to lie to murder suspects.

"Your life is over," one detective told Parrino.

Chris repeatedly denied any involvement in the murder and gave a written statement to the detectives. After also questioning Chris's fiancée and getting a signed statement from her, Parrino was released on five hundred dollars' bail for an alleged DWI charge.

At the same time as Parrino was busted, Danny's forty-year-old cousin Frank Perrone, a plumber, also claimed he was rounded up in similar fashion, surrounded by cops with guns drawn.

"What's going on?" Frank demanded.

"You know what you did," he was told.

He had been "ratted out" by a relative, a detective claimed. Soon, he was told he was charged with killing Ted Ammon and was facing twenty-five years to life—or even the death penalty. But, after questioning, he and his wife signed statements and Frank too, was released.

Danny's pal Alex Mawyer, a forty-year-old electrical worker, also alleged he was arrested at gunpoint while driving that morning and interrogated for eleven hours. Alex was told that police had a signed statement from Danny's sister Barbara that said Alex had been captured on the video system at the beach house—peeking in at Ted Ammon on the weekend of the murder. Alex believed that Barbara had never told anyone such a story. He loudly and angrily denied that he had been there or had anything to do with the crime and protested his innocence. He too, signed a statement and left.

Danny's friend Arnie Cherubino, a fifty-two-year-old real estate agent, was the last to be rounded up in the full-court press, also while he was driving. When he asked why he was under arrest, he was accused of receiving bloody clothing from Danny and using his boat to dump the incriminating items at sea. Arnie denied the charge. He was also under suspicion, he was informed, for having gotten rid of other things for Danny. Arnie said that, long before the murder, he had sold a ring and a bracelet for Danny, at Danny's request—but it had nothing to do with Ammon's death. He too, signed a statement and was released.

No one had cracked, broken down and confessed to being part of the murder plot. It appeared that the full-court press by the police had failed. But Danny's lawyers did not have copies of all the statements signed by the four arrested people, or of two other statements by a fiancée and a wife. What was in those statements? The detectives were certainly not gathering written statements for their amusement. It may have been an attempt at a "lock-in," in which detectives lock up the alibis of the suspects by documenting the times at which certain people were in certain locations—and with whom. If any of the statements conflicted, especially with Danny's alibi, would it be enough to present to a grand jury? Danny's lawyers needed to see those statements. They made a federal case out of it.

The following month, Generosa's former lawyer Mike Shaw filed an $8 million federal violation-of-civil-rights lawsuit on behalf of Tami and the four men who had been grabbed and grilled. The suit claimed that they had been ar-

rested under false pretenses and illegally questioned, despite
the fact that they had demanded to speak to their lawyers.
The lawsuit also claimed that threats and intimidation were
used and that some detectives roughed up two of the men. As
part of the federal civil case, of course, lawyers for those
who claimed that their rights had been violated would request copies of any and all statements taken. If and when
that happened, Danny and his lawyers would find out if any
surprises awaited them.

In Center Moriches, Joanne saw Generosa taking increasing
amounts of morphine for her pain, along with vodka and
scotch. She confronted Kaye about it.

"What are you doing?" Joanne demanded. "Why are you
letting her have liquor like this? She's taking morphine and
all kinds of pills. Does the doctor know this?"

"Oh, what's the difference?" Joanne later claimed that
Kaye replied. "She's going to die anyway. She's in pain, so
what's the difference if she has a few drinks?"

"But she could die."

One June morning, Joanne walked into the house and saw
Kaye dragging a limp and unconscious Generosa off the
floor, trying to get her onto the couch. Generosa was zonked.
What the hell is going on? Joanne wondered. Kaye ordered
her to leave. Joanne did as she was told but was very upset.

Alexa and Grego were spending most of their time with
Luke Johnson and his family. They were still having nightmares because they knew that, once school ended, they
would have to go back to the beach house where their father
had been killed. Grego said he was also frightened of Kaye
because she sometimes told him creepy things that scared
him. Once, he said, she described in bloody detail how she
would club live sheep over the head and then use a knife to
gut and skin them. Another time, Grego said, she claimed to
have had a violent dream about the boy:

"Grego, I had a dream last night. I dreamt that you had a

lot of money and you bought yourself a fast, red sports car and you crashed it into a tree and killed yourself."

"I hate her. I can't stand her," Grego told Luke.

Luke ran errands, including renting videos that Kaye told him to rent. Most of them were murder movies, including films about women who killed their husbands.

"My mother and Kaye are watching this stuff," Grego told Luke.

A few weeks before Danny was to get out of jail, Kaye stopped at Luke's house and walked into the kitchen, where Luke was sitting with his mother and his daughter.

"Well, Generosa's getting very sick," Kaye said. "I don't think she's going to make it through the night. If she dies in the house, I'm going to need you . . . to carry the body and put it in the car, so I can drive it in to her doctor's in the city."

Luke and his mother were flabbergasted. They could not believe what they were hearing. Luke felt Kaye was asking him to enlist another husky friend and become body snatchers.

"First of all, I think that's illegal," said Luke.

"Yes, it's illegal," Luke's mother agreed. "That's ridiculous."

Kaye pressed him but he balked.

"No, I can't do that."

He asked her why she wanted him to do it.

"I don't want the press to get wind of it," said Kaye.

"That's unethical," said Luke's mother.

"What happens if you get pulled over?" Luke asked.

"I'll worry about that," Kaye said.

"No way," Luke said.

After trying for several minutes to persuade Luke to do what she wanted, Kaye gave up and left.

"Please don't get involved with that woman," Luke's mother warned. "She's not exactly Mary Poppins."

Later, after thinking about it, Luke became more and more angry and called Kaye.

"Look, I quit. I'm here to help the kids. I'm not here to move bodies. It's getting too far out of line," he said.

But Kaye was conciliatory and asked him not to quit but just to keep on caring for the kids. She told him that she would take care of what they had discussed.

"You don't have to worry about that. I'll do the rest."

As Danny's release date Friday, June 13, approached, his lawyers told him that they expected a grand jury to be impaneled soon to look into the Ammon murder. The story broke in the papers:

AMMON PROBE AT LAST

Danny was confident that he would be acquitted of any possible murder charges but his lawyers told him that he would likely be held without bail if he was indicted in the case. That meant that he would be hauled back to rot inside the same jail he had been in—not for four months but for a year or even two—while awaiting trial. Then his lawyers gave him more bad news. Friday the thirteenth would be unlucky for him. He wasn't going to walk out of jail and be free of the criminal justice system after all. Detectives were set to arrest him on a felony theft-of-services charge—for the electric meter bypassing they had used to question Tami. They were keeping him on the hook. Danny freaked out. Like his ex-wife, he had a panic attack and perhaps something more. When the detectives from the Suffolk County D.A.'s office arrived at the jail on Friday to bust him, one of his eyes was partially closed. He thought he was having a stroke. A small group of press had gathered outside the jail to film his release. They filmed his arrest instead. Danny was cuffed and placed in a car. As the car left the jail, Danny lay down on the backseat to avoid having his picture taken by the scurrying photographers and TV crews. Later, at his arraignment, his lawyer, Eddie Burke, cried foul:

"I think the timing speaks volumes," said Burke, who made it clear that he believed Danny had been selectively targeted only because of the murder investigation. At the arraignment, the judge released Danny on ten thousand dollars' bail, took away his passport, and ordered him not to leave the state.

When he got home to Center Moriches, he hardly recognized Generosa. She was more gaunt and doped up.

There were other changes too, particularly having to do with her attitude toward him. Danny had told Generosa that he did not want to move back to the beach house in East Hampton. Now he was not invited. Generosa said that her lawyers had told her and Danny that she would never get her millions unless she separated herself from Danny, financially or otherwise. Before he went to jail, Danny's lawyers and Generosa's lawyers had been working together under a joint defense agreement. Now, it appeared, there were two different sides, as Danny had feared. He was convinced that they were trying to separate him from Generosa and the money.

That month, a special grand jury was sworn in inside a Riverhead courtroom and began hearing witnesses and evidence in the murder of Ted Ammon.

Prosecutors contacted Mike Dowd and offered the dying Generosa immunity from prosecution if she would testify before the grand jury.

"They're offering you immunity because you're dying," Danny told her. "They're on my ass. If you go in there and tell them we had nothing to do with it . . ."

"They'll never get off your ass," Dowd told Danny. "If she goes in there, they'll come after both of you."

Generosa never appeared before the grand jury. Instead, she made plans to move back to East Hampton. She had ordered workmen to begin planting a row of hemlock trees in front of the beach house. The mansion would no longer be visible from Middle Lane by the time Generosa and the kids moved in—in less than two weeks. They would also construct an automatic gate to keep out strangers—and the press. Generosa was preparing to burrow in at the beach house, without Danny.

39

RETURN TO MIDDLE LANE

Danny was convinced that the cancer was eating at his wife's brain. Generosa, he believed, was out of her mind from the disease and the drugs and drinking and had been turned against him. They would not get a divorce but it was certainly a separation, although he would deny that to others. In a rare moment alone, he told her that he loved her and asked her why she was moving away from him.

"Why?" he asked.

"You were only in it for the money," Generosa replied.

That removed any doubts in Danny's mind that Kaye and the lawyers had poisoned his marriage and Generosa's mind, in a struggle for her wealth. He did not believe that it was due to his gambling or his alleged womanizing, which he denied.

On July 1, 2003, Danny went with his lawyer Eddie Burke to Gerry Sweeney's office in Queens, to discuss Sweeney's suggestion that Danny agree to a postnuptial agreement as a way of placating the bank that was the coexecutor of Ted's estate. When they got there, Mike Dowd was with Sweeney, who said that Danny would get $2 million for a defense fund if he signed. When asked why the proposed agreement had a quitclaim provision stating that Danny was not entitled to any of Generosa's estate once he got his $2 million, Sweeney said that it was just a formality and that Danny was well taken care of in Generosa's will. Burke did not want him to sign and Danny agreed. But Danny feared that he would be arrested any day, and he wanted a defense fund so that he could not be locked up by an arrest or a lawsuit. Dowd told Danny that if he did not sign the postnup, he would be indicted, defended at trial by a free legal-aid attorney fresh out of law school, and would spend the rest of his life in prison for a crime that he did not commit. Still, Danny refused to sign.

Danny suspected that Generosa was preparing a new will but the lawyers would not let him have a copy. He wondered aloud if Gerry would get anything in the new will.

"Danny, if that will says, 'Gerry gets it all,' you can have my law license," Gerry said, with a laugh.

"Gerry, if that will says you get it all, I'll put a hit on you," said Danny, with a bigger laugh.

But when Danny would not yield, Sweeney became irate and a loud argument ensued. Danny walked out to get some air, but he soon returned. When he came back in, Sweeney was on the phone with Generosa, explaining that Danny had refused the agreement. He handed Danny the phone.

"I love you—that's why I won't sign it," Danny told her. "Gen, this doesn't mean we're not married, does it?"

"Danny, we're not divorced. Our money is divorced. I'm done sharing money with you," said Generosa. "Don't think you're just going to show up in East Hampton unannounced. If you need to see me, you call and make an appointment."

Generosa began crying and told Danny that he should trust Gerry and Mike and sign the postnup.

"They're only trying to help us," she cried.

Danny signed the agreement and walked out of Sweeney's office. Mike followed and asked to speak to Danny alone. They went into Dowd's car, where they spoke for an hour. After the private chat, Dowd took Danny and his lawyer out to dinner.

The next day, on a hot and humid afternoon, all of the

lawyers descended on the Center Moriches house. Generosa, her eyes glassy and bloodshot, was slumped in a dining room chair, staring blankly into space. She did not greet Burke or even acknowledge his presence when he arrived.

Outside, Alexa and Grego had been told by Kaye to get into Danny's sister Barbara's car for the drive back to East Hampton. They were resisting, looking to Danny to prevent their return. He moved to hug and kiss the kids goodbye, but Kaye pulled them away. She ushered them to Barbara, who drove them away to the last place on earth they wanted to go—the beach house.

"You stay away from these children, because I'm their guardian and you're *Nothing!*" Kaye screamed at Danny.

She was in Danny's face. Danny felt as if she were daring him to lose his temper and strike her, but he just stood there. He knew that he couldn't do a thing. If he was arrested for assault he would go right back to jail.

"You telling me I can't say goodbye to these kids?"

"You stay away from them! I am the guardian of these children. *You are Nothing!*"

Her tone made it obvious to observers that she didn't mean just that Danny had no authority and was no relation to the twins—he was nothing as a human being. Kaye strode to her car, a Nissan that Generosa had bought for her. As she drove by, she rolled down her window and, with a nasty smile, sarcastically said goodbye to Danny—using the term of endearment Generosa reserved for him.

"Goodbye, sweetie," Kaye intoned, with a grin of triumph.

Perhaps she was smiling because she already knew that she would receive a million dollars and the right to live in the East Hampton mansion for the rest of her life as soon as Generosa died.

Danny stood there, beaten, burning with fury and frustration, and then went into the house. In the dining room, Sweeney put the postnuptial agreement in front of Generosa and asked her to sign and she did, in a weak, illegible scrawl. Then she signed the house she was in over to

Danny. Dowd then asked Danny and Burke to leave for a while so that they could have a conference with Generosa in private. Sweeney shook Burke's hand at the door and assured him again that Danny was taken care of in Generosa's will.

He was—at least for a few more minutes. Sweeney and Dowd then presented a new will to Generosa and she signed it in her shaky hand. Danny was not even mentioned in the new document. He was cut completely out of Generosa's new will. Dowd later said he never read the new will and Sweeney was prevented from revealing its contents by attorney-client confidentiality.

Dowd felt that Danny had been harassing Generosa with demands for money and frightening her with the possibility that she might be arrested. He had spent millions of dollars of her money and brought unwanted attention and publicity. She wanted peace and quiet, not the circus that Danny always created around him. Two million dollars was not a bad day's pay for an out-of-work electrician, Dowd thought.

Generosa slept that night in the bedroom where Ted had been killed. The room had been painted, the blood-soaked bed had been replaced with a new one, as had her carpeting; but it looked eerily the same. Generosa was home to stay.

The thirteen-year-old twins returned to 59 Middle Lane, where they had so many wonderful memories. The big blue marlin was still on the wall in Grego's room but it would never be the same. Alexa was terrified of the house, as if it were haunted. She ran up to her room and retreated into her white, built-in four-poster, which was covered with her stuffed animals. She wouldn't go near the other end of the house, where her father had been killed. She tried to look ahead and hope that maybe, someday, things would go right. If they ever did, she would be thankful.

When Grego mentioned that he missed Danny, Kaye smirked.

"You'll never be with Danny," said Kaye. "He's no good.

He's a convict. If he comes to this house, I will have him arrested immediately if he steps foot on this property."

Now it was Kaye who was feeling proprietary about an Ammon mansion and estate, not Danny. Kaye later reminded Generosa that it was either her or Danny:

"If you let him into this house, I'll leave," Kaye threatened. "I'll go back to my apartment."

Alexa and Grego stayed away from the safe room, where the tea party things were still laid out and dusty. Nearby, behind the triangular wall panel, the second Rapid Eye concealed surveillance system, installed after the murder and reactivated at Danny's secret behest, quietly hummed away, recording everything they were doing in the house. Again, Danny was watching.

Because of the move, Luke was concerned. When he was at the beach house, he told Generosa that he considered Alexa and Grego part of his family and that they felt the same way. He asked her not to break that bond.

"No, no no," said Generosa. "I won't do that. You are a lifesaver to those kids."

But a few days later, when Luke's daughter Babe went with him to visit Alexa, Babe gave Generosa her usual kiss on the cheek and a hug—but got a nasty reaction.

"So, what are you doing here?" Generosa snapped. "You're not staying, are you?"

Babe ran from the house in tears. Luke was upset and started to remind Generosa of her promise not to cut the kids off from his family.

"Generosa, you told me . . ."

"I think it's time that Kaye and the kids try and get it together," Generosa said, dismissing him.

Later, Generosa regretted snapping at Babe. Luke and his kids were heartbroken. Alexa and Grego had again lost people they loved and Grego was about to be sent into exile, a boarding school in New England, after he had threatened to run away or commit suicide if he was forced to live in that house. It would be the first time in their lives that the twins would be separated. They were told that, once Grego went to school in September, they would not be able to talk to each other, except on holidays.

Meanwhile, Kaye was wearing down under the burden of caring for her sick mistress, who demanded constant attention and had become crankier since she left Danny behind. Generosa, stuck on her couch in her bedclothes, made more and more demands on Kaye. The dying woman vented and was unapologetic.

"I want a Slurpee," Generosa told Kaye late one evening.

Every night, the gourmet Generosa would demand a Slurpee, a sweet icy slush drink of bright colors from a local convenience store. Kaye got her car keys and drove to the store. She bought the colorful concoction and rushed it back to the mansion. Kaye presented the drink, along with a straw, to Generosa, who did not thank her. She also did not take one sip. It was not the first time she had sent Kaye out on a fool's errand, like a petulant child.

"I can't do this anymore," Kaye complained to Joanne one morning. "I'm sick and tired of this. Generosa's ordering me around."

Joanne noticed that Generosa was not on the couch. She had not come downstairs.

"Where's Generosa?" Joanne asked.

"Oh, she had a bad night, she's not coming down," Kaye said.

In Riverhead that month, the grand jury subpoenaed the laptop computer that had been given to Generosa's lawyer. Mike Dowd turned over what he said was a copy of the hard drive of that computer—but not the computer itself. Dowd was also subpoenaed to testify but, once on the stand, he refused to say who had given him the laptop and to whom he had given it in the month after the murder. He said that he was a lawyer and testifying about it would violate attorney-client confidentiality.

Prosecutor Janet Albertson filed papers that contended

the laptop was not covered by the lawyer-client privilege because it had accessed the Rapid Eye system on the weekend of the murder, including on Sunday, the day before Ammon's body was discovered, and was critical to the investigation because it could have been used to shut down the cameras before the killing. An examination of the original laptop hard drive might contain records of that activity, the prosecutor claimed.

The judge agreed with Albertson and ordered Dowd back before the grand jury, saying that the circumstances "suggest that the laptop was involved in the commission of the crime and was, in fact, an instrumentality of that crime."

Dowd was forced to testify that Danny had turned over the laptop after the murder. Dowd said that it had been sent out to have the hard drive copied, and then he had given it to Generosa. The laptop, he said, was destroyed in the fire at Coverwood. The grand jury continued its deliberations but it seemed that the original evidence it needed to determine who had done what with the surveillance system before, during, and after Ted's murder, was no longer available. Was the fire an accident, or a deliberate destruction of evidence?

Danny wanted to go to the beach house to see his wife but his lawyers warned him that if he went onto the property, Kaye would have an excuse to call the police and he might end up back in jail. He called the beach house and pleaded with Generosa not to let Kaye raise Alexa and Grego.

"I'm very concerned for your children. It's not good. It's not good at all," Danny told her.

"Danny, you seem to forget—I'm still alive. These are my children. I make the decisions about my children."

"They lost their father, now they're losing their mother. I'm not gonna allow the children to be raised like you were—I'm not."

"Danny, you and I disagree on how to raise children. I'm not raising my children like you raise your children. Kaye carries out my wishes with my children. Period."

Danny called Generosa again when he turned forty, on August 3. She wished her estranged husband a happy birthday.

"I'm in Center Moriches. Can I come out?" Danny asked.

"No, don't," Generosa answered. "She'll call the police on you and you'll get in trouble."

"I'm all alone," Danny said.

They talked a bit more and she mentioned that after she was dead she wanted to be cremated and have her ashes scattered on one of her favorite flower beds—her bloodred poppies. She also suggested a sentimental journey back to the Stanhope hotel, once she was gone.

"When it's all done, Danny, let's go back to where we started. We'll have a drink and we'll say goodbye."

She reiterated her intention to bid him farewell before she died.

"I'll kiss you goodbye," Generosa promised.

Later, Danny tried calling again but couldn't get through to Generosa. He suspected that Kaye, who had a cell phone, had simply unplugged the house phone. He could not believe that Generosa, despite what she had done and said to him, would not want to talk to him.

40

MORE SPIES AND PRIVATE EYES

Sandi was shocked when she read that Generosa was dying. She tried to call her and wrote a letter to her but her former sister-in-law treated her calls and letter the same way she had treated Ted's calls and the calls and letter of her doctor—she ignored them. Sandi had repeatedly tried to contact Alexa and Grego in the two years after Ted was murdered. She sent them birthday presents on their twelfth and thirteenth birthdays, as well as Christmas presents and letters. Generosa had them all sent back—no such person at that address—or threw them away. As far as the kids knew, their aunt Sandi and uncle Bob didn't care anything about them, and never thought about them. Their mother's stories were true, they concluded. The last thing Generosa wanted was for them to renew their relationship with Sandi and Bob— because Sandi was the greatest threat to Generosa's custody of the children.

In her latest last will and testament, Generosa had set up the Ammon Foundation, which ostensibly was dedicated to good works in Ted's name, but was actually dedicated to opposing all things connected with the name Ammon, according to a lawsuit later filed by Sandi and her husband, Bob. The foundation was run by Mike Dowd and Gerry Sweeney, cotrustees who were also coexecutors of the estate. They would profit from both positions and control Ted Ammon's fortune until his children were fifty years old, a rather extraordinary arrangement. Generosa, who still wrapped herself in hate like a blanket, had left instructions that her estate could spend whatever amount of money it took to deny custody of Alexa and Grego to Sandi and Bob. It was Generosa's prime directive.

When Sandi read that Generosa had made the most-recent nanny the permanent guardian of her children and was going to drag them back into the murder house, Ted's sister knew what she had to do. She retained well-known Long Island family law attorney Steven Gassman and his associate Richard Tannenbaum, who advised her to seek custody of the twins. By the time they were prepared to file suit, the news about Generosa's health had appeared in a newspaper story. It was unfortunate, but Sandi had to proceed. The children had been through so much emotional pain and loss and parental conflict and were still going through it. She had to do something.

Exhibit A in Sandi's court papers, filed in May 2003, was the psychologist's report that had concluded that Generosa was mentally ill and was a bad mother. The report said that Generosa suffered from a "paranoid world view, in which malevolent motives are attributed to others, including her own children, and reads hidden, denigrating meaning into benign remarks." It also cited her "intense hatred of Ted Ammon, her sense of entitlement, impulsiveness, self-absorption, excessive demands for loyalty from her children and others, paranoid ideation and failures in empathy." The psychologist also said that Generosa had delusional beliefs and he detailed numerous incidents in which she had berated or emotionally abused her kids.

"Should it come to pass that their own mother participated in the murder, the psychological impact on these poor, young children will require intense and careful psychological attention," Sandi said in her court papers, noting that she believed the twins had never received appropriate psychological care.

The suit also contended that the children's family was a better place for them than with a servant. Sandi said that Generosa had made a nanny the guardian simply to keep the children away from the only family they'd ever had. The papers also claimed that Danny was an unfit stepfather due to his lengthy criminal record, jail sentences, and drinking. And Sandi asked the court to consider the fact that Generosa and Danny were still suspects in Ted's murder. A final argument was that Generosa was suffering from terminal cancer and was incapacitated and unable to care for Alexa and Grego. In the legal action, filed with one judge and then moved to surrogate court, Sandi made it clear that all she and her husband wanted to do was love Alexa and Grego and raise them in their family. They did not want a dime. She pointed out that she and Bob had come to court but that Generosa and Kaye had not. Sandi said that she and her husband would not just blindly follow a script while raising Alexa and Grego—they would "make fundamental decisions concerning their lives, based on their own best interests, not to simply carry out another person's 'wishes and commands,' or to pursue a financial agenda." The twins, she said, "are deeply in need of the unconditional love and stable two-parent home my husband and I will provide." Sandi said that Generosa had lied when she claimed that she and Bob saw them only rarely.

"This is an outrageous and deceptive statement meant to falsely suggest to the court that we were only distant relatives," Sandi said, noting that Generosa had failed to mention her actions during the divorce, including her "recruiting the children to assist in her demented plots against Ted."

"Grego and Alexa were a wonderful addition to our family and have been living a nightmare that no children should have to experience. We ache for them and Bob and I want so much to raise them as our children. Family was so important to Ted and, under the circumstances, this is what my brother would have wanted for his children."

Mike Dowd's response to the lawsuit was to accuse Sandi of greed, of trying to grab the money and the kids while Generosa was sick.

"For shame," he scolded.

He was very angry that the shrink's report had been made public because it was attached to legal papers. He claimed that it was illegal and unethical that the report had made its way somehow from the psychologist and the sealed and moot original divorce and custody case file and had ended up with Sandi. He called for it to be thrown out of the case. He demanded an investigation and vowed that heads would roll and lawyers might lose their licenses if they had leaked it improperly. What he refused to do was address or discuss the diagnosis and observations in the psychological report that nuked his client.

There is a phrase taught in law school that, if you have the law on your side, pound the law. If you have the facts on your side, pound the facts. If neither the law nor the facts are on your side—pound the podium.

Sandi's lawyers asked the judge to seize the children's passports, to forestall any possible move to England or elsewhere. The judge agreed and the passports were secured in Gerry Sweeney's safe in his Queens law office. But legal cases move very slowly and it would be many months before anything at all happened.

Kaye Mayne, talking to a friend in England by phone, complained about her problems taking care of the failing Generosa and dealing with Danny and other hassles but said that she intended to tough it out—because of the $1 million bequest and the "life estate" provisions in Generosa's will, which would put her in the lap of luxury for the rest of her life.

"I have to put up with a lot of shit in America because there's a lot of infighting in the family, but I'm determined to stay because I'll get a decent pension," said Kaye.

Danny's sister Barbara, who had been paid for writing

checks, paying bills, watching Ted on the laptop computer, and helping to run Generosa's affairs, was in an awkward spot, now that her sister-in-law had broken with Danny. Generosa suddenly accused her of stealing from her, an obvious pretext, and fired her. Barbara was the last remnant of the Danny contingent to be purged. Or so Kaye and Generosa thought.

But while Kaye and Generosa were comfortably ensconced in the fortress beach house, Danny was working behind the scenes to penetrate security. Danny, it turned out, had a flair for intrigue.

After the murder, a second Rapid Eye main unit had been purchased and installed to help Generosa and Danny's private detectives in their investigation. It was still running twenty-four hours a day, with Danny watching. Now it was Generosa, not Ted, who was being spied on by the secret video system.

When Generosa took her pain pills, the hidden camera in the living room recorded the moment. As she and Kaye and the twins ate meals and watched television, other cameras recorded the images. This time, Danny was the one who was watching, remotely, and Generosa was the one under surveillance.

Joanne, the housekeeper, was secretly sympathetic to Danny and began giving him daily reports of life at 59 Middle Lane. He persuaded her also to wear a hidden recorder and Joanne began surreptitiously taping her conversations at the beach house.

Danny also quickly arranged to slip cell phones to Alexa and Grego and they began speaking secretly to him every day, something that made them very happy. Of course, neither Generosa nor Kaye knew that Danny had infiltrated their world. Between the live video, Joanne's intelligence, and the surreptitious calls from the kids, Danny knew more about what was going on at the beach house than Generosa did.

The spy kids were now working for Danny.

41

HOUSE CALLS

Danny indiscreetly spoke to someone about watching Generosa and Kaye on the hidden video system at the beach house. The word got back to Kaye, who quickly called John Kundle to rip out the system once and for all. She also had him change the burglar alarm codes and tighten up the anti-intrusion system at the beach house. Kaye also requested other security measures to protect her because she was afraid of Danny and feared for her life.

Joanne arrived at the beach house at eight on a sunny August morning. Generosa was not downstairs. Kaye was up with her. Grego was out somewhere with friends but Alexa was in the house. Joanne started cleaning. A half hour later, she saw a silver car come down the driveway. Mike Dowd got out of his vehicle and hurried up the walk. She let him in and he went right upstairs. He came back down a few minutes later.

"What's going on?" Joanne asked.

"Oh, she had a stroke, she had a stroke," Dowd said.

"A stroke?" Joanne asked skeptically. She was not aware that Generosa had a heart problem.

"She took too many pills, she took too many pills," Dowd amended.

Had Kaye left the pills out for Generosa again? Joanne wondered, shaking her head. Or was it something else? Joanne was shocked to hear that Generosa had overdosed about midnight and Kaye had called Dowd to come out from Queens. The first thing you do is call for help, Joanne thought. You don't call Generosa's lawyer to come out. Kaye and Dowd told her that they were going to take Generosa into Manhattan, to her doctor.

"Why don't you call 911?" Joanne asked.

"No no no," said Dowd. "Too much publicity out here."

"That doesn't matter. You bring her to the hospital," Joanne said.

"We're going to carry her down the stairs with your help," Dowd explained. Joanne did not know that Dowd had already spoken to Generosa's doctor.

Joanne went upstairs with them. Generosa was out of it. She didn't know who they were. She was mumbling and her head was lolling around. Joanne had never seen anything like it. They picked her up and carried her out of the bedroom. For someone so thin, she was heavy, a deadweight. At the top of the stairs, they swung her around.

"We can't get her down these stairs, we're all going to fall," Joanne said.

Dowd grabbed Generosa's feet and they slowly got her down the staircase and out to his car. They loaded Generosa into the backseat and Kaye got in beside her. Generosa was mumbling, out of her head. She seemed on the brink of death. Alexa, crying, had rushed out to say goodbye to her mother, fearing that it might be the last time. Joanne and Alexa kissed Generosa.

"Oh my God!" sobbed Alexa, as her mother was driven away.

Joanne took Alexa and the dog in her car to pick up Grego and she brought them all to her house, to await news. In the late afternoon, Kaye called.

"You have to meet me back out in East Hampton, with the children. I'm bringing Generosa home," Kaye ordered.

"How can you bring her home?" Joanne asked. "She's out of her mind; how're you going to care for her?"

"Oh, don't worry about it. Don't worry about it. And I want the kids there."

"Don't you want them to sleep over here? You want them to see their mother in this state like this?"

"No, we have to all be together."

"All right."

Joanne took the kids back to the beach house. Later, a car-service sedan pulled into the driveway. The driver carried Generosa into the house.

"Does he know what's going on here? Does he know who she is?" Joanne whispered to Kaye.

"No, I made up a name. I didn't tell him," Kaye replied.

She explained that they had brought Generosa to Dr. Mark Borelli's office.

"Why did you bring her to the doctor?" Joanne asked. "Why didn't you bring her to a hospital?"

"He gave her medication."

"She's out of her mind. What are you talking about? Medication? She needs *more* medication?"

Joanne offered to stay the night, to help, so that they could all get through it together but Kaye said no and told her to go home.

"Well, say you fall asleep, and she falls down the stairs? What's going to happen? She's going to kill herself."

"Oh, don't worry about it," said Kaye, who added that she and others "have everything figured out."

After all the anguish, things were back to normal by Monday. Generosa seemed much better.

In mid-August, a huge power blackout hit the middle and eastern United States, the worst in history. During the power failure, Danny left a peace offering in his father's driveway—a portable generator. It was a nice gesture but he made the mistake of leaving a joking note that referred to the forty thousand dollars that his father said he had spent on Danny's bail and lawyers over the years. Danny's note said his father could "take it off my bill."

Danny felt that his father was harsh and inflexible. Bob Pelosi felt his son was using money to try to buy his way back into his good graces. Neither father nor son could say or do anything right for the other. Bob Pelosi loaded the generator onto his truck and dropped it off in Danny's driveway, unused, along with his own note:

"I never asked you for anything except respect and I didn't get that."

In late August, while Joanne was cleaning at the beach house, Kaye ordered her to hurry up because Mike Dowd was coming out again. They were going to take Generosa to the hospital. Obviously, Joanne thought, they did not want her around this time.

When Generosa departed a second time, Kaye told Alexa and Grego to give her a hug and a kiss.

"Say goodbye to your mother," Kaye told the kids. "This is probably the last time you'll see her."

The twins sobbed and kissed their mother.

A security tape captured Generosa later that day walking into Lenox Hill Hospital in Manhattan under her own power, with Kaye at her side, ready to assist her. Generosa was signing in to the hospital under a phony name—to hide from the press and Danny.

"Mary Tyler Moore," suggested Generosa, who had always loved the actress.

Since the real Mary Tyler Moore lived not far away in Manhattan and it was a name that would also generate unwanted publicity, it was shortened and changed slightly:

"Mary Taylor."

"Mrs. Taylor" was admitted for treatment of advanced breast cancer. Mike Dowd later took the kids to his house in Queens. By Friday night, Generosa was near death.

"Don't let Danny be alone with my children," Generosa said to Mike Dowd, the last words he heard her speak.

Generosa Ammon died at 8:15 Friday evening, August

22, 2003. She was forty-seven years old. Dr. Todd Spelling, the hospital resident on that floor at the time of death, had not attended to Generosa at all—simply signed the certificate and filled in the information from her chart. She had been attended by her personal physician, Dr. Mark Borelli, who had admitted her. The immediate cause of death was certified as "cardiopulmonary arrest," due to or as a consequence of "metastatic breast cancer." The form directed that no autopsy be performed and said that her profession was "homemaker."

She had certainly excelled at the difficult tasks of building and transforming houses and grounds but Generosa had never been able to master the simple art of making a house a home.

Her lawyers arranged for her body to be transported to a funeral home and for her remains to be cremated. Mike Dowd notified Danny several hours after she passed away.

Later, Joanne had questions about the way Generosa had died. Kaye claimed that she had bedsores, but Joanne never saw any or heard anything about it. She thought Generosa had been improving and, from talking to her, Joanne believed that she had a year or two left. To Joanne, she appeared to be in better shape than she had been in in weeks when they took her to the hospital, and then, by Friday, she was dead. Was it possible that a hospital would participate in an assisted suicide? Joanne wondered. Or, had someone else slipped her an overdose? What had happened? Alexa and Grego, who had witnessed some of their mother's suicide attempts and other incidents, were also suspicious and were asking the same questions as Joanne was.

When Joanne expressed surprise at the death to Kaye, considering how relatively well Generosa had seemed, Kaye smiled.

"I knew she wasn't coming back, honey," Kaye said.

"How did you know? I thought she was coming back. She was perfectly fine."

Kaye did not answer. Instead, she told her that she had something for her.

"You're not in the will, but Generosa wanted you to have this," Kaye told Joanne, handing her a check. Generosa had not told Kaye to give money to the housekeeper, but Kaye decided that Generosa would have wanted Joanne to be rewarded for her service.

Surprised, Joanne looked at it. It was one of Kaye's personal checks. On the Pay to the Order of . . . line, Kaye had written "Joanne Matheson." The amount was ten thousand dollars. Joanne's eyes widened.

"Don't you dare say anything about any of the incidents that took place in this house," Kaye warned her.

PART THREE

Autumn

42

HOLDING THE BAG

Danny found out about Generosa's death when Mike Dowd passed on the news on Friday night, several hours after the fact. Generosa's body was already at the same Manhattan funeral home, Frank Campbell's on the Upper East Side, that had received Ted's body after his murder.

Danny knew that Generosa had not wanted to die like her mother. She could have undergone chemotherapy and survived another two years but she had preferred death to sharing her mother's fate.

After his initial shock and tears, Danny went into overdrive. He was convinced that those around Generosa had conspired to help her kill herself. By two on Saturday morning, he had arrived at the Madison Avenue funeral home. He rang the night bell and asked for her under the fake Mary Taylor name.

"I want to see my wife," Danny said.

He was admitted into a viewing room and paid his last respects. He saw no bedsores, which had been the alleged reason she went into the hospital. Danny was upset that there had been no autopsy, which would have established the cause of death and documented the amount of drugs that might have been present in her bloodstream and if they had played a part in her death. No autopsy meant no proof, and even if there had been a mercy killing, the licenses of the doctors and lawyers involved were safe. Danny was convinced that the people around Generosa wanted her dead before she could change her will again.

He kept a vigil with her until after the sun came up and they took her body to the crematorium in New Jersey. Danny went with her. After the cremation, he called Mike Dowd and told him that the cremation was complete; Danny had been told that the ashes would be shipped to the funeral home in Manhattan. He said that he would return there on Monday to claim them. Danny believed that Generosa had asked to see him—to give him that goodbye kiss—but those around her would not allow it.

The *New York Post* broke the story on Monday morning:

AMMON WIDOW DIES OF CANCER

In the story, Danny's new lawyer, Gerald Shargel, who had a reputation as an excellent murder defender who sometimes represented mobsters, said it was "a sad day for Danny Pelosi. It's a sad day for the children. . . . Right up to the end, she strongly expressed her love for Danny."

Another source said, "She went away painlessly. All her wishes were carried out. But she may have taken the truth with her."

"We are saddened to hear of Generosa's passing," Sandi Williams said.

On Monday afternoon, Danny was driven into the city by Luke. Danny went back to the funeral home to claim Generosa's ashes. He was dressed in dark slacks and a short-sleeved shirt the color of rum punch. He sported a gold chain around his neck, dark sunglasses, and a thin gold watch on his left wrist. He was wearing his gold wedding band. The ashes were in a plastic bag inside a sealed cardboard box, a brown eight-inch cube with a white mailing label on one side. The box was placed in a large white shopping bag with the name of the funeral home on the out-

side and Danny left with the small remnant of Generosa
Ammon. He felt that he had a promise to keep. As he walked
the five blocks from the funeral home to the Stanhope Hotel
carrying the shopping bag containing Generosa, Danny
thought about the spot he was in. Ted had been murdered.
Danny's brother Jim was dead. Generosa was dead. Danny
had a $2 million defense fund from the postnuptial agree-
ment and believed that he would need every penny. Danny
and his circle were already the focus of the Suffolk County
Homicide Squad and the grand jury, but, with Generosa
dead, Danny felt that he had been left holding the bag.

He strode into the familiar hotel with Luke and stopped at
the front desk and asked for room 1406, the presidential
suite, where Danny had first regaled Generosa with his tool
belt. They told him it wasn't available but they might have it
ready for him later. As Generosa had suggested, he walked
her back to the corner banquette in the bar where they had
spent so much time at the start of their relationship. Danny
sat at the round table and ordered a Bud Light for himself
and Generosa's favorite drink—a Cosmopolitan in a rocks
glass. He took the box reverently out of the bag and placed it
next to him on the table, where Generosa used to sit. The
cardboard box looked tacky, like a UPS box, something that
Generosa would have detested. And, of course, her actual
ashes were in contact with *plastic*. In an effort to add a bit of
style and respect, Danny draped a white linen napkin over
the box, which looked much better, like an altar. He placed
Generosa's gold wedding ring atop the napkin. When the
drinks arrived, the Cosmopolitan was placed in front of the
white shroud and Danny's brew, in a tall beer glass, was put
before him. He clicked glasses, toasted his dead wife, and
sipped his beer. Only one more thing was needed to complete the tableau. Danny lit two Marlboro cigarettes. He
placed one of them on the corner of Generosa's untouched
drink, where they made a small ash and then burned out. He
took a drag from his. Danny was breaking the law—the New
York City public smoking ban—but he didn't give a damn.

When Mike Dowd discovered that Danny had retrieved
Generosa's ashes from the funeral home, he was furious.
Generosa's will specifically stated that the ashes were to go
to Kaye, despite the fact that Danny and Generosa were still
married. Danny had snatched his wife's remains and placed
them in the center ring of his circus. Dowd felt that, once
again, Danny was thinking of himself and not of the children. When reporters called him at the office to ask for a
comment about his client's death, an angry Dowd told them
that Danny had kidnapped his estranged wife's ashes.

"It's terrible that the tragedy of her death has been com-
pounded by her husband's illegal removal of her ashes,"
Dowd said.

The reporters, pleased that they had a much better story
than just following the *Post*'s accounting of that day, quickly
called Danny's lawyers. They asked for comment about
Danny's alleged hijacking of the ashes.

"He didn't steal anything," said Danny's lawyer Gerald
Shargel. "By custom and tradition, the ashes go to the husband, not the lawyers or the nanny. This is pretty bizarre.
Danny Pelosi wants to honor his wife's ashes. We haven't
even seen the will yet. He wants to have an appropriate service and mourn his wife."

Shargel then called Danny, who became enraged at the
claim that he had stolen his own wife's ashes. The funeral
home had given him a valid, signed receipt, and Generosa
had given him verbal instructions before she died.

When a *New York Post* reporter called Danny on his cell
phone at the Stanhope, he unloaded, and gave the reporter an
exclusive that would go national.

"The Stanhope is where it started and this is where it
ends," Danny said. "She told me, 'It all started here. We'll
have a drink and say goodbye.'"

He denied that he had purloined the remains.

"Stole what?" Danny demanded. "I didn't steal nothing.
I'm here with her now, saying goodbye. Now, I hear her
lawyer says her remains should go to Kaye, the toilet bowl

cleaner. I'm gonna have a ceremony, as she wished, with her children, my children, and a few family friends, and I will dispose of her remains the way she wanted."

Generosa had told him that she wanted her remains used as fertilizer for the flower beds outside her beloved East Hampton beach house. Generosa wanted her ashes to be watered by rain and soak into the dirt, where they would do some good. There, in the dark, they would nourish the roots of her plants and help grow her perfect petals, in the ideal shade of color—such perfect flowers that people passing in the sunshine on Middle Lane might think that the blooms had been carved out of stone.

"She wanted her ashes to go on the poppies, so that we will remember her every year when the poppies come up," Danny said. "I hope this is the end of it, for these kids. I hope they can put it all behind them and live their lives. I want for them what their parents wanted for them—when they were together and happy."

The reporter hung up and called his office, but at first they thought he was joking. Photographer Bob Kalfus was dispatched to race up to the Stanhope and catch Pelosi before he could leave. He found Danny in the mirrored corner bar table, with two drinks, two cigarettes, and something under a white napkin. He started taking pictures, his flash strobe glinting off Generosa's gold wedding band.

"Are those the ashes?" Kalfus asked Danny.

"Yeah."

The photographer asked Danny to lift the shroud so that he could see what was underneath. Danny did not want to do it, until Kalfus explained that he did not want Danny to open the box, he simply wanted to confirm that they were actual remains.

"I mean, you could have your hat under there," Kalfus said.

Danny lifted the napkin for a moment and the photographer saw the label, which was from the crematorium to the funeral home. That was good enough for him.

He fired off a few more shots and left. The frame of

Danny lifting the veil and revealing the box of ashes, a
Marlboro dangling from his lips, would run above the story
on page 3 the next day in the *Post*:

TO YOU, GENEROSA
PELOSI TOASTS ASHES OF WIFE IN BAR WHERE THEY MET

When the photographer left, Danny took Generosa for a
walk and a talk in Central Park, just as they had done when
they were living at the hotel. As the sun set, he returned to
the hotel and picked up the key to room 1406, the presidential suite. They rode up in the elevator together, as they had
so many times, and Danny carried her ashes over the thresh-
old and into the room.

"This is not the first time I carried you," he told her, with
a chuckle.

He closed the door behind them and Danny and Generosa
were alone.

43

CAUGHT DEAD

Mike Dowd and Danny stopped talking as soon as Generosa was cremated. Before her ashes were cold, their rift went public in the press and, later, in court. Although Dowd maintained that Danny and his late wife were not involved in the murder, he felt that Danny's published photo, which showed him having a drink with Generosa's ashes in a bar, proved his point about the widower.

"That picture says it all," Dowd told a reporter. "It's Danny with the two things he loves most in the world—himself and alcohol."

In answer to a reporter's question, Dowd denied that Generosa's death was an assisted suicide. Neither the doctor who had signed the death certificate nor her doctor would comment when asked the same question by a reporter. Dowd said that he had spoken to Generosa "about not wanting to go on in a vegetative state, while the pain was unbelievable, and I didn't disagree with her." He said that he knew nothing about Kaye Mayne's ten-thousand-dollar payment to Joanne, the housekeeper, but had believed that Generosa wanted Joanne to receive money, even though she was not mentioned in the will.

A crop of lawsuits would spring from the Ammon case, which was becoming a growth industry for attorneys. More and more lawyers went to different courts to argue related cases, seeking or spending the money Ted Ammon had left behind and, in some cases, both. The bizarre case became even more absurd when some of the lawyers hired lawyers themselves. It began to appear that Ted's entire fortune would be gobbled up by lawyers engaged in litigation for years to come but no one would ever be charged with his murder.

A court made Kaye the permanent guardian of the Ammon twins. She would not allow Alexa and Grego to attend a church memorial service for their mother, because it was organized by Danny and his family. Instead, the twins and Kaye planted a tree outside the beach house for their mother. After the lawyers discussed it, Danny returned the ashes to Generosa's lawyers. But they were not given to Kaye—they were held, in limbo, until a final disposition by the court. The last remains of Generosa Ammon, after their detour to the Stanhope and a trip back to Center Moriches, were driven to Gerry Sweeney's law office in Queens and placed in his locked safe. Generosa was trapped on Queens Boulevard, near where she and Danny had married—a place in which she would not want to be caught dead.

Unlike Generosa, Kaye, on the advice of her lawyer Mike Dowd, allowed the twins to be questioned by a homicide detective and a prosecutor. But the kids refused to see Danny as a suspect.

"What about Mark Angelson?" Alexa asked.

Prosecutor Janet Albertson replied that Mr. Angelson had been cleared of suspicion.

"You gotta be kidding me," said Grego. "I heard he was wearing gloves."

"How do you know about the gloves?" Albertson asked.

"Didn't he stop at a hardware store and buy gloves?" Grego pressed.

"And you don't find that a little weird?" Alexa asked.

"No," the prosecutor replied.

"I'm only thirteen years old and I find it a little weird," Grego insisted.

Grego was sent away to a private boarding school but Alexa remained in East Hampton with Kaye and went to an exclusive local private school.

Danny declined to seek custody because he was advised that his background would guarantee that he would not win, especially while he was still a murder suspect. Sandi Williams was still trying to end the nightmare for her niece and nephew. In court papers, she said she was concerned that the kids "will not see their money during their lifetime" because Generosa's lawyers controlled the estate and the so-called Ammon Foundation.

"The children's money will be, for all practical purposes, controlled by two complete strangers to them, with no accountability or oversight and exoneration from any conflicts of interest," she told the court. Dowd and Sweeney denied the charges.

Alexa and Grego wrote a letter that wound up with Judge Czygier in the custody case. The letter said that they disliked Kaye Mayne and did not want to live with her in the house where their father had met his fate. The event was covered by the *Post* and included a picture of Kaye.

NANNY DEAREST
AMMON ORPHANS TRY TO BOOT GUARDIAN

Kaye had brought a book of short stories to court. One of them, "Erie's Last Day," by Steve Hockensmith, was about a detective investigating a long-unsolved murder of a white-collar husband who had been bludgeoned to death in his home by an unknown intruder. The killers turned out to be the merry widow and her younger, blue-collar boyfriend. After the murder, the boyfriend told coworkers that he was set for life, and he quit his job. Then, the killer boyfriend died and the widow went to jail. The thug was killed in a

shootout when his shotgun exploded. The detonation was the
result of a shotgun barrel that had been plugged by the dis-
enchanted widow—because her boyfriend had beaten her.

Judge Czygier ordered a hearing to determine whether
Kaye Mayne would retain custody or whether Sandi and
Bob Williams could become the children's guardians. In
court papers, Sandi said that the decision to split up Alexa
and Grego so soon after their mother's death was one that
might cause serious psychological harm.

Generosa's will left Kaye Mayne a "life estate," the right to
live in the East Hampton beach house for the rest of her life,
and left Danny nothing, a fact also noted in the newspapers:

$1 MILLION NANNY
NANNY SPANKS DANNY

Danny filed a lawsuit seeking to overturn the postnuptial
agreement and Generosa's final will, claiming that lawyers
Mike Dowd and Gerry Sweeney had committed fraud.
Danny claimed that Dowd and Sweeney had lied to him
about being taken care of in Generosa's will, a trick that he
said had induced him to sign the postnup. Also, he argued,
Generosa was drugged and not competent when both documents were signed. Generosa's estate, as filed by Sweeney
and Dowd, totaled $35 million, causing Danny's lawyers to
charge that the estate was being underreported. Others also
wondered where half of Ted Ammon's fortune had gone,
even after taking into account debts and trusts. Danny was
using $2 million of Ted's money to defend himself and his
friends as suspects in Ted's murder and he was also using
the money to seek more of Ted's fortune from Generosa's
estate.

Dowd felt that Danny was manipulating the Ammon children to advance his aims and wanted to gain control of Generosa's money through them. As soon as Danny filed the
lawsuit, the will was held up. Kaye Mayne did not get her $1

million. Kaye then testified before the grand jury. As Danny had feared, Kaye told the jurors that he had confessed to the murder. After her testimony, Joanne, the housekeeper, asked Kaye what she had told the panel.

"Well, I told them that Danny told me that he killed Ted," Kaye said, not saying whether she also told the jurors about the details of the "confession" that were wrong or whether she thought that Danny was joking or saying it to scare her.

The two sides took off the gloves and charges and countercharges flew. Mindy Trepel, a lawyer associate of Sweeney's, told the court that Generosa had told her that Danny was physically abusive to her—a charge he angrily denied. Dowd, accused of serious misrepresentations, hired a lawyer. At least one other lawyer in the case also hired a lawyer for advice. Judge Czygier eventually dismissed all of Danny's claims except the fraud charges against Dowd and Sweeney. The court ordered that Danny's lawyers could depose witnesses and present evidence of the alleged fraud before a decision was handed down.

Danny began to broadcast his innocence on numerous network television shows and several local TV stations. On one show, he said that before he met Generosa, he had dreamed of finding a wealthy woman to take care of him, prompting the *Daily News* to label him:

IT'S PELOSI, THE GIGOLOSI

Danny was still facing jail time for the felony electricity-stealing charge and went to court several times. He had paid the forty-one thousand dollars for the juice he allegedly stole, but the criminal charge remained. He complained that the power company had charged him at a very high rate. His ex-wife, Tami, still faced her misdemeanor charge resulting from the same meter bypass. Tami and Danny's pals, including Alex Mawyer and Chris Parrino, were still pursuing their federal lawsuit, claiming that their civil rights had been vio-

lated in the full-court-press roundup by police. Chris was
still facing a charge of making a false written statement in
connection with Danny's DWI bust.

J.P. Morgan Chase bank filed a $20 million wrongful
death action against Danny, claiming that he had murdered
Ted Ammon. The bank successfully argued that the case
should be held in abeyance until the criminal matter was
completed, just as in the O. J. Simpson case. Besides again
declaring his innocence, Danny wished them luck. He
claimed that he was broke, allegedly having spent his $2
million postnuptial nest egg on lawyers.

As the months wore on, summer became fall, and the second anniversary of Ted's murder came and went. Fall became
winter and the year 2004 arrived without any indictments.

Despite his claims of relative poverty, Danny had found a
new, sexy girlfriend, Jennifer Zolnowski, and he took her
and an entourage of friends and family to Hawaii for a winter vacation in January 2004. The day after they arrived at
the Maui Marriott, an eighteen-year-old cheerleader went
off a balcony on the high-rise and fell to her death. Danny
joked that he would probably become a suspect.

Jennifer was blond, beautiful, and blue-eyed. She was a
bank teller. To some it was an odd coincidence that Danny
called his new love by the same-sounding nickname he had
used for Generosa—Jen. Danny had surprised Jennifer with
a marquise diamond engagement ring, and sometime during
their stay at the romantic tropical resort she became pregnant. Of course, Danny the widower wanted to keep his new
romance away from the press, so he was trying to stay low-
key. On January 16, 2004, Danny and his group took a sun-
set booze cruise out of Lahaina for dinner and drinks, but all
was not smooth sailing. Before dinner, a crew member told a
woman in Danny's party that, because of her behavior, she
would not be allowed to have any more alcohol until the
meal. Words were exchanged. Later, Danny removed his
shirt and gave it to the lady, who was cold. The same crew

member told Danny to put his shirt back on. More words were exchanged and a reference to Danny's infamy was made: "Hey, movie star, put your shirt on. This isn't *Prime Time Live,*" the first mate told Danny.

As the passengers disembarked on the gangplank, someone sucker-punched the first mate, breaking his nose and knocking him down. The Pelosi party left the decked first mate and resumed their vacation.

At four the next morning, Danny was roused from sleep in his hotel suite by a banging on the door.

"Police! Open up!"

"Are you Dan Pelosi?" one detective asked.

"Yeah."

They informed him that he was under arrest for assaulting the crew member. Danny denied the charge and said that someone else must have slugged the guy. Danny claimed that the victim was simply looking to cash in with a civil lawsuit, but said that the joke was on him—because he was broke. At a later court date on the Hawaiian Punch, a judge ordered Danny to stop drinking and to throw out all the alcohol in his house, an unusual ruling before a conviction. Danny protested, and sparred with the judge, claiming that Maui authorities and the Suffolk County D.A.'s office were working "hand in hand" to get him. He fired his local lawyer.

"The Suffolk County D.A.'s office is working through the Maui prosecutor's office because they cannot arrest me for murder," Danny declared after court.

Danny and his associates, particularly his pals Alex and Chris, were still the targets of the Suffolk County special grand jury, who were slowly being taken through the prosecution's largely circumstantial case. The grand jury sent Danny a letter asking him to testify before them. His lawyer Gerry Shargel said that Danny would be glad to do that—if he was granted immunity. He was not and he did not.

The already bizarre case took another weird turn, with

Danny and a friend making charges of corruption against the
police. Danny's friend Alex, who was living in the basement
apartment at Danny's house, claimed that as he was driving
to Riverhead to tell the grand jury that the police had tried to
bribe him to finger Pelosi in Ted Ammon's murder, he was
stopped by cops and arrested for driving a vehicle with
stolen license plates. Alex and Danny told the press that
Alex's arrest was a sinister move by Suffolk County cops to
prevent Alex from telling his bribery story.

"Obviously, I'm not going to make it to the grand jury
today," said Alex, as he emerged from a Patchogue police
precinct after posting sixty dollars' stationhouse bail.
"C'mon, man, this is harassment or fear tactics. Obviously,
anything that I'm going to say is going to hurt them. First
off, Danny had nothing to do with any of this bullshit, and
neither did I. I want to go back to my life. Since the day he
met her, my life hasn't been the same."

He claimed that after he was arrested in the roundup, detectives had offered him fifty thousand dollars in cash inside
a paper bag to name Danny as Ted's killer.

"When I'm leaving, they offer me cash money to inform
on my friend," said Alex.

Requests from the grand jury also resulted in several legal battles, more lawyers, and more delays. The grand jury
subpoenaed outtakes from a TV show on which Danny had
appeared. They also issued a subpoena for the defense
files—the private detectives' interviews of seven people the
prosecution considered witnesses, potential suspects, or out-
right targets, including Chris Parrino. It was the first time
that the prosecutors declared their suspicion that Danny
"and a small entourage of friends and relatives had participated in the murder," a judge noted. But the judge quashed
both subpoenas. Danny's lawyer Gerald Shargel said that
the moves smacked of desperation on behalf of the prosecution. Another defense team member, Paul Bergman, called it
"a fishing expedition."

Suddenly, it appeared as if Danny's brother Jim was still

helping him after death. On February 16, 2004, Danny was helping Jim's widow, Lee, clean out her house when he claimed to have found the Taser his dead brother had taken from the Manorville house. It had not been melted down. Danny said that he had found it on the top shelf of his brother's bedroom closet. He turned it over to his lawyer, Gerald Shargel, who had it tested before turning it over to the grand jury. Danny's legal team believed that the prosecution had made much of the missing weapon before the grand jury. Shargel hoped that the rediscovered stun gun would convince the grand jury that Danny was not involved.

If the prosecution had made the missing stun gun the linchpin of their case—proof that Danny had destroyed a weapon used in the murder—then its sudden discovery might ruin their case. If Danny had used it on Ted, why would he turn it over to police?

"This is your get-out-of-jail-free card," Shargel told Danny.

The question was whether the grand jury would consider Danny's fortuitous discovery evidence of his innocence—or evidence of a clever attempt to throw a monkey wrench into the investigation at a crucial juncture.

In April, Alexa and Grego, along with a new court-appointed psychologist, went to Huntsville, Alabama, to visit their aunt Sandi and uncle Bob. They both loved it there. It was warm and their aunt and uncle had a big house. They were concerned that they were going to be forced to go to church and were relieved to hear that it would be entirely their choice. They were happy to learn that they could redecorate their rooms and that their weeknight curfew would not be until eleven-thirty. It didn't hurt when they discovered that they could get their learners' permits a year earlier than in New York. They both decided that they wanted to live there—if Sandi agreed to let them communicate with Danny and his family. Sandi and the psychologist agreed that this would be okay with supervision, which made the twins very happy.

The news came just a few days before their fourteenth birthday. The problem would be selling the plan to Kaye Mayne and her lawyer, Mike Dowd.

That same month, the grand jury granted Danny's nephew Jeff Lukert immunity, and he testified before the panel. Jeff, who had once been suspected in the alleged murder plot as a driver, was a cornerstone of Danny's alibi and key to his defense.

Prosecutors usually insist on hearing what a witness will say—and how it will help indict and convict their targets—before granting immunity. This was a strange move because Jeff had not agreed to testify against his uncle. Under ordinary circumstances, that would have been the price of immunity. But these weren't ordinary circumstances. Prosecutors suspected that their case might be won or lost on the strength of Danny's alibi. The more details they knew about that, the more they could lock in, the better the chances they'd find a hole—if there was one. So Jeff, by testifying before the grand jury, would help them establish an alibi that, they hoped, might be knocked down in the year before the trial.

Outside of the secrecy of the grand jury room in Riverhead, it seemed as if nothing was happening. Justice had been long delayed. Would it be denied?

44

A TRUE BILL

Danny darted among the loud, laughing Saint Patrick's Day Parade crowds on the slushy Manhattan sidewalk along with his friend. He kept glancing behind him, looking for the plainclothes detectives he was sure were following him. A light, wet snow was falling, and the boom of the bass drums and the wailing of bagpipes resonated off the stone and glass buildings lining Fifth Avenue. One color dominated at the annual Wearin' o' the Green: emerald clothing, hats, scarves, flags, banners, carnations—even some green faces and green hair.

The tens of thousands of people and the circuslike atmosphere were perfect for Danny's mission. He had been walking for dozens of blocks to shake any cops on his tail. He thought he had lost them. He and his pal stopped at a gleaming stainless-steel storefront with a Burger Heaven sign over the door, one of several locations of the popular gourmet fast-food chain. They went inside and Danny ordered a big juicy sirloin burger, with cheese, pickle, onions, and red relish, along with French fries, lettuce, tomato, coleslaw, and a large soda.

Danny had begun that snowy Wednesday, two days after the twins' fourteenth birthday, at home in Center Moriches with his newly pregnant fiancée, Jennifer. His lawyers called and told him that they had received a tip that it was the grand jury's last day. If true, it was finally crunch time. Danny's stomach clenched and he went into action. He gave it five-to-seven odds in favor of an indictment. He gave his old cell phone to his daughter Rachelle. He told her to drive east while using the phone. If the cops followed that signal, it would buy him some time—because he was heading west. He had a new, never-used cell phone that he was sure authorities could not bug or trace. Danny had already decided to hide from the police—so that he could surrender. He did not want to be hauled out of his house in handcuffs, in front of his fiancée, family, and neighbors, like a common criminal. He wanted to beat the cops one last time, as a matter of personal dignity. He and his friend drove into Manhattan, where Danny walked among the Midtown crowds while waiting for news. He walked faster and faster and sometimes broke into a trot, as if he thought he could outrun the indictment. He checked in to a hotel and, after weaving through the parade throngs again, he and his buddy went to Burger Heaven for lunch.

Just as he finished his cheeseburger and fries, his new cell phone chirped. It was one of his lawyers. Danny was told that they had a further tip—that the grand jury had voted one or more indictments and looked like they were ready to close up shop—but the lawyers were unable to confirm the information. The D.A. was not returning their calls. It was likely that Danny had been charged with murder. In shock, now that the moment had finally arrived, he set up an appointment to meet with the lawyers and hung up. Surrounded by smiling Irish eyes and celebrating diners, Danny's face registered panic. He feared incarceration because he detested being alone. When he had been in the Riverhead jail for his last four-month DWI rap, he was locked up alone for twenty-three hours a day and it drove him nuts. The thought of a year or more in a cage—not to mention the possibility of twenty-five years in that hellhole, or a worse prison—made his stomach churn. Hit with a wave of nausea, Danny bolted outside and vomited his lunch into the gutter. On any other day, a man who looked slightly green and was retching into the street might have turned a few heads, but it was Saint Patrick's Day. Nobody looked twice.

Later in the day, Danny met with his lawyers. One of them, Paul Bergman, became convinced that undercover detectives were staking out his office, and may have picked up Danny's trail when he left. If Bergman was correct, that could only mean one thing—they were about to arrest Danny. If he was not correct, it proved that paranoia was contagious. Danny returned to his hotel to wait for news. When he stepped outside for a smoke, he spotted a familiar-looking man across the street. Was he a homicide detective? Danny ducked back into the hotel restaurant and hid in a waiters' station while the man he believed to be a detective pulled up to the hotel in an unmarked car with another man. The man got out, came inside, and walked past Danny without noticing him. The man went toward the front desk. Danny fled out another exit and quickly left the area to change hotels—glancing over his shoulder as he ran. If the man was a detective, he might have gotten the wrong impression from Danny's surreptitious activities—that he was on the lam, for example.

But no one was following Danny—except his own fear.

He lost his imaginary pursuers by mingling again among the throngs watching the parade. When he spotted a live TV van belonging to a local station on which he had previously professed his innocence, he popped inside and sat in a chair, startling the producer.

"Who are you?" the producer asked.

"I'm Dan Pelosi," he said, glancing around nervously.

That night, Danny appeared on TV, and became weepy when discussing the possibility that he might go to jail. He insisted on his innocence and said that he did not "have the luck of the Irish" on that day. A newspaper story the next morning also said that Danny feared he was about to be indicted, although a law enforcement source told the paper that no such indictment had yet been handed down. In the story, Danny noted the well-known lawyers' saying that any prosecutor could get a grand jury to indict a ham sandwich—and offered a new twist: "It's a Dan sandwich," he said with a smile.

"I just pray that the judge allows me to go home after my bail hearing—I'm not going anywhere," Danny said.

In East Hampton, after hearing that Danny might have been indicted, Kaye Mayne turned to an unhappy Alexa Ammon and said, "See, I told you Danny's going to jail."

Danny and his lawyers decided to go to court on Thursday, March 18, to try to surrender—as a way of finding out if there was an indictment or not.

A grand jury can do one of four things: it can indict, which is called a "true bill," or it can fail to indict—"no true bill"—or it can simply disband without reaching any conclusion. Grand jurors may also issue reports, particularly in cases of public policy. If the grand jury disbands without action, because the evidence was not there for an indictment, the prosecutor can always revisit the case in the future. If the grand jury votes "no true bill," the case is essentially over—barring spectacular revelations—because the prosecution would have to start all over again.

"Is this my last cigarette?" Danny asked his lawyers outside the Riverhead courthouse that morning, remembering that the adjacent county jail was a nonsmoking facility.

"It could be, so enjoy it," Gerry Shargel told him, as they walked through a light snowfall to the courthouse entrance where the press was waiting. The cameras following them, they went to the third-floor courtroom of the judge who was the adviser to the grand jury.

"What's up, Eddie?" a court officer asked Burke, who explained that the unexpected media event was due to the rumor that Danny had been indicted.

"News to me," the officer said, before going back to the judge's chambers to ask. A few minutes later, Suffolk

County D.A. Thomas Spota arrived and denied that his office wanted to lock up Pelosi:

"I don't know why Mr. Pelosi is here," Spota said. "I was just called down to this courtroom."

Later, after a conference with Pelosi's lawyers, Spota emerged and announced to the press, "An indictment has not been filed." He said that the twenty-three-member special grand jury, which was scheduled to run until August, was still at work and had not voted "no true bill"—a nonindictment. It seemed that the tip to the lawyers had been wrong. Shargel said that Pelosi's trip to court was not wasted, because it demonstrated that his client "is ready to surrender on a rumor" and was not a risk of flight, if arrested. "He is ready to face these charges anytime they're brought." In other words, it was a demonstration that they hoped would get Danny out on bail after an arrest. On the way out of the building, Danny turned to Burke.

"I can't handle this roller-coaster ride anymore, Eddie; it's too much of an impact on my kids."

Paul Bergman told the press that Spota had agreed to give the defense lawyers a call if their client was indicted—to avoid a repeat of the odd spectacle of someone surrendering for a crime with which he had not been charged. Several press outlets speculated that the "surrender" had been nothing more than a publicity stunt.

But just four days later, on Monday morning, Spota's office faxed a letter to Danny's lawyers informing them that the grand jury had, indeed, voted a true bill and that Danny had been indicted. The letter did not mention the charge, but everyone assumed that the charge was murder. Now it seemed that the tip to the defense was correct, but a bit premature. After almost two and a half years of being the prime suspect, Danny had finally been charged with Ted's murder. Later that day, Danny told a reporter that he wanted Alexa and Grego to know that he had not killed their father.

"I didn't do this, guys," Danny said. "There's nobody who knows me better than my children and Alexa and Grego, because they became part of my family. No matter how the media places a spin on this—you believe in the person you know, the person who will always be there for you. They know I had nothing to do with it."

Danny gave several TV interviews and spoke to a host of reporters, getting his story out. The next morning, he put on an olive pin-striped suit and tie. Before he went to court, he said goodbye to his three children and family. When he and Eddie Burke stopped for coffee on their way to court, a woman Danny did not know pressed rosary beads into his hands.

"Just pray by these and you'll get bail," the woman told him.

Danny, not generally noted for excessive piety, saw it as a sign from God. He thanked her, and prayed as he fingered the beads on the way to court. A crowd of TV crews, reporters, and photographers were waiting outside on the cool, sunny morning. The somber suspect told the reporters that he hoped to talk to them on the way out. He and his lawyers, Burke, Shargel, and Bergman, rode an elevator up to the fifth floor, to the D.A.'s office.

"Let's do this," Danny said as they entered the office.

He was photographed, fingerprinted, and processed before being taken in handcuffs to the third-floor courtroom of Justice Robert Doyle. Before the arraignment, the lawyers met with the judge. Danny's defense team asked if Danny had, indeed, been indicted the previous week and they were told that he had—but the judge had not received or signed the indictment until Monday. When Danny was escorted from the prisoner holding area into the well of the court, with his hands cuffed behind him, he saw a full house. On Danny's left, the whole side of the gallery was filled with reporters. On his right, he saw his beautiful blond fiancée, Jennifer, sitting in the front row, wearing a low-cut designer dress suit that revealed an amount of cleavage not usually seen in court, along with other supporters, including friends Alex Mawyer and housekeeper Joanne Matheson.

The lawyers waived the reading of the unsealed indictment against Danny, which was only two sentences long:

> *THE GRAND JURY OF SUFFOLK COUNTY, by this indictment, accuses the defendant DANIEL PELOSI, of the crime of MURDER IN THE SECOND DEGREE. The defendant, DANIEL PELOSI, on or about October 21, 2001, in Suffolk County, State of New York, with intent to cause the death of R. THEODORE AMMON, caused his death.*

Prosecutor Janet Albertson, her long, straight brown hair falling to the shoulders of her dark dress suit, stood with her right hand on her hip and told the court that the special grand jury was still in session and that further charges against other individuals might be forthcoming. She said that the nine-month grand jury investigation had called fifty-one witnesses and examined more than a hundred exhibits before handing down an indictment. She said that the killer "applied a stun gun on the victim's neck and back." The fatal assault inflicted "defensive injuries" in the form of fractures to Ammon's hands and arms, said Albertson. He also suffered "fractured ribs, punctured lungs, and thirty blows to his head," she said. Albertson said that the defendant "had purchased numerous stun guns" before the murder. After the slaying, Pelosi made statements that "implicated himself, as well as others" in the killing. On the night of the murder, Albertson said, the defendant "had the capability to look inside the house for twenty-one minutes at approximately two o'clock in the morning." He was the only one who knew how to unplug the secret surveillance system that spied on Ted and was one of the few who knew it existed and where it was—behind the wall, inside the secret safe room.

The Rapid Eye unit "was hidden within the recesses of that home, in a location which was known to very few people, outside of the installers. . . . One of the only individuals who was aware of the location of that hard drive unit, as well as the power source—which was a simple plug—was Daniel Pelosi," she said.

After the killing, the unit, with its hard drive containing thousands of photos, was removed from the mansion—"a key piece of evidence that strongly points to the guilt of Daniel Pelosi," Albertson said.

Danny reacted to that information with a look of shock and he whispered to his lawyers, who also looked surprised at the news that the surveillance unit had been removed.

Albertson noted that Danny faced twenty-five years to life behind bars, if convicted, and asked Justice Robert Doyle to hold him without bail. She told the judge that Danny had a long arrest record for DWI and assaults, including his pending assault charge in Hawaii. She said that he was mentally unstable and had a long history of drug and alcohol abuse. If any bail was granted, she argued, it should be no lower than $3 million. She claimed that Danny cared more about his freedom than he did about money—especially since it was not his.

"It's not his hard-earned money," said Albertson. "It's really the money of the victim, whom he is accused of murdering."

Gerald Shargel then argued on Danny's behalf for bail. He told the judge that the long investigation and the long witness list of the grand jury proved the opposite of what Albertson claimed. He said that it showed they had "a weak, circumstantial case. I suggest to you, Your Honor, that it is not an overwhelming case."

Shargel reminded the judge that Danny had always shown up for court in his recent cases and had come to the same courtroom six days earlier—to surrender on a rumor that he had been indicted. Shargel said that Danny was ready to post $1 million bail. He said that his client was innocent and they wanted to prove it by going to trial in record time—three months later, in June.

But Doyle said only that he was mindful of the seriousness of the charges and quickly ordered that Danny "be remanded without bail."

It happened so quickly, Danny looked stunned. His lawyers later said he was scared, but desperate would have been a more accurate description. He had really believed he would get bail. Tears welled in his eyes and he looked over to Jennifer in the front row. She also burst into tears, dabbing at her eyes with a tissue, as Danny was led out of the courtroom.

Danny's pal and tenant Alex Mawyer—himself still a possible suspect of the grand jury—was also there to support Pelosi and called the proceedings "a joke. Let my 'brother' go. We just want our lives back."

In the sunshine in front of the courthouse, Shargel, flanked by Burke and Bergman, stepped up to a porcupine of microphones on a stand and announced, "We are looking forward to trying this case in June and we're looking forward to our client being free again. Our case can defeat their case, period." The only thing Shargel would say about the defense case was that it was "going to be very much about how the evidence in this case was obtained."

Outside the courtroom, D.A. Thomas Spota said that he too, was ready for trial—and claimed that the case took so long to bring due only to defense delays. They "obstructed in any way they could," said Spota. He gave, as an example, the prosecution's attempt to get the laptop that Barbara and Danny had used to spy on Ted, saying that it "resulted in three months of litigation and delay." He said that the grand jury was continuing its work and that others might also be indicted in Ted's murder. Pelosi's millions, which had been earned by Ted, had enabled Danny to hire the best lawyers money could buy—but the D.A. vowed that it would not thwart justice:

"He may have three lawyers, five lawyers—they will certainly meet their match," Spota promised.

After dreading it for years, Danny was finally in custody and facing a murder trial and possibly the rest of his life behind bars, a fate he considered nothing less than a living death in hell. Danny was ushered into a courthouse holding area and was taken downstairs into the subterranean passage leading to the jail. He was headed for an eight-by-twelve-foot cage with no window. He would have to strip out of his expensive Italian suit and silk tie. A corrections officer would wrap his clothing and belongings up in a large, brown paper bag and stick it on a steel shelf where it would stay until his release or transfer. He would be issued underwear, socks, a green shirt and green elastic-waisted pants, and sneakers without laces. He had been through the same drill at the same jail several times before, enough to know he hated it. He dreaded the lockdown he knew he would have to endure, the twenty-three-hour confinement in a small cell, with only one hour a day to shower or to exercise outside. But he and his lawyers were certain that no jury would ever convict him. They would present the results of their own investigation to the jury and he would be acquitted. That was why they were pushing for an early trial. But once inside the lockup, with the curses of the jailed echoing in his ears, it would be harder to believe in that day.

Except for his childhood and a nine-year dry spell, Danny had struggled with alcoholism, drug dependence, infidelity, bankruptcy, and criminal charges for most of his life. He finally hit it big with Generosa in October 2000 and rode the green wave to the high life he felt he deserved. He paid off his debts and threw cash, cars, gifts, and jobs to his friends and family. Danny lived in mansions in Manhattan, East Hampton, and England. He wore expensive, fine clothes, sported gold and diamond jewelry, drove hot cars, and was waited on by servants. He went on Caribbean vacations and took his crew on high-rolling junkets to Atlantic City and

Las Vegas casinos, where he stayed in luxury suites, and claimed to have dropped huge sums at the gaming tables.

Three and a half years later, it was all over. He was manacled and heading for a cage, where he would eat stale cheese and baloney sandwiches in a cell that contained a sink, a smelly toilet, and a hard bed. He could neither smoke nor drink nor have sex with a woman, perhaps his strongest addiction. Danny was jumping out of his skin. If, somehow, it all went wrong at his trial and he was convicted and served a full sentence, he would not walk free again until he had reached retirement age, sixty-five, when he would be much less able to cut a dashing figure to older ladies of means. Danny Pelosi had protested that he was an innocent man, and now he was about to enter a jail filled with men who also claimed to be innocent. He blamed it all on detectives and prosecutors. He felt that they had bungled the investigation and had targeted him only because of his record, his background. He had been framed.

As Danny reached the end of the tunnel, the huge steel bars, covered with pale, flaking paint, rumbled to one side and he entered the prison. Once inside, the heavy metal gate began rattling back into place, as he was led down the hall. That was when Danny remembered with a chill what day it was on Monday, when he heard about the indictment: March 22. It was Generosa's birthday.

Happy birthday, Danny thought. He decided that it was not a coincidence. It was a message from Generosa to him, that he would be acquitted—that he would be going home.

The jailhouse bars loudly clanged shut behind him.

45

"THERE'S A MONSTER INSIDE ME!"

Janet Albertson, clutching her trial files, made her way through the crowd gathered outside Judge Doyle's fourth-floor courtroom for the beginning of Danny's murder trial in the autumn of 2004. The prosecutor was scheduled to kick off the trial by making her opening statement to the jury of nine women and three men. Family members, reporters, and other observers jostled for position, hoping to get a seat in the courtroom when court officers unlocked the doors. Albertson joined her co-counsel Ming Liu Parson at the prosecution table in front of Suffolk Supreme Court Justice Robert Doyle.

The grinning defendant was clad in a crisp blue suit and tie, chatting with his lawyers, Gerald Shargel, Paul Bergman, and Danielle Shalov at the defense table, craning his neck around to wink at a reporter and smile at his family. He was anxious to start. The sooner they began, the sooner he would be free. He had already confidently predicted: "I'll be out for Halloween."

"All rise!" a court officer shouted. Everyone came to their feet, as black-robed Justice Robert Doyle took the bench, and then sat down. But, before the judge could bring in the jury, Albertson rose at the prosecution table. She did not go to the podium to make her opening statement. Instead, she dropped a bomb.

She told the court, the media, and the stunned onlookers, that the talkative Danny had "made direct admissions of the murder" to two jailhouse informants, one of whom had made recordings of Danny's indiscreet words. She said he had been plotting from his jail cell, in an attempt to influence a potential juror and assault witnesses against him. There was evidence, Albertson said, of "various threats made to my own children."

An angry Shargel was on his feet, loudly objecting to the "outrageous" claims, saying his client could not get a fair trial and he might have to ask for a mistrial.

"They engineered it. They staged it to delay this trial," Shargel charged. "This was a charade. This was a game."

"I don't have to have the defendant threatening my own children. I didn't engineer that," Albertson shot back.

The trial was delayed for weeks, while the sides battled over the new charges. Danny was quickly charged in a new indictment with attempting to influence a juror, attempting to intimidate witnesses, attempted assault, criminal solicitation, and conspiracy. He faced as much as fifteen years in jail on the heaviest count alone. Danny was charged with directing his fiancée, Jennifer, who had just given birth to their son, to take part in his plot. He allegedly ordered her to deliver $500 in cash to a woman at a McDonald's, as a down payment in the scheme to assault several snitches. Jennifer was caught on a prosecution videotape, handing over the money. She testified against Danny at the grand jury and received immunity. The next time Danny saw her in court, he mouthed the words "I love you" to her. But Danny's words for the prosecutors during a hearing on the new charges were not as pleasant.

"Jerk-offs," Pelosi muttered to a reporter in court. "We're going forward. They ain't got no goddamned case. If they had a murder case, they wouldn't use this bullshit."

Opening statements were finally delivered on October 13. Albertson told the jurors that the only person in the world who took up with Generosa and wanted to take over Ted's money by violence through "the brutal murder of Ted Ammon, is in fact, the defendant Daniel Pelosi," and straightened her arm to point the finger of blame at him.

"The evidence will show he had a monster in him and it was unleashed on Ted Ammon," she told the hushed courtroom. She said Generosa's $3 million townhouse building loan was about to become due just after Mr. Ammon's murder and the woman was desperate for cash. Danny and Generosa "believed they were being cheated out of their fair share. It's very simple. This is all about money," Albertson said. "It's not the bogeyman, it's one man—that man," she said, pointing at him again. When the trial is over, Albertson told them, "You will find him guilty and you will feel good about it."

In his opening statement, Shargel, more passionate and folksy, stood proudly behind his client, his hands affectionately on his shoulders, and told the folks in the jury box, "ladies and gentlemen, you're looking at an innocent man." Timing was critical in the case, he said. Albertson's case was physically impossible. Cell phone records, he told them, would prove that Danny was still en route from Manhattan to Center Moriches when Ted was already dead.

"You know," he smiled at the jury, "I could sit down right now."

But he did not. The real killer left "calling cards" at the murder scene, especially a stray pubic hair found on Ted's naked shoulder. "It was not Danny Pelosi's hair." He told them about Ted's last phone call, in which he said he was at Two Mile Hollow Beach, a known gay spot, and he was afraid of some men there. The pubic hair, he said, was the result of a gay sexual encounter Ted had just before his death.

"Danny Pelosi is not a murderer."

Later, Albertson told reporters that Shargel had "besmirched" Ted's reputation by using the gay theory "or, at least attempted to." The contention that Ted had a secret gay tryst at a gay beach and that "it caused his death or played a role in his death is not only untrue, but offensive."

Many prosecution witnesses made an impact on their direct testimony but were possibly weakened by items on cross-examination by the defense. Several experts testified about forensic pathology, DNA, fingerprints, and other evidence, but most of the testimony failed to incriminate or exonerate Danny. Prosecution witnesses made a huge impact and were not checked by cross-examination and became the focus of the trial.

Albertson announced "call Robert Pelosi," and Danny's father Bob entered the courtroom. Dressed in a gray suit, the retired banker took the stand against his own son, who stared, stone-faced, from the defense table. In the audience, Bob's wife, Dorothy, Danny's daughter, Rachelle, and Danny's fiancée, Jennifer, watched together from the second row.

The prosecutor began the direct questioning and quickly brought him to the weekend of the murder, when he saw Danny at a family wedding. On that afternoon, Ted was already dead, but his body had not been discovered. Albertson wanted to know if Danny had said anything at the affair that later seemed significant.

"He asked me that 'If someone wanted to get rid of something, what would you do?' "

The retired banker was asked if he inquired why his son was asking such a strange question. Bob answered, "I didn't ask him. I didn't want to know."

Later, when he found out that Ted Ammon had been murdered and his son was a suspect, he said he had a question for Danny.

"Whatever happened to that stuff you wanted to get rid of?"

"Arnie took care of it," Danny replied, meaning Danny's

pal Arnie Cherubino, who was briefly taken into custody but never charged.

On cross-examination, Shargel immediately went after Bob, grilling him in a loud, accusatory tone calculated to bait a man with a temper. Shargel probed, trying to prove that Bob only told police about the alleged exchange after his beloved son Jimbo died, and that he blamed Danny and was seeking revenge.

"I don't know what you're implying. I don't blame him for Jimbo's death. I love Danny. I'll love him until the day I die. I don't like what he's gotten involved in," Bob said. "He was a good son, and there were times I was ashamed of him. My relationship with Danny was very see-saw. He was in and out of jail. I felt Danny disgraced me and disgraced the name Pelosi, a very proud name. I love you, Danny— whether you know it or not," Bob said directly to his son, who stared coldly back, his face flushing, eyes moist. Shargel was drawing to the end of his questions but had not dented Bob's testimony. He claimed that Bob had been ashamed of Danny all of his life.

"Baloney," Bob replied.

"Oh, yeah?" Shargel shot back. "Then how did Danny break his nose?"

"You told them that I—?" Bob exploded indignantly, ignoring Shargel and scolding his son directly. "Shame on you! I broke your nose?"

"You couldn't!" Danny snarled defiantly from his seat, showing the jury their first glimpse of his temper. The jurors' heads jerked back and forth, from father to son, as if they were at a tennis match. Danny's daughter, his fiancée, and his stepmother were all sobbing. The judge halted the proceedings, ordering Shargel to control his client. When the jury had filed out and Danny was being handcuffed, he looked at his father, still sitting on the witness stand and loudly growled, "I hate him!"

The following week of testimony began with Danny's old pal Dale Cassidy, who told the jury that a full year before the crime, Danny got drunk and said he wanted to kill Ted to get his millions.

"Danny said 'I have a plan.' He said he was going to leave his wife, marry Generosa, get the money, and go back to Tami,'" said Dale. "Danny said, 'I'll bash in his brains while he's sleeping.'"

One of Danny's former girlfriends, Tracey Riebenfeld, told the jury that three days after Ted's murder Danny came to her Center Moriches apartment and "asked me to lie for him because Generosa was framing him for the murder of Ted Ammon."

She said she also agreed to lie and give him a phony alibi by saying "we were having sex in the back of his Bronco" on the night of the murder—even though they had not yet had sex. She said she was in love with Danny and thought they had a future—until she saw Generosa's wedding ring on Danny's finger.

"He told me what took place that weekend," said Tracey. She said Danny claimed Generosa was present during the murder, along with Chris Parrino, and Danny's nephew, "Little Jeff," who drove the getaway beach-house car.

"I bashed his fucking brains in, and he cried like a bitch" and begged for his life.

Danny told her "he had used a flashlight and a lamp" in the killing. "I said 'why did you do that?'" and Danny dramatically thumped his chest and, wild-eyed, yelled, "BECAUSE I HAVE A MONSTER INSIDE ME!"

"I was scared," Tracey told the hushed courtroom. Then, she said Danny twisted her arm painfully behind her back and, "quiet and smiling," looked down into her face and warned her that if she ever told anyone what he had confessed, that "I would never see my kids again." She broke off the affair but later saw him at the wake for his brother, Jimbo, where Danny told her, "I'm counting on you, kid."

Albertson's last question was whether she was still in love with Danny.

"No."

After a week of pummeling testimony, Danny still seemed oddly confident of his ultimate victory. When officers, who escorted him to and from court, noted Danny's new pink dress shirt and pink tie, he responded with sarcasm.

"I'm trying to look bisexual."

The only news that dented Danny's bulletproof confidence was when juror number four told a court officer that Danny was glaring at him in a strange way. For Danny, it was an eerie echo of his civil court jury—when jurors were frightened by Danny's gaze and voted against him. For two days, Danny seemed subdued and depressed before returning to his usual cocky self.

Across the parking lot at the court complex, in Surrogate Court, where Danny was trying to overturn Generosa's will, Kaye Mayne's lawyer Mike Dowd testified in a sworn deposition that Danny told him, "I want you to know that there was a time that she [Generosa] had some guys in the house . . . that she was talking to about killing Ted, and I went into the beach house the weekend Ted was murdered and took the hard drive for the surveillance unit." Mike said Danny claimed he had removed the spy-system computer to protect Generosa—because it showed her planning her husband's murder with shady men.

"Look, I've done my best to protect her and I want you to understand that, on [the] fear that someone would see the tapes, what is on the hard drive . . . that is missing from the house where Ted was killed, that I went in that weekend and removed the hard drive," Danny said, according to Mike's testimony.

After that meeting, the month before Generosa died, Danny's postnuptial payoff jumped from $1.3 million to $2 million.

Back at Danny's trial, the crucial defense claim that a pubic hair, belonging to someone else, was found on Ted's body—and then went mysteriously missing—was shattered by a forensic scientist, who testified that a hair on Ted's shoulder appeared to be loose, but when he grasped the strand with a pair of tweezers, he could "see that it was growing out of the skin."

Danny's sister, Barbara Lukert, was next on the stand and testified about spying on Ted with Danny's laptop on the weekend of the murder from her Center Moriches home. Barbara said that Danny first called her on Saturday night, October 20, 2001, and asked her to get a bag he had stashed in her attic and leave it outside her garage for his friend Chris Parrino to pick up. She refused. Danny arrived at 1:20 on Sunday morning and retrieved the mysterious bag that he had secreted in his sister's attic. Then he went outside and met Chris. Barbara followed and saw Chris getting behind the wheel of Ted's station wagon. Danny claimed they were going to a bar.

"I gave him a hug, and I felt something hard where he hugged me." Because of the rush and the odd middle-of-the-night activity, she asked her brother, "What's going on?"

"Just go to fucking bed, Barbara, and mind your business!"

She said Danny did not return until after sunup. Barbara admitted that after the slaying she received a Jeep Cherokee and a check for $45,000 from Generosa, some of which she testified was past wages. She also admitted that Generosa paid for her divorce lawyer and Danny paid her mortgage and gave her a total of more than $222,000. Shargel cross-examined Barbara and brought the trial to a screeching halt by asking her if some members of her family "thought that Generosa had put a spell on the family?"

"Objection!" Albertson said.

The judge hustled the jury out of the courtroom and the lawyers argued hotly in the well of the court. Albertson told Doyle that Shargel's claims were "ridiculous" and hearsay evidence that should be excluded. The defense lawyer argued that he had the legal right to cross-examine Barbara

about the alleged witchery and his claim that some in the
Pelosi family believed "that Generosa Ammon was the
devil . . . that Danny Pelosi had married the devil" and that
"through some sort of mystical spell, caused the death of
their beloved Jimbo."

The prosecutor then told the judge that Barbara had
changed her trial testimony from her earlier grand jury testimony. The sister of the defendant "is in the custody and control of the defense," Albertson argued. She also said Barbara
told family members just after the murder that "she was terrified of this defendant . . . she said she was afraid that
Danny was going to kill her because of what she knew." Albertson said that, just after the slaying, Barbara told family
members that on the laptop she had seen a specific friend of
Pelosi's lurking outside the mansion where Ted was slain—
Alex Mawyer. She also said that when she hugged her
brother on the morning of the murder, "she felt what she felt
were two guns" under his jacket. But in her court testimony
that day, Barbara said it could have been Danny's cell phone
or almost anything. Judge Doyle ruled against the witchcraft
line of questioning.

"It's just too stupid to talk about," Albertson said to the
press with a smile. "If Generosa Ammon was a witch, she
was a good witch—because she gave him an awful lot of
money. If anyone's going to be haunted by it, it's not going
to be me."

A prosecution forensic accountant testified that Danny
had control of $6.6 million of Ted's money and spent at least
$3.8 million on the high life for himself, his pals, and fam-
ily—before and after the murder. More than a million went
for alleged gambling debts and $15,000 was spent on cigars.

Danny's archenemy, British nanny Kaye Mayne, was the
next witness to receive Danny's cold stare. She told Albertson that Danny's drinking and gambling created a constant
stream of cursing, screaming, and demands to the ailing
Generosa for more and more money, and the couple were
like "thunder and lightning."

One day, she found Generosa "on the couch crying, curled up, very tiny by this stage and she said 'I'm trapped! I'm trapped!'"

Late one night, while Kaye was napping on the couch in the living room, a drunken Danny staggered in.

"I sat up and he came and sat right next to me and whispered in my ear, about Ted's murder—how he had beaten and beaten and beaten him, and the blood, and he had begged for his life. And it was just horrible and I was very, very scared . . . and I was thinking, 'What is he doing?' and I thought he was trying to frighten me, to frighten me away. So, when he had finished speaking, I said to him, 'Did Ted know it was you?' and he said, 'You fucking hard bitch!' and he got up and stormed out."

"And then what happened?" Albertson asked in the silent courtroom.

"The next day . . . I was in the garage, doing wash, when he came into the garage and he said, 'I have talked to my lawyer about you and he agrees with me. You are a fucking hard bitch and I'm going to kill you.'" She said Danny also confessed a second time.

"I was out in the garden, reading a book under the tree, and he said, 'I gave this woman money—I killed her husband, and now she won't give me a few hundred thousand!'"

While Danny served his four-month jail sentence for drunk driving, there was peace in the house and respite from the chaos. When he got out, Generosa issued an ultimatum that he get a job, keep regular hours, and straighten up or get out.

"He did it for about three or four days," said Kaye.

"Then what happened?" asked Albertson.

"The weekend happened," Kaye replied, with a smirk. She said Danny got drunk and shouted abuse and obscenities and threw things. Later, he apologized and asked for more cash. Kaye sobbed and wiped her eyes with a tissue when she recalled the suffering and death of Generosa. She said that as her employer lay dying in a Manhattan hospital, she purchased a bouquet of orchids. "I put notes on it, 'From Danny,' saying that he loved her and that they were 'soul mates,' that was his thing, that they were soul mates, and I gave her that and said it was from Danny."

Generosa was moved by the fake token. "It's a shame because I really loved him, but I couldn't live with him in all that chaos," Generosa told Kaye.

Clayton Moultrie, a large, muscular crackhead and criminal, was one of the jailhouse snitches against Danny. His dark beard and shaved and glistening brown head emphasized his thug-like appearance as he towered in the witness stand and took the oath with a huge right hand. He told the jury that Danny had confessed to savagely bludgeoning Ted, explaining he was "trying to break every fucking bone in that asshole's body."

During a blistering cross-examination by Shargel, Moultrie protested he would not lie to get a deal from prosecutors.

"So you did it for the good of the Republic?" Shargel scoffed, sparking laughter.

The tough guy broke down in the face of the sarcasm and cried. The defense lawyer was in a logical bind in front of the jury. On one hand, Shargel said repeatedly that Danny had a big mouth and made up stories and even confessed to crimes he did not commit—because he was a goofy braggart. On the other hand, Shargel attacked any witness who said Danny confessed to them. Which was it? Why not just admit that Danny had said it all? Every time the bearded lawyer expertly savaged a witness, he was also proving that he feared them.

The prosecution called two pathologists to the stand. Both testified that the series of double red spots on Ted's neck and lower back were from a stun gun. There was extensive testimony about the time of death, based on the digestion of Ted's last meal. The prosecution witnesses said Ted died four to ten hours after dinner. He finished dinner no later than 9:30 that Saturday night. If Ted had died only four hours later, Danny was in the clear. Cell phone records introduced by the prosecution proved that. Only if Ted died six to ten hours later would Danny be in the picture. The prosecution also called two stun gun experts to testify that the red marks were the result of a skin reaction to the high-voltage shocks of a stun gun.

Albertson rested the people's case on the day before Thanksgiving. Before he was handcuffed and led away, Danny issued a scathing review of Albertson's case to a reporter in the front row, who pointed out he had boasted he would be out by Halloween. "Fuck Halloween. I'll be home by Christmas."

For some reason, the prosecution did not call a witness who claimed that just after 6:00 A.M. on Monday morning, eleven hours before Ted's body was found, he actually saw two men fleeing from the scene of the murder. Adam Moriarty* told police and others that he was driving in his truck with his lights off in the pre-dawn pitch-darkness on Middle Lane. Moriarty later told people he was illegally hunting, "jacking deer," which involved flipping on his lights when he saw movement in the dark. When he saw two shadows moving in the Ammon driveway, Adam popped on his headlights, ready to shoot. Instead of game, he saw two men. One of them instantly jerked his hand up and covered his face, but the second guy just stared, like a deer caught in the headlights. Adam got a look at his features. It was a good bet that the guys were up to no good, but Adam could hardly call the cops with a rifle on the seat. If he had known the pair might have been killers, he could have held them at gunpoint and been a hero, but he did not hear about the murder until two days later. When detectives later showed him an array of photos he failed to pick out a picture of Danny. When the defense began its case, Shargel, of course, wanted to call Adam to the stand. He was subpoenaed and told to report to court to testify the following day. Shargel introduced himself to Adam and asked if he would submit to a pretestimony interview. Adam refused and Shargel told him to go home. The lawyer had no intention of violating the first commandment of trial lawyers—never call a witness unless you first know exactly what they are going to say. The only person who claimed he might have seen the killers of Ted Ammon rode the elevator down to the lobby alone and walked out of the courthouse.

Danny's Ted-was-bisexual-and-was-killed-by-gays defense began and ended with their second witness—Sam Wagner, the gay man who had lived with rich friend Barton Kaplan down Middle Lane from the Ammon estate. On direct questioning, Wagner told Shargel the unusual story that, two years before the murder, he spotted Ted one morning, as the multimillionaire was jogging towards him—with a full erection. Wagner said he did not know who his sex partner was until he saw his photo in the newspaper after the murder. Wagner could not supply a date or a month for the event and was even confused about the year. He also claimed to have learned about the murder on the wrong day—before Ted's body had been found.

On cross-examination by Albertson, Wagner admitted that a *New York Post* reporter was the first person he told about the alleged tryst and that he was only "75 percent sure" that the man was Ammon—but later claimed he was 100 percent certain on television.

"As it was reported in the paper, you met and, the next thing you knew, you were doing 'boom-boom' in the woods?" Albertson asked, quoting Wagner from the article.

"Right," said Wagner.

"And, during some of this 'boom-boom,' I guess you weren't concentrating on the man's face?"

"I was not in the process of doing that, looking at him directly in the face, no."

Shargel also called a forensic pathologist to disagree with the prosecution pathologists on the time of death and the stun gun. After a defense huddle, Shargel decided to cut the brief defense case short after two more witnesses. If the trial was winding down, that meant that Danny would not take the stand, something he always had said he would do. It appeared Shargel would only call seven witnesses in a five-day defense. Albertson had called forty-one witnesses over two months.

The best thing Danny had going for him was not his defense. It was the perceived holes in the prosecution's case, such as their failure to place him at the scene. Were the holes big enough for Danny to slip through?

EPILOGUE

Danny's case appeared to be over. It was late in the afternoon and the judge had scheduled closing statements for the next day. But, after the last defense witness stepped down, Danny turned from the defense table and announced to his family in the third row, "I'm testifying."

"Are you kidding me?" replied an amused Judge Doyle from the bench. Albertson's response was also to laugh and turn around to look at Pelosi—who gave her a big confident grin. His lawyers were not so confident. They had advised Danny to stay away from the witness chair. Danny, wearing an expensive, black Italian suit, took the stand, raised his right hand, and took the oath, giving his full name as Daniel John Pelosi.

"Mr. Pelosi, on October 20, 2001, were you in the Town of East Hampton?" Shargel asked his client.

"Absolutely not," Danny replied in a loud, defiant voice.

"On October 21, 2001, were you in the Town of East Hampton?"

"Absolutely not."

"Mister Pelosi, did you murder Ted Ammon?"

"Absolutely not."

"Did you participate in any way in the murder of Ted Ammon?"

"Absolutely not."

"Pass the witness," said Shargel, with a dramatic wave of his hand, finished with his questions, as if the case were over and they could all go home. Everyone went home for the night, but in the morning, the courtroom was filled to over-flowing, as Albertson rose to begin a heated cross-examination that would last more than five hours. Danny agreed at first that both he and Generosa mistakenly be-lieved Ted was hiding $300 million to $500 million from them. Then, minutes later, Danny denied believing that Ted was concealing assets. He admitted that he bought a stun gun but claimed it was for Generosa. When confronted with the testimony of his pal Dale that a year before the murder he had a plan to bash Ted's brains in to get his millions, Danny's response was less than a ringing denial.

"I don't believe so."

Danny tried to portray himself as a working class hero, a regular guy who was fighting in court to overturn Gen-erosa's will so he could help Alexa and Grego.

"I don't want none of Mister Ammon's money. It belongs to the children," Danny claimed.

"And you're still suing in Surrogate Court to set aside your postnuptial agreement so that you could get a piece of the estate, aren't you?"

"So I can give it to the children," Danny explained.

"The children already have it, Mister Pelosi. That's what's in the will, right?"

"I don't understand the question."

Later Danny even made a few jokes and tried his big smile but none of the nine women and three men was laughing. Albertson questioned him about zapping his workmen at the townhouse job site with his new toy, the stun gun.

"So, did you try it out when you got it?"

"Absolutely not."

"Did you offer your workers a hundred bucks to try it on them?" Albertson asked, surprised at Danny's denial.

"I paid them a hundred dollars and tried it on them," Danny said, reversing his answer.

"Did you try it on guys you didn't pay a hundred dollars?"

"Yeah, I hit the guys on the job. I was fooling around. I was being me."

"And being you was stunning people with a Taser? That is being you?" Albertson pressed.

"I'm a good guy. I would hit you, just like when they got it, and they hit me. It was all in fun."

"That is what you did to Ted Ammon?"

"Not at all."

"No, that wasn't fun?"

"I didn't do nothing to Mister Ammon."

"You didn't enjoy beating him?"

"Where are you going?"

"Did you tell Tracey that you bashed his brains in and he 'cried like a bitch'?" Albertson asked, her voice rising.

"No, I did not."

"Did you tell Tracey he begged for his life?"

"No, I did not."

"Did you tell Tracey you did it because you had a monster in you?" she demanded loudly.

"No, ma'am."

"You got a monster in you?" she asked, sarcastically.

"No, I had sex with Tracey and said I was Tarzan. That is about the only thing I could relate to pounding on my chest."

Danny did not deny being full of anger and rage.

"It would depend on the scenario, the situation that I was in. Just like anybody," Danny replied.

"And you are capable of flying into rages?"

"As you are," he shot back.

"I'm sorry?" Albertson said, taken aback. "Do you know me outside of this courtroom?"

"Through the papers."

"Did you read the newspaper article about me and my family?" Janet asked, referring to his alleged threat against them.

"Yes I did."

"Did you make any statements about the children, when you read that article?" Janet demanded, trying unsuccessfully to get Danny to admit that he had threatened her two young children. Danny also did not deny that he was very angry on the Saturday of the murder, pacing and yelling, "This has got to stop. Ted needs to be a man. He has to give her half. Someone needs to knock some sense into his head." He admitted they were his words but said they sounded more sinister when they came out of the petite prosecutor's mouth than when they had emerged from his.

"So, when you said somebody needs to 'knock some sense into him,' you weren't the guy who went out that very night and did just that?" Albertson asked.

The jurors' heads turned to Danny, who replied, "It's a phrase that I use, okay? I'm a . . . 'I'll knock some sense into you. Wake up.' It's a phrase. It's part of my language." Danny gave long, rambling, unresponsive answers. Over and over, the judge scolded him for not answering the questions. At one point, Danny bragged that he had won his 1996 civil accident case.

"Actually, the jury awarded you nothing," Albertson said, incredulous.

"But I won the trial 100 percent," Danny insisted.

"Did you get enjoyment when you were stunning the people at work with that stun gun?" Janet asked, trying to catch Danny off guard.

"I never . . . Yes, I did," said Danny, changing his answer in midsentence.

"What part of it did you like?" she asked.

"I liked the way they jumped and reacted and said, 'You fucking asshole!'" Danny chuckled, unable to keep the sadistic glee from his face.

Several jurors were wearing expressions of distaste and most of them turned away from him when he talked, keeping their eyes on Albertson instead. Danny said it was true that he crushed up a sleeping pill and slipped it into Generosa's beer on that Saturday, but he claimed he had nothing to hide. Then

Danny claimed that the hard object that his sister Barbara felt under his jacket was a box of marijuana he retrieved from Barbara's attic, not a stun gun. His only uncorroborated alibi was driving around, looking for someplace to buy beer with Chris Parrino. He admitted that he was one of a very few people who knew where the missing hard drive unit was hidden in the attic of the murder mansion but claimed word got around because "I have a real big mouth."

On redirect questioning by Shargel, Danny said that on the Saturday of Ted's murder, Generosa was drunk and "in a raging fit. She was all pissed off about Ted." He said Generosa wanted to kill herself, and he had to break down the bathroom door of the apartment to prevent it. He said he left the kids alone in the apartment at 11:30 Saturday night after Generosa had already left to go to her former butler Steven's apartment. On Sunday, after the murder, he claimed he could not locate Generosa.

"Mister Pelosi," said Shargel, "did Generosa Ammon ever ask you to murder her husband?"

"Yes . . . Generosa wanted to know if I knew of anybody who would kill her husband, or if I could do it myself." Danny said he never agreed to either request.

Albertson rose again to quiz Danny about what she felt were incredibly convenient discoveries—a note written by Ted supposedly showing he was hiding assets, and the stun gun Danny claimed he found in his dead brother Jim's closet. But Danny said his forensic experts concluded, "guess what? It didn't have anything to do with Ted Ammon."

"Because that is not the stun gun!" Albertson retorted. "You wouldn't give us the one you actually used. You're too smart for that—aren't you?"

"Objection!" said Shargel.

"Sustained."

She asked him if he ever told a psychiatrist that he "continued to drink, drug, and lie my ass off?"

"I have a habit of telling stories," Danny admitted.

"And when you told those stories, were they lies?"

"Yeah."

Albertson finished and Shargel stepped up again and brought up Danny's greatest fibs, his bogus claims to be in the witness protection program and an imaginary shootout with federal agents.

"You are a bullshitter, right?" Shargel asked.

"Absolutely." He again denied killing Ted, and Shargel sat down.

"Are you bullshitting the jury right now with that answer?" Albertson asked.

"No, I am not," Danny said. He was the last to speak but Albertson had the last word. In his closing statement to the jury, Shargel said all the witnesses that testified against Danny had an axe to grind, or something to gain, or hated his client.

"Where was Generosa Ammon that night?" Shargel asked. "It was Generosa Ammon, not Danny Pelosi, who was filled with hate and anger. This was a woman who was out of control."

The lawyer then focused on Generosa's butler Steven, who "got a gift of one million dollars" after Ted was killed. "Where were Generosa and Steven that night?"

In her closing, Albertson ridiculed the defense's claim that all of the witnesses were conspiring to frame Danny, the "mysterious gay man" defense, and Shargel's suggestion that Generosa's servant was involved.

"It's not any man, not some man—but that man who committed this murder," the prosecutor intoned loudly, pointing an accusing finger at Danny.

The jury returned the following morning to begin their deliberations. Their final request, read back on the third day, was of the first half hour of Danny's cross-examination. Just after noon on Monday, December 13—three months to the day from opening statements—the jury sent a note saying they had reached a verdict. Danny, his hands cuffed behind him, was led to the defense table. Four large court officers formed a human barrier between him and the gallery.

Nervous, Danny shook hands with all three of his lawyers and crossed himself. The jury filed in and his eyes darted desperately from one to the other, looking for a clue—but they did not return his gaze. Courtroom superstition holds that jurors do not look at defendants they have convicted.

"It's guilty," said a reporter in the front row, after looking at the jury and the officers.

The judge asked the jury if they had reached a verdict.

"Yes, we have," said jury forewoman Deborah Erickson. "Guilty."

Danny, whose hands had been steady in front of him, began to shake visibly. His face turned red and, as the jurors were polled and replied "Guilty," one by one, he put his face in his hands and struggled to hide his sobbing. Danny then stared blankly at the floor, stunned. Danny stood up, his chin on his chest, and his hands were cuffed behind him, all hope of being home by Christmas gone. Gone also was his usual banter and winking at friends, family, and reporters. He began to cry again, hiding his tears from the spectators as he was led away.

In front of the cameras and microphones, Albertson said that Danny, essentially, was her best witness, that his decision to testify had been disastrous, especially when he admitted he got a charge out of zapping people.

"He particularly enjoyed stinging people—that was my smoking stun gun," Albertson grinned.

She revealed that before the trial the first jury she faced was Alexa and Grego. She presented some of her case to them and convinced them that Danny had lied to them and had betrayed them.

"Pelosi fed them a lot of stories. I think they realize they were being used."

A disappointed Shargel told the press that Danny was crestfallen because "he was optimistic right up to the last moment."

The jury tossed out the experts as self-canceling, but completely believed Bob Pelosi and Tracey Riebenfeld. They also suspected that more than one person killed Ted.

"Money and rage, those were the two major things," juror number seven, Patricia Campbell said. Danny "went nuts . . . when he found out he would only get half—he wanted it all. Nobody could handle the way he spoke. The look did not match the mouth."

News of the verdict spread quickly. Mike Dowd told a reporter Danny "was clearly undone by his mouth and his insatiable greed."

"Thank God this is over for the children," said his client Kaye Mayne.

Danny also spoke to a reporter.

"I'm still in shock. I don't know what went wrong," the convicted killer said from his cell. "I'm appealing. I'm an innocent man."

Before the trial, Danny had told a reporter he would be happy "to pull the switch" to execute whoever "really killed Ted," because of all the pain it had caused Alexa and Grego. But first, he said, the killer's "skin should be peeled off" and salt should be applied to torture the person who ended Ted Ammon's life.

Some who had known Danny for a long time, however, were no longer convinced of his innocence. One such person said that Danny was subject to violent alcoholic blackouts for years, as he had admitted in court documents, and may not have even remembered killing Ted. That person recalled an incident in which Danny allegedly choked and assaulted a woman close to him in a drunken fury—and then later denied and genuinely seemed not to remember the assault.

"I think, when he's drunk, he turns into this monster and I've seen it and the family has seen it. He blacks out and he gets in such a fit of rage, he's like a split personality. It's almost like his eyes go black."

The events of Generosa Ammon's childhood—especially the alleged molestation by a trusted adult—were never mentioned at the trial but were partially responsible for the kind of person she was. The family of the man Generosa said had sexually abused her as a child denied the claim. He was never charged with any crime and died before anyone in the family heard the charge. He is not identified by name because there is no way to prove—or disprove—Generosa's claims, which were made independently, over many years, to several people.

Danny's defense claim that Ted was a closet bisexual killed by random gay men he met at a local gay beach was laughed out of court. If Ted had been bludgeoned by unknown "rough trade" gay killers for some unknown reason, how would strangers committing a crime of opportunity magically know of the existence of a hidden video surveillance system and just where to find it—behind a ceiling beam, which is behind a wall panel, inside a hidden safe room, reached only inside of a closed closet? They certainly could not have tortured Ted to get that information—because he did not know it. If he had known about the spy system, Ted probably would have ripped it out with his bare hands, those who knew him say. Also, statistically, most such "rough trade" attacks are made in the course of robberies. Why, then, did the killers ignore two grand in cash and the keys to a new Porsche on their way out the door? The women who knew Ted knew the self-serving defense scenario was a lie. They knew Ted was a man who loved women.

The defense also tried, unsuccessfully, to pin the murder on Generosa and her servant, causing the *New York Post* to print a mocking front page headline, THE BUTLER DID IT. Without a doubt, Generosa had guilty knowledge before, during, or after Ted was killed. Danny testified that she asked him to go out and hire killers or do it himself. After the guilty verdict, Generosa's lawyer Mike Dowd said that Danny confessed to Generosa. There is no reason to disbelieve either story. However, it is more likely that a man, or men—rather than a petite woman—inflicted the horrific injuries. Perhaps Generosa sobered up after dispatching Danny to do the deed and felt a flood of remorse and fear after the event, as her sobbing in Central Park would indicate.

If so, she could never have dropped the dime on Danny because he could tell police she had ordered the hit, even if she did not. As Generosa sobbed to Kaye, she was trapped. Once she received her death sentence from the doctors, she did her best to keep her kids away from Danny, although it seemed as if it was too late. He had won their hearts. Or, did Generosa actually exact her revenge with her own hands, and take Ted's life—up close and personal—while he saw who was doing it, as her accomplice kept Ted helpless with one or more stun guns? Danny claimed she tried to kill him twice, once with a knife and once with a dog bowl while he was asleep, just as Ted had been sleeping when he was attacked.

It is possible that someone remotely watched on the hidden video surveillance system, as Ted was murdered, but it would have been a terrible risk—especially to the actual killers—to have generated a record of the crime. It is more likely that the system was shut off before the murder—either remotely, by turning off the cameras with a laptop, or by simply unplugging the power connection in Ted's study, as Danny knew how to do.

If Generosa knew before the murder that she was dying of cancer, she may have plotted to kill Ted, knowing that her illness would claim her before the State of New York could. The single overriding factor in the case was Generosa's overwhelming hatred of Ted. She and Danny may have known that her husband had not changed his will, despite their performance for her lawyers. Generosa may have done exactly what she told Ted she would do—had him killed. Generosa was a hands-on person, especially in the garden, but she let others do the heavy lifting.

Generosa attempted suicide several times but died in a hospital, of natural causes, according to the death certificate. Even so, she died by her own hand—because she refused to undergo treatment that would have allowed her to live with her kids for up to two more years. Did she surrender and die years before her time just to save her pretty blond hair—or was something else eating away at her soul that she could not live with? Her marriage to Ted, their life with the kids—the perfect stone flower she had carved in her mind, their perfect lives—had shattered forever and could never be put back together.

When he heard about the guilty verdict and Danny's reaction, Bob Pelosi felt his son was convinced that he could charm the nine women jurors because he believed he could woo any woman in the world, part of his lifelong propensity for scheming and lying.

"I could never believe that my son could kill someone for money. If it's true, it's nauseating," Bob told a reporter, choking back tears.

In his anguish, Bob's thoughts wandered back to Danny's childhood, when the boy found an old go-cart frame and a busted motor. Danny worked hard to fix it up and repair the engine but the machine would never work more than a few minutes, despite all of his talented tinkering. One afternoon, Bob saw his son zipping around on the cart and congratulated him on a great repair job. But, when he went to start his lawn mower, Bob kept pulling and pulling the cord and it wouldn't start. He opened it up and realized that Danny had switched engines. The good motor was now on Danny's cart. Danny was a good son but he would not admit his guilt. Even when confronted with irrefutable evidence, he continued to lie, as if he really believed his own ridiculous story.

"I'll always remember him as a little boy," Bob said sadly. "I'm sorry he grew up."

INDEX